Power and Protest in the Countryside

Power and Protest in the Countryside

Studies of Rural Unrest in Asia,
Europe, and Latin America

Edited by Robert P. Weller
and Scott E. Guggenheim

Duke Press Policy Studies

Durham, N.C. 1982

© 1982, Duke University Press

Printed in the United States
of America on acid-free paper

Library of Congress Cataloging in Publication Data

Weller, Robert P. (Robert Paul), 1953-
  Power and protest in the countryside.

  (Duke Press policy studies)
  Bibliography: p.
  Includes index.
  1. Insurgency Congresses. 2. Peasant uprisings—
Congresses. I. Guggenheim, Scott E. (Scott Evan),
1955-   .II. Title. III. Series.
JJ328.5.W44   1982   305.5'63   82-12991
ISBN 0-8223-0483-X

Contents

Figures

Power and Protest in the Countryside

1. Introduction: Moral Economy, Capitalism, and State Power in Rural Protest

Scott Evan Guggenheim and Robert P. Weller

This book originated in the Symposium on Peasant Rebellions held at the Johns Hopkins University on January 24–25, 1980.[1] Yet partly as a result of the Symposium, the revised papers collected here are not limited either to peasants or to rebellions. A full understanding of peasants means knowing how they articulate with other classes, and a full understanding of rebellions means knowing how they relate to other forms of protest (or to the lack of any protest). This book thus addresses some important questions that an approach toward "peasant rebellions" alone would bypass: when do peasants act as a class, and when do they act separately? When do people rebel, when do they choose a less violent form of protest, and when do they remain quiescent?

The essays collected here examine the forms rural violence has taken through the past three centuries of social and economic change. Each essay is independent, yet each also corrects and refines earlier conceptions about three shared theoretical concerns, which we discuss in detail below. The first shared concern is moral economy: several of the authors examine how people use accepted forms of standardized protest in particular historical contexts. The second is the growth of capitalism: each essay clarifies how changes in the class structure may lead to the loss of old forms of protest or to the creation of new forms. Third is the influence of the state: many of the essays stress the independent role the state plays in determining particular forms of rural action or inaction. The authors, who include anthropologists, historians, political scientists, and sociologists, root their treatment of these theoretical, social scientific ideas in concrete historical cases; this book is an interdisciplinary attempt to challenge some of the traditional theories of peasant rebellion.[2]

Moral Economy

Moral economy concentrates on the system of rights and obligations that surround interpersonal and interclass relations in rural societies. Although moral economy may be taken to include as diverse a variety of theorists as Eric Wolf and Jim Scott (see Popkin, 1979: 5–8), moral economists agree that we should examine shared normative standards of what constitutes proper behavior.

Scott (1976) and his students have popularized what we shall call the strong version of moral economy theory. In this version, social obligations permeate the transfer of surplus from the peasantry to the nonproducing classes, and economy is thus inseparable from morality.

> Woven into the tissue of peasant behavior, then, whether in normal local routines or in the violence of an uprising, is the structure of a shared moral universe, a common notion of what is just. It is this moral heritage that, in peasant revolts, selects certain targets rather than others, and that makes possible a collective (though rarely coordinated) action born of moral outrage. . . .
>
> We can begin, I believe, with two moral principles that seem firmly embedded in both the social patterns and injunctions of peasant life: the *norm of reciprocity* and the *right to subsistence*. . . . Reciprocity serves as a central moral formula for interpersonal conduct. The right to subsistence, in effect, defines the minimal needs that must be met for members of the community within the context of reciprocity. Both principles correspond to vital human needs within the peasant economy (Scott, 1976: 167).

The peasant is obligated to pay his rent, and the landlord is obligated to guarantee the peasant a minimum level of subsistence; peasants have rights as well as duties, though this is not to say that these rights have never been violated. Indeed, peasants throughout the world have evolved many forms of protest to violations of their customary rights, ranging from emigration, to joining the priesthood, to food riots, to outright rebellion (see, for example, Adas, 1981).

Scott (1977b) has suggested that peasants create and sustain ideologies intrinsically opposed to the dominant world view. Peasants, in this view, develop their own concept of justice to interpret their basic conflict with their landlords. This folk ideology is often a specific reversal of elite ideology: "Any moral order is bound to engender its own antithesis, at least ritually, within folk culture" (Scott, 1977b: 33). Peasants may subordinate themselves to the elite ideology, or they may dissent from it; which alternative they choose depends on the material relation between the peasants and the elite. In either case, peasants understand that their interests differ from the interests of their masters.

The strong version of moral economy argues that peasant ideologies and institutions provide useful building blocks for constructing revolutions. In times of structural change, landlords will no longer meet peasant expectations, and peasants will attempt to reassert the traditional morality. According to Scott, because the peasants' alternative universe "represents the closest thing to class consciousness in preindustrial agrarian societies" (1977b: 224), reassertion of the traditional moral economy may be an effective ideology for rebellious organizations. Indeed, such an ideology may be truly revolutionary, by seeking to alter the new structural conditions.

Thaxton's essay, "Mao Zedong, Red *Misérables*, and the Moral Economy of Peasant Rebellion in Modern China" illustrates several aspects of the strong version of moral economy. Thaxton attributes much of the success of the Chinese Communist Party in organizing peasants to the Communist offer of a renewed traditional system of rights and duties. In contrast to the usual stereotype of outside organizers who easily turn peasants to their purposes, Thaxton offers a picture of outsiders who must adapt to the "alternate symbolic universe" of the peasantry.

Wasserstrom's "Indian Uprisings under Spanish Colonialism" also fits parts of the strong version of moral economy. He shows how Mexican Indians in the eighteenth century adapted Christianity to protect their way of life. They rebelled to protect a traditional moral economy. Wasserstrom concludes that "not economic exploitation alone, but rather the destruction of their way of life itself prompted these people to reject colonial rule and to try their hand at a desperate throw of the dice."

The milder version of moral economy generally takes a more negative position on the possibilities of a truly peasant-based revolution (see, for example, Hobsbawm, 1971; Wolf, 1969a). This version assumes neither peasant solidarity nor class consciousness. The breakup of peasant societies under capitalism may lead to violent outbursts, they say, but these outbursts are never politically effective. Peasants may take part in genuine revolutions, but only as the allies of other groups.

Although the mild version of moral economy sees a less stable and a less unified peasantry than the strong version (especially under capitalism), it also recognizes that peasants may have an array of traditionally sanctioned types of protest. Hobsbawm (1959), for example, treats social banditry as a traditional response to violations of accepted norms. Tilly has also discussed ritualized protest among European peasants. He writes elsewhere, for instance, that food riots "occurred not so much where men were hungry as where they believed others were unjustly depriving them of food to which they had a moral and political right" (Tilly, 1975: 389). His essay in this book also stresses that violations of the moral economy were a major cause of contention in seventeenth-century France. Adas's essay also mentions a traditionally sanctioned repertoire of unrest including petitions to officials, transfer of allegiance to new patrons, flight from unacceptable situations, entry into religious groups, cooperation with bandits, gangs, and, of course, rebellion (see also Adas, 1981).

Samuel Popkin (1979) has criticized moral economy theories, without differentiating between strong and mild versions. He faults moral economists primarily for romanticizing and idealizing the peasantry. Using Vietnam to illustrate his case, Popkin argues that many of the institutions moral economists claim promote village redistribution of wealth actually accentuate stratification. He shows furthermore that commercialization of the economy under capitalism did not threaten the subsistence base of peasants as a unit; instead, some peasants benefitted from capitalist expansion by finding alternatives to local forms of exploitation. Villages, according to Popkin, "are best viewed as corporations, not communes, and . . . patrons with multistranded ties are best seen as monopolists, not paternalists" (1979: 4).

Several of the essays here make similar criticisms, concentrating especially on the stronger version of moral economy. Skocpol examines Scott's work in detail, and agrees that he romanticizes the peasantry. Adas writes that Burmese uprisings under the British stemmed from frustration with the market, not from threats to a subsistence ethic—the very abundance of rice was causing problems for the Burmese. Roseberry also argues that Venezuelan peasants experienced no subsistence crisis. More importantly, Venezuela had no precapitalist peasantry; there was no traditional peasant moral economy because the peasantry was created by capitalism (see also Roseberry, 1978).

Other authors emphasize the exploitative (rather than the mutualistic) nature of ties between elites and peasants. Traditional peasant institutions such as marriage and inheritance, labor arrangements, and ritual hierarchies may contribute to exploitation of peasants (Cancian, 1965; Cole and Wolf, 1974; Terray, 1972). All of this evidence casts doubts on the idea of a traditional moral economy of mutual rights and duties.

Yet Popkin's alternative itself has problems. He argues that we can best understand peasant life as a series of decisions about the possible rewards of various types of investments. Peasants decide to join collective action based on (1) expenditure of resources, (2) positive rewards, (3) probability of success, and (4) leadership viability and trust (Popkin, 1979: 24). In contrast to the moral economists, Popkin does not stress shared norms. Instead, "norms are malleable, renegotiated, and shifting in accord with considerations of power and strategic interaction among individuals" (Popkin, 1979: 22).

One problem with decision-making theories is that the criteria for making decisions are not created by isolated individuals, nor are they objective givens. They are instead the "malleable" and "shifting" norms that Popkin mentions. Individuals' decisions may indeed change social norms, but at the same time, social norms affect individuals' decisions. We agree with Alavi that "men do not act or think in isolation from other men, nor are their goals formulated entirely by private contemplation" (1973: 34). Furthermore, the structural factors which limit choice must be considered. "The constraints built into a structure . . . never enter into choice; individuals may not only be unaware of them, but they may be systematically excluded from consciousness" (Silverman, 1975: 120).

Thus, while Popkin's criticism of moral economy may have validity, his alternative is difficult to accept. Furthermore, not all aspects of moral economy can be rejected. We gain from the moral economists' emphasis on shared norms, even though they may have romanticized the norms they discuss. Shared norms need not be a romanticized subsistence ethic; they may instead be a repertoire of accepted forms of protest—including food riots, social banditry, rebellions, and so on—in response to violations of various kinds of values. Shared norms also need not be entirely traditional; they may instead be flexible reactions to new structural conditions.

Many of the essays here substitute a more "malleable" and "shifting" view of norms for the romanticized moral economy that Popkin effectively criticizes. Tilly, for example, shows how standardized forms of protest extended throughout seventeenth-century France; they arose in response to similar pressures created throughout the country by the state and its apparatus of war. That is, the French repertoire of unrest was not simply part of a tradition-bound moral economy; it was also a creative reaction to new structural conditions.

Wasserstrom makes a similar point: high taxes and a low standard of living under Spanish colonialism had created a *new* moral economy in southern Mexico by 1620. The communal solidarity of the Indians was a reaction to the Spanish, not a reflection of their peasant tradition. The traditional Burmese moral economy that Adas discusses also adapted to the changing effects of British rule in the nineteenth and early twentieth centuries. Saya San, for example, the most famous modern Burmese rebel, combined nationalist party politics with traditional Buddhist themes of rebellion. Roseberry treats the same theme, showing how a very "traditional" Venezuelan uprising—a caudillo war in 1929—was in fact part of a tradition that extended back only to the latter half of the nineteenth century, and that resulted from the growth of coffee plantations. Mintz, in his afterword, also advises us to reconsider exactly what the apparently backward-looking goals of rebellious peasants really meant in particular historical situations.

This volume thus offers a revised view of moral economy. Many of the essays specify agreed-upon repertoires of unrest that clarify why peasant action takes particular forms. Yet it cannot be assumed that these repertoires are bound by peasant traditions—instead, they must be viewed as the result of tradition interacting with the objective conditions of particular situations. Peasant norms must not be idealized in defiance of real historical differences, and investigators must not be blind to flexibility of norms in light of ongoing structural changes. The following sections explore how two crucial causes of structural changes—capitalism and the state—influence rural action.

Capitalism

Capitalism has created an increasingly integrated world system. The major changes in world trade that Wallerstein (1974) documents for the sixteenth century affected the forms of protest in many parts of the world. Continuing changes in the structure of the world system, especially in the nineteenth century (see Migdal's essay), have also meant continuing changes in rural unrest. We have arranged the essays here in roughly chronological order to reflect and clarify the historical development of this system.

All of the essays illustrate the results of commercialization of the economy under capitalism.

The spread of the market has torn men up by their roots and shaken them loose from the social relationships into which they were born. Industrialization and expanded communications have given rise to new societal clusters, as yet unsure of their own social positions and interests but forced by the imbalance of their lives to seek a new adjustment. Traditional authority has eroded or collapsed; new contenders for power are seeking new constituencies for entry into the vacant political arena. Thus, when the peasant protagonist lights the torch of rebellion, the edifice of society is already smoldering and ready to take fire (Wolf, 1969a: 295).

Tilly examines one effect of commercialization in seventeenth-century France: the state promoted commercialization to support its war machine, and the market thus became a major focus of contention by the end of the century. Migdal analyzes the extensive commercialization of much of the world in the late nineteenth century. He discusses in turn: (1) changes in land tenure, which were intended to increase yields and to increase planting of cash crops, and which often resulted in the consolidation of large landholdings; (2) changes in taxes, which were increased and collected in cash, forcing peasants into the market, and often overwhelming them with debts; and (3) construction of railroads, which helped the market expand into previously inaccessible areas.

The essays which follow Migdal's confirm his scenario. Adas, for example, shows how newly market-bound peasants in nineteenth- and twentieth-century Burma reacted against the new economy with attacks on moneylenders and with antitax campaigns. Thaxton also points to the problems that increased tax demands and the related increase in cash cropping caused for twentieth-century Chinese peasants.

Ties to the world market could also affect the tactical advantages peasants held in some conditions (see Wolf, 1969a: 290–294). Land ownership had traditionally provided many peasants with the resources to maintain rebellions, but the new economy often left people landless. Mountainous (or otherwise marginal) geographic locations made it difficult for authorities to exert control, but improved transportation to feed the market also limited this advantage for peasants.

While the increasing commercialization of rural economies tends to limit the tactical advantages of rural dwellers, capitalism also produces radical alterations in the class structure that can result in new allies for peasants. Traditionally, privileged groups could increase their power where colonial states relied on village elites for local administration; new economic elites—entrepreneurs, middlemen, brokers, etc.—could arise by performing vital market functions; and so on. In time, these groups could use their positions to acquire and consolidate political and social power, often threatening groups more closely bound to the precapitalist economy. This process creates more than just new class interests, it also creates possibilities for new class alliances.

Much of the material in this book illustrates how changing fields of power under capitalism affect the forms of rural unrest. In Tilly's essay, the growing demands of the French state often threw nobles and peasants into an alliance against the central authority and its representatives. Yet alliances can shift according to particular conditions: intendants (who represented the crown) sometimes appealed to local lords for military help; tax farmers (also creations of the crown) sometimes conflicted with army smugglers who cut into their profits.

Wasserstrom's example of the 1712 Tzeltal rebellion in southern Mexico also reveals new class alliances forming under the pressure of capitalism, through a process that may have been very common. Whereas the major schism in precolonial and early colonial Tzeltal society was between Tzeltal elites and commoners, Spanish rapacity caused the Tzeltal to redefine class interests as ethnic interests against the colonial government. Just as in France, old enemies became new allies. Further, Adas's Burmese case is very similar to the Mexican case. Officials of the traditional Burmese state, displaced by the British, allied with peasants. New ethnic groups, especially Indians, took vital positions in the new market economy. As a result, much unrest took the form of ethnic nationalism, which was opposed to alien overlords and foreign ethnic groups rather than to class exploitation.

Yet peasants need not always ally with groups opposed to the state. Conflicts within the state, or between the state and other political brokers, may lead to alliances between the state and the peasantry. Many land reform movements in Latin America reflect an alliance of state and peasants against other powerful groups.

Some scholars, including Marx, argue that capitalism destroys the peasantry as an autonomous class. Marx and Engels thought that the peasantry would be an untrustworthy ally of the proletariat at best. At worst, class enemies of the proletariat could mobilize the peasantry, as in the countercoup of Louis Napoleon (Marx, 1973b [1852]). Why were Marx and Engels (and Wolf, 1969a; and Hobsbawm, 1971) so skeptical about peasants? One reason was the problem of property. Most peasants controlled small landholdings, and therefore could not be expected to support fully a proletarian revolution dedicated to the overthrow of private property. Second, peasant social structure inhibits class action. Because peasant production is based on small landholdings, peasants are isolated from one another. Many groups with differing, often opposed interests exist within the peasantry; these range from relatively large landholdings that employ hired labor, to tiny family farms that barely provide subsistence. The peasantry may differentiate even further under capitalism. Wealthy peasants may see their interests more with regional and national entrepreneurs than with their poorer neighbors. Poor peasants may ally with urban industrialists to break the power of landlords, or they may be forced into the proletariat. At the same time, class exploitation in peasant communities is often hidden by ties of kinship, community loyalty, or ethnic solidarity (Mintz, 1974). As a result, in this view peasants rarely act as a solidary unit, and effective rural rebellion must depend on nonpeasant leadership. This limits the forms rebellion can take.

Several of the essays support this view of peasants under capitalism. Migdal describes the growing frailty of traditional ties which united peasants in the nineteenth century; he cites, for example, the weakening of the pueblo in Mexico, and of the joint family in India. Roseberry explicitly compares the disunited peasantry of nineteenth-century Venezuela to Marx's (1973b [1852]) description of the fragmented French peasantry under Louis Napoleon.

Yet other scholars disagree with this prognosis on the peasantry under capitalism. The stronger version of moral economy, in particular, argues that capitalist expansion may consolidate peasant unity and increase the potential for peasant revolution. Thaxton's analysis of China argues that the revolution succeeded because it relied on traditional peasant demands that were strengthened under capitalism. Although Adas (1980) criticizes moral economy, he also stresses the continuity of traditional forms and goals of protest in Burma.

A third position, stemming primarily from Arthur Stinchcombe (1961) and later developed by Jeffery Paige (1975), examines in more detail than the others the particular types of cultivating classes that exist under capitalism. Paige argues that the relative dependence of both cultivators and noncultivators on land versus either capital or wages is the most important determinant of the forms of rural unrest (see Skocpol's essay for a fuller summary). His work reminds us that we must distinguish among different types of cultivators with different types of relations to other classes.

Paige himself, however, does not offer a sufficiently dynamic approach to the peasantry, and the essays that follow criticize him repeatedly. Adas points out that much rural upheaval in Burma stemmed from a mixture of tenants, smallholders, and landless laborers—thus combining categories that Paige assumes are separate. Skocpol criticizes him at length, concluding that we need a more social-structural approach. Tilly's criticism of theories of peasant rebellion that ignore labor and capital to concentrate only on land is also relevant to Paige's argument.

The essays in this book illustrate a more flexible approach to the effects of capitalism than any of the three we have just characterized. Capitalism may or may not destroy the peasantry as a class; Roseberry shows that capitalism may even create a peasant class. Similarly, Paige's static economic categories do not reflect the complexities of actual unrest in the countryside. Roseberry discusses this most explicitly, insisting that we analyze both the forces that promote class homogeneity and the forces that promote class heterogeneity. This approach combines well with Skocpol's distinction between peasant rebels who mobilize themselves (as in China or Vietnam) and those who are mobilized from above (as in Russia, France, or Mexico). We cannot understand such differences in the forms of unrest simply by realizing that capitalism dislocates peasants, or that it changes class structures. We must look, in addition, at how these general processes affect particular groups in particular historical conditions.

States and Politics

The third major theme running through this book is the role of state formation and operation in creating the conditions for rural violence. States have administrative control over national territories, and they try to monopolize the coercive machinery; these factors guarantee the importance of the state to any social movement. Furthermore, states, like any large-scale organizations, require large and continuous inputs of resources to support state development and operation. They achieve this primarily through taxation, and taxation provides one of the most frequent grievances of rural rebels.

Most of the essays here argue with the tradition that identifies state interests with dominant class interests. Skocpol (1979) makes the strongest case for treating the state as a potentially autonomous institution:

> State organizations necessarily compete to some extent with the dominant class(es) in appropriating resources from the economy and society.... As Marxists have pointed out, states usually do function to preserve existing economic and class structures, for that is the smoothest way to enforce order. Nevertheless, the state has its own distinct interests vis-à-vis subordinate classes. Although both the state and dominant classes share a broad interest in keeping the subordinate classes in place in society and at work in the existing economy, the state's own fundamental interest in maintaining sheer physical order and political peace may lead it—especially in periods of crisis—to enforce concessions to subordinate class demands (Skocpol, 1979: 30).

Tilly's essay also emphasizes that the state can be an independent actor. The rebellions of seventeenth-century France were not the direct result of capitalism (which developed late in France), nor were they the result of running large estates using land-poor labor (which was rare). Instead, Tilly attributes the numerous uprisings of that period to state construction of an army. The new army and its wars meant vastly increased state demands for money, food and other resources, and these new demands led directly to rural violence. Wasserstrom provides a similar example, where increasing church and state demands on Indian resources helped create the conditions for revolt.

Roseberry's essay provides an interesting contrast to Tilly and Wasserstrom. Creation of a strong state in Venezuela also required increased resources. Yet the new demands of the state created little unrest because they were met through the new oil industry, not through the agricultural sector. State construction can lead to varying results in the countryside, depending on how it is carried out.

The essays in this book thus do not reduce the state to a reflection of the economy; they seek instead a more interactive understanding of the mutual effect of state and economy. Several papers, for example, show the influence of the state on the development of capitalism. Tilly discusses how the French state fostered commerce in order to tax it. Migdal emphasizes how capitalism relied on the state to give access to raw materials and to guarantee production of needed commodities in the Third World. The state could also move at cross-purposes to capitalism, for example, when the state preempted railroads to move troops instead of commodities. Roseberry makes the strongest claims, warning against treating the state and capitalism as independent entities.

Conclusion

The essays in this volume suggest some initial distinctions which may lead to varying forms of unrest. First, some groups act in response to violations of a moral economy that provides them with a repertoire of appropriate forms of unrest. Food riots, social banditry, and the rest of this repertoire are not contests for state power; they are responses to local conditions. Other violence was a contest for state power, as for example when Burmese nobles or Venezuelan caudillos attempted to assert total local autonomy. Under the influence of the changes in capitalism and the state that we have just discussed, moral economy protests may develop new means of organization and new grievances, which lead it to vie for control of the state. The essays here begin to clarify these issues, but we clearly need more studies of the various forms of action short of rebellion: riots, banditry, religious conversion, emigration, and simple stoicism may be reactions to the same influences which lead to rebellion.

The essays that follow agree that the general processes of capitalist expansion and state operation affect both the repertoire of unrest which moral economists discuss, and the organizational possibilities for various types of action. They are concerned with understanding each case in its historical, social, and economic context, and they generally criticize studies that concentrate on a single class (e.g., peasants) or a single cause (e.g., income source) in order to facilitate broad generalizations. Mintz mentions in his afterword that use of accepted categories of analysis is often usefully followed by critical reexamination which questions the established categories to look anew at process. The essays here are a beginning of this reexamination of historical process in the light of social scientific theory.

2. Routine Conflicts and Peasant Rebellions in Seventeenth-Century France

Charles Tilly

Bumpkins Against Taxes

> Au Bolonnois, ces jours passez,
> Pluzieurs Paysans ramassez,
> Grands mangeurs de choux et de raves,
> Faizoient les mutins et les braves,
> Etans plus de cinq mil cinq cens,
> La plus-part hors de leur bon sens. . . .

Thus read a trio of couplets in Jean Loret's doggerel newspaper, *La Muze historique*, for 15 July 1662:

> Around Boulogne these last few days
> Many peasants formed a crowd.
> Great chompers of cabbage and turnips,
> They posed as brave rebels—
> Five thousand five hundred strong,
> And most of them out of their senses.

The verses continued:

> But M. D'Elbeuf, the noble prince,
> Governor of the province,
> Scattered them easily
> With a few royal troops
> And settled for their flight;
> Thus, by a sensible decision,
> Avoiding a lot of killing
> And preserving women and girls
> From the ravages of the mercenaries. . . .

In those years of the 1660s, Jean Loret had plenty of chances to versify about rebellious peasants. After Louis XIV assumed personal power at Mazarin's death in 1661, he sought at the same time to extend France's military conquests abroad and to lay down a net of control over his own roisterous land. It took Louis and his agents well over a decade to contain the French rural population's inclination to respond to grievances through large revolts. Even then, the proscribed Protestant countrymen of southeastern France repeatedly resisted royal control, and held troops at bay, well into the following century. The French peasantry of the seventeenth century certainly had the will to rebel.

The particular rebellion on which Jean Loret lavished his art has come to be known as the Lustucru War, most likely by analogy with a comic clod of the time, Lustucru. The War of the Bumpkins, we might call it. It was one of the three or four largest rural revolts of the decade. Like the others, it began with the royal effort to impose new taxes. The long war with Spain had ended, with France the gainer, at the Treaty of the Pyrenees in 1659. But it was still necessary to pay for that war, and prepare for the next. In 1661 Louis XIV and his minister Colbert sought to raise some of the missing revenue by rescinding the fiscal privileges of a number of provinces, and imposing taxes which were already being collected elsewhere.

One of those provinces was the Boulonnais, the region surrounding Boulogne-sur-Mer, the channel port near France's northeastern frontier. In return for its maintenance of a defense force, the province had long enjoyed exemption from major taxes. During the last phases of the Spanish war, however, the crown had imposed an ostensibly temporary special tax for the support of a local regiment, and the provincial estates had reluctantly agreed to make an annual payment for that purpose "until the war was over." Although the province did, indeed, enjoy two or three years of fiscal respite after the treaty of 1659, by May of 1661 the royal council was decreeing a new, special but permanent annual tax of 30,000 livres. The estates' protests drifted away in the wind. By early spring 1662, the hapless new intendant Colbert de St. Pouenges (a cousin of the royal minister) was attempting to have the tax collected, in the face of total noncooperation from the provincial authorities: the seneschal and the lieutenant general, he reported on 2 April, refused to help: "Neither of them was willing to aid me, wanting as much as possible to block the King from levying any taxes in the Boulonnais, since they claim that would be contrary to the region's rights." (*BN MC*, 108). Resistance grew. At the end of June, the military governor, the Duke of Elbeuf, was writing that:

> I have just received a letter from M. Esmale, the agent accompanying the troops in the Boulonnais, a region which is offering insolent resistance to the King's orders and wishes. He tells me that he has informed the Court. But while I am waiting for news from you I have sent one of my guards to him, and if he needs reinforcements I will send all my boys while the Estates are in session. This looks serious to me. Let me inform M. Le Tellier that the Bishop of Boulogne is stirring up all this disorder (*BN MC*, 109, Elbeuf to Colbert, 28 June 1662).

Although he was wrong to blame the bishop, Elbeuf was right to take the movement seriously. Mainly peasant bands formed in dozens of villages, and consolidated into a makeshift army; eventually they found a nominal leader in a petty local lord, the sieur du Clivet. The irregular forces attacked tax-collectors, beat back the few troops who were on the scene, pillaged, then—at word that regular troops were on the way—retreated to the castle of Hucqueliers.

Le Tellier, the great builder of the French army, did not hesitate: he dispatched soldiers, a military commander, and a hanging judge. On 11 July, a few rounds of cannon fire sufficed to bring the irregulars in the castle to their knees. The military commander immediately hanged four of them as a warning. Then began the mopping-up and the summary trials.

Colbert saw possible advantages in the quickly checked rebellion. As he wrote to the special judge, Machault, on 11 July:

> I should tell you in secret that this revolt might well give the King the idea of abolishing all the province's privileges, which are very extensive. These people are exempt from the land-tax, excise taxes, salt-taxes, and generally all sorts of imposts. That is why it is important that you carry on your investigation and your trials in such a way as to make it clear that the King would have every right to act on that thought (Clément, 1861–69, 4: 2).

Despite strenuous efforts, Machault failed to discover any telling evidence of direct involvement on the part of the rich and powerful; with the exception of one small landlord, all those charged were commoners, and mainly peasants. Eventually all the prisoners who were condemned to death had their sentences commuted, except for three leaders—two of whom were broken on the wheel, and the third hanged. More than 360 of the rebels went off in chains to serve their lives as galley slaves. That was the end of the Lustucru, and the characteristic closing of a seventeenth-century peasant rebellion.

But was Lustucru really a "Peasant Rebellion"?

On reflection, the armed resistance to taxation in the Boulonnais raises some difficult questions. What happened to the vaunted localism of peasants, to their supposed obsession with land, to their famous lack of involvement in politics? How could these poor people have aligned themselves with magnates such as the seneschal, the lieutenant general, and the bishop? How could a peasant rebellion form around a question of taxes?

Since Lustucru really happened, and since the royal imposition of new taxes did play a part in its appearance, these questions suggest that common conceptions of peasant rebellion are faulty. To put it more prudently and precisely: standard ideas framed by twentieth-century students of peasant rebellion do not apply very well to the seventeenth-century experience of the Boulonnais. In fact, they do not apply very well to any of the major rebellions in which the peasants of seventeenth-century France took part.

To clarify what is at issue, let us look at a well known analysis by Hamza Alavi. Alavi seeks to uncover the objective bases of peasant involvement in revolution. To do so, he follows the experiences of poor and middle peasants in Russia, China, and India. "Rich peasants" he regards as something of a misnomer for capitalist farmers. As such, according to Alavi, they are unlikely candidates for peasant revolution; they belong to the enemy. Middle peasants, in contrast, "are initially the

most militant element of the peasantry, and they can be a powerful ally of the proletarian movement in the countryside, especially in generating the initial impetus of
the peasant revolution" (Alavi, 1965: 275). They have a strong enough material
base to stand up against the great landlords. But that very material base, translated
into class position, makes them unreliable carriers of revolution in the long run: it
gives them a stake in the existing system of property.

The poor peasants, despite their vulnerability to pressure from landlords, therefore carry the ultimate hope of peasant revolution. Here is the core of Alavi's
argument:

> When in extreme and exceptional cases the exploitation and oppression is car-
> ried beyond the point of human endurance, the peasant may even be goaded into
> killing his master for his departure from the paternalistic norm. But he is still
> unable to rise, by himself, against the system itself. His dependence on the master
> thus undergoes a paternalistic mystification and he identifies himself with his
> master. But this backwardness of the peasantry, rooted as it is in objective depen-
> dence, is only a relative and not an absolute condition. In a revolutionary situa-
> tion, when anti-landlord and anti-rich-peasant sentiment is built up by, say, the
> militancy of middle peasants, his morale is raised and he is more ready to re-
> spond to calls to action. His revolutionary energy is set in motion. When the
> objective pre-conditions are realized the poor peasant is a potentially revolution-
> ary force. But the inherent weakness in his situation renders him more open to
> intimidation and setbacks can easily demoralize him. He finally and irrevocably
> takes the road to revolution only when he is shown *in practice* that the power of
> his master can be irrevocably broken and the possibility of an alternative mode
> of existence becomes real to him (Alavi, 1965: 275).

Alavi's stimulating analysis of revolution deserves discussion for its own sake. In
two crucial regards, however, it holds to the conventional opinion. First, the word
"peasant" stretches to include all sorts of rural cultivators. Peasants, for Alavi, include far more than the classic type: land-controlling agricultural households that
produce most of what they consume, supply the bulk of their labor requirements
from the household itself, and yield a significant portion of their production to
others outside the household. They also include specialized cash-crop farmers,
sharecroppers, agricultural wage workers, and others. Second, the interests around
which they are likely to organize and act—if they organize and act at all—concern
control of land. Uncertain access to land and exploitation by others who control
land provide the incentive to revolt. The landlord is the enemy.

Gerrit Huizer's *Peasant Rebellion in Latin America* differs from Alavi's analysis
in emphasizing frustration, resentment, desires for vengeance, and other states of
mind. When it comes to the definition of peasant rebellion, nevertheless, the two
analyses coincide. Like Alavi, Huizer adopts a broad definition of the peasantry,
and centers his analysis on control of the land. After a review of many concrete
cases of agrarian conflict in Latin America, Huizer concludes:

On the whole it seems that the means used by the peasants were usually such that, with a minimum of extralegality, a maximum of concrete benefits of security could be achieved, mainly the possession of the land which they tilled. As soon as the peasants' demands were satisfied, and the land they worked was in their possession, in most cases they lost interest in the political movement as a whole. . . . It seems, however, that the landlords have so much fear of change that they take a stand which provokes the peasantry to use increasingly radical means. Thus the peasant movement became in some cases a revolutionary factor in the society as a whole, in spite of originally limited demands and the moderate attitude of the peasants. In those areas where the peasants took to radical forms of action, their civil violence occurred generally as a direct response to landlord intransigence and violence, and because no other ways were open to them (Huizer, 1973: 140–141).

Thus land and the behavior of landlords become the pivots of peasant rebellion. Even Henry Landsberger (1974), in his cautious, comprehensive, classificatory approach to "peasant movements," takes essentially the same line. Most writers on peasant rebellion have something like this in mind: land-poor cultivators band together and carry out sustained, large-scale violent attacks on people who control local land, or who are making visible efforts to gain control of the land.

If that is peasant rebellion, then seventeenth-century France had no significant peasant rebellions. Attacks on landlords were rare, and the theme of access to land was virtually absent from the major movements which did involve cultivators. The closest approach to a full-fledged peasant rebellion was the series of conflicts in Brittany called the Bonnets Rouges [Red Caps]. From April and, especially, from June to July 1675, the rural movement coupled with a series of urban struggles, which came to be known as the Révolte du Papier Timbré [Stamped-Paper Revolt]. Seeking to raise the funds for armed forces sufficient to battle Spain, Lorraine, and the German Empire, while intimidating Holland and England, Colbert had recently tried a whole array of fiscal expedients, including the imposition of stamped paper for official transactions, the establishment of a profitable tobacco monopoly, and an inspection tax on pewterware. In Brittany, quite plausibly, word spread that a salt tax was next. Unlike the innumerable other rebellions which reacted somehow to fiscal pressure, however, the revolt of the Bonnets Rouges involved rural attacks on landlords and tithe collectors. As two historians of the revolt sum things up:

> Under the influence of a collective feeling, and in holiday excitement, people went off to attack a variety of objects—castles, offices or monasteries—which gave immediate, concrete satisfaction to their anger, and sometimes ended in orgy. It was only later, when the movement had spread contagiously in the void left by the weakness of repressive forces, that some parishes tried to coordinate their efforts better, and even started conceiving a measure of strategy under the leadership of improvised chiefs (Garlan and Nières, 1975: 206).

At a certain point, some local rebels were able to impose treaties involving such matters as abolition of corvees and feudal rents, limitations on legal and ecclesiastical fees, freedom to hunt on noble land, and abolition of the tithe; abbots, lords, and bourgeois signed in fear of their lives. The rebel victories were brief, the repression terrible. Although the Bonnets Rouges did not seize the land, they did sound some of the standard themes of peasant rebellion, and did anticipate some of the issues which emerged as salient rural grievances during the Revolution, twelve decades later.

Yet the revolt of the Bonnets Rouges is marginal to the category of peasant rebellion as described by most twentieth-century analysts. And it stands out as an exception in seventeenth-century France. Why? If we take the structural approach adopted by Alavi, Huizer, and many others, we will stress how rarely seventeenth-century French landlords ran their estates as large farms, and how little cultivation involved the labor of land-poor cultivators on other people's large estates. To find the conditions for peasant rebellion in seventeenth-century Europe, following this line of thought, we would have to move out of France and into Spain, England, southern Italy or, preeminently, Russia and Eastern Europe. If, on the other hand, we take the expansion-of-capitalism approach adopted by Eric Wolf, Eric Hobsbawm, and many others, we will stress the tardiness of French landlords in adopting capitalist strategies for the use of their land. We will then call attention to the proliferation of land invasions, struggles over common use rights, and attacks on landlords during the eighteenth century as the landed classes did, indeed, take up the capitalist game. Either way, we arrive at a rationale for treating seventeenth-century France as a negative case.

War, Statemaking, Taxes, and Peasant Rebellion

If Lustucru, the Bonnets Rouges, and the host of other substantial rebellions of seventeenth-century France which heavily involved peasants do not fit the standard model, we have a right to suspect that the model is wrong—or at least too narrow. The effort to confront model with reality brings out three serious inadequacies in the model. The first is to overemphasize land, at the expense of other factors of production, such as labor. The second is to suppose that rebellion is a phenomenon sui generis, distinct in form and content from everyday struggles over interests. The third is to reason from the predominance of economic interests to the predominance of manifestly economic actors, especially landlords, as the targets of rebellion.

To the emphasis on land, the French seventeenth century replies that peasants often act collectively to save their labor power, their seed, their livestock, or the income from their crops. To the supposition that rebellion is sui generis, the French seventeenth century replies that the main differences between everyday struggles and great revolts do not lie in the form or content of the individual actions which make them up, but in the connections and coalitions among local groups. To the reasoning from economic interests to manifestly economic actors, the French seventeenth century replies that anyone who ignores the role of national states in precipitating peasant rebellion will misunderstand a good deal of agrarian history.

The analysis that follows makes these three points rather indirectly. Instead of reviewing the great rebellions of the seventeenth century, I examine the relationships between a variety of smaller-scale conflicts and the processes by which the French statemakers of that century increased their power. That means concentrating on the effects of war. My discussion sketches the impact of warmaking, and preparations for warmaking, on the dominant forms of contention in seventeenth-century France. The analysis not only neglects peasant rebellion, but also treats the peasantry as but one of several classes affected by the French state's monumental effort to build a war machine. In compensation, it draws attention to a phenomenon that students of peasant movements have neglected unduly: the strong impact of the effort to gather the resources for warmaking on the interests of ordinary people, including peasants.

Once brought out into the open, the strong impact of war on peasants is not hard to understand. It is not just that seventeenth-century armies ravaged the countryside on their way to besiege the cities. Far more important, in the long run, is the fact that the bulk of the resources required for the waging of war were somehow embedded in the land. Directly or indirectly, the men, animals, food, clothing, shelter, and money committed to armies came largely from the countryside. The great majority of the seventeenth-century French population lived in villages. Although a substantial number of industrial workers, landless agricultural laborers, rentiers, priests, notaries, and other nonpeasants plied their trades in the countryside, a comfortable majority of the villagers were probably peasants in a narrow sense of the word: members of households that drew their main subsistence from working land over which they exercised substantial control, and for which they supplied the bulk of the essential labor. When authorities stepped up the demand for men, animals, food, clothing, shelter, and money in order to build armies, somehow the wherewithal had to come mainly from peasant stocks. Some peasants yielded some of the warmaking requisites willingly, just so long as they fetched a good price. But on the whole the following things were true of those requisites: (1) They were not so fully commercialized and readily supplied as to allow the everyday operation of prices within the market to make them available to warmaking authorities. (2) Those that were under the control of peasant households were entirely committed either to the maintenance of the household or to the household's outside obligations. (3) Both households and communities invested those commitments and obligations with moral and legal value. (4) The conditions under which landlords, priests, local officials and other authorities could claim resources which were under the control of peasant households were matters of incessant bargaining and bickering, but were also stringently limited by contracts, codes and local customs. (5) Authorities who sought to increase their claims on those resources were competing with others who had claims on the same resources, and threatening the ability of the households involved to meet their obligations. (6) At the extreme, demands for resources threatened the survival of the households involved. (7) Ordinarily, demands for cash required households to forego crucial purchases, to sell more or different resources than they were accustomed to doing, to borrow money, and/or to default on their cash obligations.

The impressment of a peasant's son for military service deprived a household of essential labor, and perhaps of a needed marriage exchange. The commandeering of an ox reduced the household's ability to plow. The collection of heavy taxes in money drove households into the market, and sometimes into the liquidation of their land, cattle, or equipment. Existing claims on all these resources were matters of right and obligation. We begin to understand that expanded warmaking could tear at the vital interests of peasant households and communities. We begin to understand that conflicts of interest could easily align peasants against national authorities as well as against landlords. We begin to understand why local power-holders, with their own claims on peasant resources threatened, sometimes sided with rebellious peasants. And we begin to understand why seventeenth-century rebellions could begin with disputes over something so amoral as taxation, and yet proceed with the passionate advancement of legal and moral claims.

All these are justifications for taking a circuitous path to the analysis of conflicts involving the seventeenth-century French peasantry. In this paper, I propose to trace out the connections between the French crown's strenuous and growing involvement in war and a series of standard forms of conflict. Peasants will appear and reappear in the analysis, if only because they constituted such an important share of the total French population. But the analysis itself centers on the confrontation between French statemakers and the whole population from which they were striving to wrest the means of warmaking. This analysis will, I think, clear the way to a consideration of forms of rebellion which do not fit twentieth-century conceptions of peasant revolts, but nevertheless involve peasants vitally.

The Burden of Government

In his *Traité de l'économie politique*, published in 1615, Antoine Montchrestien had reflected on the cost of war. "It is impossible," he mused, "to make war without arms, to support men without pay, to pay them without tribute, to collect tribute without trade. Thus the exercise of trade, which makes up a large part of political action, has always been pursued by those people who flourished on glory and power, and these days more diligently than ever by those who seek strength and growth" (Montchrestien, 1889: 142). That money was the sinew of war was by then an old saw. But making the full line of connections—from war to troops to wages to taxes to cash and thence back to trade—was a special concern of seventeenth-century statemakers. Montchrestien and his contemporaries did not draw the obvious conclusion: that cutting off trade would be desirable, since it would prevent war. The French conventional wisdom, instead, settled into something like these propositions: (1) In order to make war, the government had to raise taxes. (2) To make raising taxes easier, the government should promote taxable commerce. A large part of what we call mercantilism flowed from these simple premises. Both the raising of taxes and the promotion of commerce, however, attacked some people's established rights and interests; they therefore produced determined resistance. Thus began a century of army-building, tax-gathering, war-making, rebellion, and repression.

Much of the royal domestic program consisted, in effect, of undoing the Edict of Nantes. The 1598 edict had pacified the chief internal rivals of the crown—the Catholic and Protestant lords who had established nearly independent fiefdoms during the turmoil of the religious wars—while Henry IV was bargaining for peace with a still-strong Spain. The edict had granted the Huguenots the right to gather, to practice their faith, and even to arm and to govern in a number of cities of France's south and west. It also absolved those officials who had raised troops, arms, taxes, and supplies in the name of one or another of the rebel authorities (Wolfe, 1972: 225–230). The Edict of Nantes had frozen in place the structure of forces which prevailed in the France of 1598, while restoring the ultimate powers—including the powers to raise troops, arms, taxes and supplies—to the crown. For a century, subsequent kings and ministers sought to unfreeze the structure, to dissolve the autonomous centers of organized power that remained within the kingdom.

Protestants were by no means the only threat. Great Catholic lords also caused trouble. As seen from the top down, seventeenth-century France was a complex of patron-client chains. Every petty lord had his *gens*, the retainers and dependents who owed their livelihood to his "good will," to his "protection" against their "enemies" (to use three of the time's key words). Some of the gens were always armed men who could swagger in public on the lord's behalf, avenge the injuries he received, and protect him from his own enemies. The country's great magnates played the same games on a larger scale. They maintained huge clienteles, including their own private armies. They held France's regional military governorships, and kept order with a combination of royal troops and their own. Indeed, at the century's start France did not really have a national army, in the later sense of the word. In time of war or rebellion the king fielded his own personal troops. He also recruited the armies of the great lords whom he could both trust and persuade to take the field on his behalf.

Great Catholic lords, including such members of the royal family as the successive princes of Condé, tried repeatedly to strengthen their holds on different pieces of the kingdom. In the summer of 1605, according to a contemporary account:

> The King, being in Paris, was warned by a certain captain Belin that in Limousin, Perigord, Quercy and other surrounding provinces many gentlemen were getting together to rebuild the foundations of rebellion that the late Marshal Biron had laid down. Their pretext was the usual one: to reduce the people's burdens and to improve the administration of justice. In any case, their plan was simply to fish in troubled waters and, while appearing to serve the public good, to fatten themselves on the ruin of the poor people (*Mercure*, 1: 12).

The king gave Belin a 1,200-livre reward, then saddled up for Limoges. There he convoked the nobles and hunted down the rebels. Five were decapitated in person, six more in effigy. That stilled the threat of noble rebellion in the southwest for a few years.

Limousin's abortive rebellion never reached the stage of popular insurrection. Only half of the potent seventeenth-century combination—noble conspiracy plus popular response to royal exactions—came into play. But in those insurrectionary years the gentlemen conspirators had a reasonable hope that if they kept fishing in their region's troubled waters, people's grievances against royal taxes, troops, laws, and officials would sooner or later coalesce into disciplined resistance. More than anything else, the popular contention of the seventeenth century swirled around the efforts of ordinary people to preserve or advance their interests in the face of a determined royal drive to build up the power of the state.

The France of 1598 was, then, a weakened country—weakened by internal strife, but also weakened by threats from outside. Three remarkable kings spent the next century reshaping the French state into an incomparable force within its own borders and a powerful presence in the world as a whole. Henry IV, Louis XIII, and Louis XIV made the transition from a leaky, creaking, wind-rocked vessel which alternated among mutiny, piracy, and open war, which had either too many hands on the wheel or practically no steering at all. They ended their work with a formidable, tight man-of-war.

The Prevalence of War

Remember how much war the seventeenth century brought. To take only the major foreign conflicts in which French kings engaged, there were:

1635–1659: war with Spain, ending with the Treaty of the Pyrenees
1636–1648: war with the Empire, ending with the Treaty of Westphalia
    1664: expedition against the Turks at St. Gothard
1667–1668: War of Devolution, ending with the Treaty of Aachen
1672–1679: Dutch War, ending with the Treaty of Nimwegen
1688–1697: War of the League of Augsburg, ending with the Peace of Ryswick

If we included the minor flurries, the list would grow much longer. In 1627 and 1628, for example, the British temporarily occupied the Ile de Ré, on France's Atlantic coast, and sent a fleet to support besieged La Rochelle. In 1629 and 1630, while still battling domestic rebels, Louis XIII was sending expeditionary forces into Italy. In 1634, the king occupied and annexed Lorraine. War had long been one of the normal affairs of the state. Now it was becoming the normal state of affairs.

One of the century's ironies is that the two great guides in the early decades of French militarization were men of the Church. Richelieu and Mazarin fashioned a policy of conquest. That policy required in its turn the recruiting, organizing, supplying, and paying of unprecedented armies. The effort brought to prominence such financiers as Fouquet, adept at the creation of *combinazioni* or the quick mobilization of credit. It called forth such administrative virtuosos as Le Tellier, indefatigable in the creation of armies and the large support structures essential to keep them going. The consequence was the reshaping of the state into an administrative apparatus oriented increasingly toward the production and use of armed force.

If the dominant process in seventeenth-century France was the militarization of the state, its paradoxical effect was a civilianization of royal administration. Increasingly the representatives of the crown with whom local people had to deal were full-time civilian administrators. The administrators owed their livelihood not to the protection of a great regional lord but to the support of a minister in Paris and to the sustenance of the royal apparatus as a whole.

That happened in two ways. The first was the long drive to disarm every place, person, and group that was not under reliable royal control; the drive took the forms of bans on duelling, dismantling of fortresses, and dissolutions of civic militias as well as the incorporation of private forces into the royal army. The second was the expansion of the numbers and powers of royal officials—most obviously, the intendants and their staffs—who were charged with raising the revenues, controlling the supplies, and securing the day-to-day compliance necessary to build and maintain a big military establishment. Over the century as a whole, the crown was successful in both regards: it greatly reduced the possibility of armed resistance within the kingdom, and it enormously increased the resources available for royal warmaking. Yet success came at the price of bloody rebellion, of brutal repression, and of expedients and compromises which committed the crown to an immense, exigent clientele of creditors and officials. These statemaking processes stimulated the large-scale contention of the seventeenth century.

War and the Means of Warmaking

Seventeenth-century statemakers who wished to expand their ability to make war had to do more than organize armies. They had to find the essential resources: men, food, horses, wagons, weapons, and the money to buy them. Although military commanders seized the materiel of war directly when they could, French armies acquired the bulk of their resources through purchase—not always from willing sellers, as we shall see, but purchase nonetheless. The government raised money for its military purchases in a variety of ways: through forced loans, through the sale of offices and privileges, through fines and confiscations, and through a number of other devices to which officials applied their ingenuity increasingly as the seventeenth century wore on. But in the long run one form of taxation or another provided the great majority of the essential funds. The seventeenth century brought spectacular increases in the French fiscal burden, and the prime reason for those increases was the rising cost of waging war.

Figure 2.1 combines some information concerning France's seventeenth-century tax burden with some speculative computations concerning the impact of the tax burden. The curve for "gross tax revenue" traces Clamageran's estimates of total receipts from regular taxes in selected years. Since the latter half of the seventeenth century became the great age of raising money by irregular expedients—borrowing, selling privileges, forcing contributions, and so on—the curve probably underestimates the increase for later years. For lack of a figure near the Fronde (1648–1652), it also disguises the fact that taxes kept rising into the 1640s. Nevertheless, the graph displays the fierce increase in total taxation after the 1620s, the lull of the 1650s, and the new acceleration after Louis XIV's accession to full personal power in 1661.

The other curves suggest two different ways of thinking about the impact of rising taxes. Expressing taxes as the equivalent of a volume of wheat has the clearest meaning for those who actually had wheat to sell: large farmers, landlords, tithe collectors and some rentiers. For them, the general trend of taxes ran upward, the year-to-year fluctuations in the impact of taxes were dramatic, yet years of high prices could actually be advantageous—just so long as their supplies did not decline as rapidly as the price rose. When it came to people who had to buy wheat or bread to survive, however, the years of high prices were never advantageous; in those years, their tax obligations rarely declined, but much higher proportions of their incomes went into the purchase of food. Unless the government remitted taxes, those became terrible years of squeeze for consumers. Our curves for hours of work disguise that year-to-year variation, since they depend on conventional wage figures for an idealized semiskilled worker. Nevertheless, they indicate that a) on the average and over the long run, the rising national tax burden could easily have tripled the amount of work time that the taxpaying French household devoted to the government and b) the reign of Louis XIII (effectively 1615–1643) brought a spectacular rise in the per capita tax burden.

The surges in taxation corresponded closely to quickening preparations for war. In the later 1620s and 1630s they register the effects of Richelieu's shift from the quelling of domestic enemies to the challenging of Spain and the Empire. In the 1640s, Mazarin continued to drive for more taxes and bigger armies. In the later 1660s and the 1670s rising taxes signal the start of Louis XIV's great wars. Taxes were, indeed, the sinews of war.

Given the formidable growth of state power and the decreasing support of popular movements by great lords, the persistence of rebellion and resistance through the seventeenth century offers a measure of the interests at stake. The fact that ordinary people should have the urge to resist is itself perfectly understandable. Warmaking and statemaking proceeded at their expense. Warmaking and statemaking placed demands on land, labor, capital, and commodities which were already committed: grain earmarked for the local poor or next year's seed, manpower required for a farm's operation, savings promised for a dowry. The commitments were not merely fond hopes or pious intentions, but matters of right and obligation; not to meet those commitments, or to impede their fulfillment, was to violate established rights of real people.

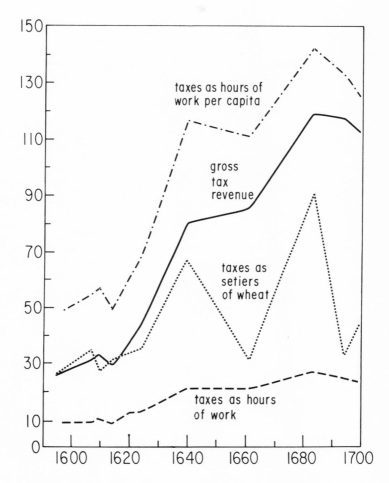

Figure 2.1. France's gross tax revenues, 1567–1699: raw figures and equivalents

Key: **taxes as hours of work per capita:** taxes as hours of work, divided by an interpolated figure for total population, as estimated by Reinhard, Armengaud, and Dupâquier (1968); the figure shown estimates hours of work per year per capita. **gross tax revenue:** *impôts: revenue brut:* expressed in millions of livres, as reported by Clamageran (1867–1876). **taxes as setiers of wheat:** gross tax revenue expressed as the number of units of 100,000 setiers of first-quality wheat it would buy at Paris prices, as reported by Baulant (1968); divide by 10 to get millions of setiers of wheat. **taxes as hours of work:** gross tax revenue expressed as a multiple of the hourly wage of a semiskilled provincial worker (*manoeuvre de province*), as reported by Fourastié (1969: 44–49); the wage figure is an interpolation of a very general estimate, and therefore tells nothing about year-to-year fluctuations; shown in hundreds of millions of work hours.

In addition to local and customary rights, raising new resources often meant abridging or rescinding privileges the state itself had ratified. Exemptions from taxation, rights to name local officers, established means of consent, and bargaining over financial support to the crown—all gave way as statemakers made the claims of the government supplant the rights of individuals and communities. Popular indignation was the greater because of a standard seventeenth-century tactic: offering privileges and profits to the tax farmer, venal officeholder, or other entrepreneur who was prepared to give the crown ready cash in exchange for the opportunity to draw future revenues from the local population. It was bad enough that a rich man should profit from other people's sacrifices. But when his privilege actually increased the local burden (as regularly happened when a newly-exempted official stopped paying his share of the local tax quota, or when the office in question involved new or expanded fees), the rich man's neighbors were commonly outraged.

Not that the middlemen were the only objects of popular resistance. Ordinary people often felt the military effort quite directly. Soldiers and officials wrested from them the wherewithal of war: food, lodging, draft animals, unwilling recruits. People hid those resources when they could, and defended them against seizure when they dared. On the whole, however, the military got what they wanted.

The direct seizure of the means of war from the people lagged a distant second behind the extraction of money. In a relatively uncommercialized economy, demands for cash contributions were often more painful than demands for goods. They required people either to dig into the small stores of coin they had saved for great occasions or to market goods and labor they would ordinarily have used at home. The less commercialized the local economy, the more difficult the marketing. Taxes, forced loans, the sale of offices, and other means of raising money for the state and its armies all multiplied during the seventeenth century. Directly or indirectly, all of them forced poor people to convert short resources into cash, and then to surrender that cash to the state.

When rights were at issue and the force available to the state was not overwhelming, ordinary people resisted the new exactions as best they could. Tax rebellions, attacks on new officeholders, and similar forms of resistance filled the seventeenth century. Nevertheless, French statemakers managed to override rights and resistance alike; they succeeded in increasing enormously the financial burden borne by the population as a whole.

How did the statemakers succeed? By dividing their opposition, by using force, by routinizing the collection of revenues, by multiplying the specialists devoted to the extraction of those revenues, and by expanding the number of people and groups having a financial interest in the state's survival. The definitive settling of the intendants in the provinces, accomplished after the Fronde had forced the temporary withdrawal of the intendants from the land, was no doubt the single most important stratagem. The intendants of Richelieu and Mazarin were still serving, by and large, as temporary troubleshooters; after the Fronde, however, Mazarin, and then Colbert, expanded and regularized their service. The intendants supervised the collection of revenues, applied coercion when necessary and feasible, kept watch over the local expenditure of state funds, and stayed alert for new opportunities to tax, to sell offices, to preempt local revenues and to borrow, borrow, and then borrow again.

Although the borrowing eventually increased the share of state revenues which went to service debts, it also expanded the number of people who had financial interests in the state's survival. It created a large class of officials who served their own advantage by helping to pay the expenses of the state. The tax farmer advanced cash to the crown in return for the right to collect taxes at a profit. The purchaser of a new office made a substantial payment to the crown in return for an annuity, for the right to collect the office's revenues and, frequently, for some form of exemption from taxation. A guild paid over a sum of money—usually borrowed from its members and from local financiers—and received a royal guarantee of its monopolies and privileges. That became the standard royal expedient: in order to raise current revenue, the king's agents found someone with capital, then induced or coerced him to advance money now in return for a claim on future income and the assurance of governmental support in collecting that income. Such a routine deflected the indignation of ordinary people from the statemakers to the tax farmers, officeholders, and other profiteers who fattened themselves at the people's expense.

In order to reduce the political risks of this fiscal strategy, however, the crown had to tame and supplant its internal rivals. Otherwise, each new round of popular resistance would provide an opportunity for some set of magnates to offer themselves as champions of the people's rights. In parallel with its external warmaking and its internal fund-raising, the crown undertook a massive effort of co-optation, neutralization, and suppression. After the failure of the Fronde, the great princes and their clienteles fell into line. With some important exceptions, the major blocks of Protestant autonomy gave way under the continuous grinding and blasting of Louis XIII and Louis XIV. The parlements, the other "sovereign courts," the provincial estates, the guilds, and municipalities all finally lost significant shares of their ability to resist royal demands and to ally themselves with ordinary people against the crown, as the intendants used a combination of force, fragmentation, and fiscal advantage to bring them into acquiescence. Thus the intendants and other royal officials became freer to use their growing repressive power when ordinary people dared to resist governmental demands directly. These changes had predictable effects on the character of popular contention: a decline in the involvement of major powerholders in big rebellions, an increasing focus of popular resistance on the exactions of tax farmers and officeholders, a decreasing readiness of royal officials to negotiate with groups protesting the violations of their rights.

Routines of Seventeenth-Century Contention

Anyone who digs into the materials of seventeenth-century contention notices some recurrent traits. There is the importance of the exactions of troops, the demand for taxes, and (toward the end of the century) the failure of local officials to apply proper controls over the food supply in times of shortage, all as objects of contention. There are the standard sequences in which existing communities respond to violations of their rights and privileges by assembling, electing leaders and spokesmen, issuing protests and demands, and then (if not satisfied) retaliating against their enemies. There is the frequent collective appeal to an influential patron, a powerful judicial authority or, preferably, both at once. There is the use of established festivals and ceremonies as occasions for communicating approbation or reprobation of public officials. There is the mutual modeling of crowds and officials, with the crowd sometimes borrowing the execution in effigy from the official treatment of absentee felons, and with officials sometimes borrowing the selection of a single spokesperson to state the crowd's grievances. There are the elementary forms of collective action: the sacking of private houses and tollgates; the expulsion of miscreants, including tax collectors, from the community; the deliberate blocking of the gates or the streets; the seizure of a disputed commodity, especially grain or salt; the staging of ritual mockery; much more rarely, the mustering of armed men for an attack. There are the sustained rebellions that resulted from coalitions between aggrieved groups of ordinary people and disaffected or ambitious clusters of the privileged. There is the visible rupture of this pattern of coalition with the royal victory over the Fronde and the Frondeurs. All these features appear clearly in the seventeenth-century contention of Anjou, Flanders, Burgundy, Languedoc, and the Ile de France.

Some patterns of contention were common to many regions because the same sweeping processes were affecting the interests of ordinary people throughout France. Warfare, statemaking, and the development of capitalism dominated the seventeenth-century patterns. Through the century as a whole, war and preparation for war set the master rhythms.

War is a form of contention that creates new forms of contention. We might order the different ways in which ordinary seventeenth-century people acted together by increasing distance of the various sorts of action from the fact of war itself. Thinking only of those occasions on which people actually gathered together and made claims of one kind or another, we might prepare this rough scale:

1. Direct participation of civilians in combats among armies.
2. Battles between regular armies and armed civilians.
3. Resistance to direct exactions by the military: impressment and the commandeering of meat, wine, bread, sex, and lodging.
4. Resistance to official efforts to raise the means of support for armies: especially taxation, but also the commandeering of corvee labor, wagons, horses, food, and housing.
5. Resistance to efforts, official or unofficial, to divert resources—especially food—to armies.
6. Conflicts emerging as by-products of the presence of troops: soldier-civilian brawls, clashes over military smuggling and poaching.

7. Resistance to attempts of officeholders to exact new or larger returns from their privileges and official duties.
8. Local and private vengeance against violators of everyday morality, including established rules for the marketing of commodities.
9. Conflicts between followers of different religious creeds.

These were the major occasions for contention on anything larger than an entirely local scale. Most items on the list had a substantial, recurrent connection to war-making. Resistance to officeholders' exactions, for instance, linked to war: the offices in question were commonly created, or preempted by the crown, as part of the drive to raise military revenues. Indeed, of the larger recurrent forms of contention in seventeenth-century France, only the struggles between Protestants and Catholics, and some of the conflicts over food, were not obviously related to the creation, maintenance, and maneuvering of armed forces. Even food riots and religious conflicts, as we shall see later, had their links to war.

Civilians in Combat. Let us go down the list. If we include the forces of princes and great lords, then all five of our regions experienced army-to-army combat at various points of the seventeenth century. In battles of French forces against French forces (I speak of their current allegiances, not of their origins; the forces of the Prince of Condé and other grandees were often Swiss, Croatian or something else), Languedoc was no doubt the champion. As early as 1621, the Duc de Rohan, using the Cevennes as his base, had Protestant armies in the field against the royal forces in Languedoc. The king's pacification of Languedoc in 1622 was only the first of many royal pacifications in that rebellious province. In Languedoc peace came unstuck easily.

When it came to clashes between French forces and those of foreign crowns, on the other hand, Burgundy and Flanders had much more experience of seventeenth-century war than did Anjou, Languedoc, or the Ile de France. Especially Flanders. After all, most of the region began the century as Spanish territory, and came to the French crown only as the result of conquest, reconquest, and military occupation. In 1641, we find the civic militia of Lille (still a Spanish possession) turning back the French troops who arrived to besiege the city (Liagre, 1934: 113). In the village of Rumégies, near Valenciennes,

> In 1660–1661, it was necessary to whitewash the church, "the walls having been blackened and damaged by the wars, since both inhabitants and soldiers fired their guns there, on account of which the whole church—roof, glass and paint—was run down." In 1667, toward Ascension (16 May), the curé, fearing the approach of the armies of Louis XIV, sent the church's ornaments and his parish register to Tournai. Part of the population evacuated the village. The rest stayed there and, in order to protect themselves, fortified the cemetery and dug a trench all round: a means of defense by which the inhabitants had profited "many times during previous wars" (Platelle, 1964: 504).

Rumegies' people did, in fact, take a reluctant part in war after war. They dug their trench of 1667, however, on the eve of a crucial change. With the end of the War of Devolution in 1668, the province of Tournai, and thus Rumegies, became French territory. From that point on, the marauders and occupiers most to be feared were the village's former masters, the Spaniards. The nearby frontier did not become relatively secure until the Peace of Utrecht, forty-five years later.

Armies vs. Civilians. Some of Rumegies' wartime ravaging may have resulted from battles between regular army units and armed civilians. Most of the time, however, armies chased each other through the village; the villagers defended themselves and their property as best they could. For a clearer case of civilian involvement in combat, we may turn to Burgundy in April 1637. That was the second year of France's direct participation in what later became known as the Thirty Years War. According to the *Gazette* (see abbreviations list in References):

> The peasants from around St. Jean de Lône, Auxonne and Bellegarde, to avenge themselves for the burning that the garrisons of Autrey and Grey were doing along our frontier, recruited a few soldiers to lead them and, on the 21st and 22nd of this month, threw themselves into three big enemy villages, including 400-household Joux. After they had killed everything, they reduced the villages to ashes. They are determined to deal with all the other villages in the same manner, so long as the enemy gives them the example (*Gazette*, 1637: 263).

Even this tale, to be sure, does not show us armed civilians confronting enemy units. Except when householders defended themselves against invading troops, such encounters were rare or nonexistent.

Resistance to Military Exactions. The most frequent struggles between soldiers and civilians did not arise from military actions, as such, but from the attempts of military men to seize precious resources from the civilian population. The agents of Louis XIII and Louis XIV created armies much faster than they created the means to satisfy those armies' wants. They nationalized the troops at the same time, transforming them from private retainers of great lords to public employees of the national state. But only toward the end of Louis XIV's reign did something like a national structure for supplying, paying, and containing the growing armed forces begin to take shape. By that time, the armies were in almost perpetual motion—at least for the two-thirds of the year that the roads could support the artillery the seventeenth-century military had started to drag around with them.

The consequences were predictable. Pay was usually late and sometimes never. Commanders often lagged a year or more in paying their troops. Food supplies frequently ran low. Military housing was practically nil. Few young men willingly became soldiers; impressment and emptying of jails became common devices for recruitment. Mutiny and desertion were rarely far away. Commanders who wanted to keep their regiments intact threatened and coerced when they could, but only survived by promising or arranging rewards. They regularly promised booty from a captured city . . . sometimes at the same moment as they took ransoms paid by the city fathers in order to avoid pillage. In theory, they were supposed to pay the populace for the labor, food, lodging, and supplies their armies required. In practice, they tolerated or even encouraged their soldiers' commandeering of food, drink, lodging, services, goods, money, and sexual experience. Many generals and supply officers had it both ways: they pocketed the royal funds and let the troops forage. Only when the rapine threatened to call forth popular rebellion, or retaliation from military superiors and royal officials, did the commanders commonly call a halt.

The soldiers involved in snatching what they could get from the population thought the commandeered sex, meat, wine, bread, labor, and lodging was no more than their due. The victims, however, disagreed. Hence an unending series of local conflicts in which demanding soldiers faced indignant householders. One of the rare successes of the householders occurred during the 1632 rebellion of the Duke of Montmorency in Languedoc:

> The sieur d'Alsaux, who during the rebellion seized a place called Montreal, between Carcassonne and Toulouse, had gone out to forage; the residents chased out the soldiers he left behind; at his return, they locked the gates and fired many musket rounds at him. Peasants of the region around Carcassonne knocked a number of his foreign troops off their mounts; and the 25th of September, when some of his Croats were passing close to a little village four leagues from the same city, the villagers went out and killed twenty-six of them, took all their baggage and treated the rest of them in such a way that they are not likely to feel the urge to return to France for a long time (*Gazette*, 3 October 1632: 410–411).

More often, however, the reports which survive from the century run like the laconic note of March 1678 concerning the intendant of Burgundy: "M. Bouchu took care of the complaints he received from many localities about violence committed on the occasion of, and under the pretext of, the recruitment of soldiers" (*A N*, G[7] 156). On the whole, "taking care" of such complaints meant hushing them up.

Resistance to Official Efforts. The intendants faced a sharper dilemma when it came to popular resistance stimulated by official efforts to raise the means of support for armies. When ordinary people fought back against the demands of troops, troops were there to put them down. But when ordinary people rose against civilian demands for taxes, corvees and supplies to support the army, the troops were often far away. The *maréchaussée* (the state police, one might say loosely) could deal with an individual or two but was usually helpless in the grip of a determined crowd. The *gardes des gabelles* (salt tax guards) and other armed forces in the service of the tax farmers acquired plenty of experience in small-scale crowd control, but likewise fell apart in the face of substantial risings; in any case, they generally confined their work to the particular purposes of the tax farmers. Municipal constables and militias, where they existed, tended to limit their efforts to their home bases, and to be unreliable allies for royal officials.

What was the intendant, faced with determined opposition, to do? He could try to face it down with moral authority, threats, and the thin armed force at his disposal. Or he could call on the military governors of provinces and regional capitals to send in royal troops to back him up; in that case, he not only confessed visibly to his inability to keep order on his own, but also acquired obligations to a significant rival within his own bailiwick. Small wonder, then, that the intendants' reports to Paris often swing between utter silence about a resistance movement and detailed reports, appeals for aid, and cries of vengeance. Small wonder that the intendants often explained popular resistance as the result of plots, treason, and barbarism.

The very process of establishing French administration after conquest was full of the risk of resistance. In the part of Hainaut recently taken from the Spanish, the intendant Faultrier was busy organizing the collection of taxes in 1686. That meant negotiation and coercion, village by village. The village of Estrun, near Cambrai, had put up more than the usual resistance to the elimination of the privileges it had enjoyed under Spanish dominion. In the process of bringing the villagers into line, the intendant had exiled their curé and put one of their notables in jail. By January of 1686, however, Faultrier thought his decisive action and his threats of more jailings had sufficiently intimidated the people of Estrun (*AN*, G⁷ 286, letter of 3 January 1686 [see abbreviations list in References]). The tax farmer and the villagers came to a compromise agreement. Yet on 7 July the intendant was writing that:

> they have since presented a declaration to the farmer's agent which I find very insolent; when people are only insolent on paper, it isn't hard for an intendant to punish them. I therefore didn't give their action much weight, but they went much farther. For when the agent tried to collect his taxes, they sounded the tocsin on him and the men he had brought to help him. The women began with stones, and their husbands finished with clubs. All of them said that until they saw an order signed by the King they would not pay, and that my signature was not enough for a matter that important.

At that point, predictably, the intendant requested the dispatch of troops to enforce the royal prerogative (*AN*, G⁷ 286). Over the seventeenth century as a whole, some version of this encounter between tax collectors and citizens was no doubt the most frequent occasion for concerted resistance to royal authority. That was true not only in Hainaut and Flanders, but also in the rest of France.

Resistance to the Diversion of Resources. As the century wore on, nevertheless, the locus of conflict moved increasingly to the market. The reasons for the shift are simple and strong: royal officials turned increasingly toward the promotion of taxable trade and the use of the market to supply the needs of their growing state. The army, in particular, moved away from direct commandeering of its supplies (with the exception of troops: the free labor market never supplied enough soldiers), and relied increasingly on *munitionnaires* to buy up its necessaries. The new strategy regularized governmental demands somewhat, and thus probably made them easier to sustain. It diverted indignation from intendants to merchants and *muni-tionnaires*. But it created new grievances.

The grievances, for the most part, concerned food. The other resources (always excepting manpower) required by the armed forces were sufficiently commercialized and abundant for the market to supply them without great stress most of the time. The simultaneous growth of cities, bureaucracies, armies, and a landless proletariat, on the other hand, placed great strains on the French food supply. In times of shortages and high prices, the new strategy led intendants, merchants, and local officials to challenge the established ways of assuring that local communities would have prior access to their means of survival. It challenged the inventories, exclusive marketing, price controls, and other tight regulations which had long been standard responses to shortages. Ordinary people responded to the challenge by substituting themselves for the delinquent authorities. They seized, inventoried, marketed, controlled, and punished on their own. The closer the authorities were to the local population, the more they hesitated either to suspend the old controls or to punish those who attempted to reinstate them. Hence many "disorders" involving the "complicity" of local authorities.

The conflicts rose to national visibility with the subsistence crises of 1693–94, 1698–99 and 1709–10. The feeding of the army was only one of several factors in these crises, but it was an important one. Probably more so than it had to be, because the army contractors had lush opportunities to speculate with the stocks they bought up by royal authority. In Buxy, Burgundy, at the beginning of September 1693, local people seized the grain which had been purchased by Burgundy's *munitionnaire*. The intendant accused a judge, a royal prosecutor, and other officials of having encouraged the populace. Yet the root cause of the conflict, he reported, was that the *munitionnaire* was stockpiling old grains and buying new ones. "Allow me to tell you," he wrote to the *contrôleur general*, "that we've never before seen in Burgundy what we're seeing now. It isn't usual for a munitionnaire to spend the whole year here getting his supplies, and even less so to employ a thousand persons who commit all sorts of irregularities in their purchases and in commandeering transportation, without our being quite able to speak openly about it for fear of slowing up the supply service" (*A N*, G⁷ 158, letter of 13 September 1693; cf. G⁷ 1630). In short, the intendant had a strong presumption that the contractor in question was not only exceeding his authority, but also profiteering in the grain trade.

Rarely was the impact of military procurement on conflicts over food supply so unmixed and visible; it is the market's genius to mix motives and diffuse responsibilities. In a more general way, nevertheless, the recurrent patterns of conflict reveal the sore points in the system. High prices, shortages, and hunger as such did not usually call up popular action; serious conflicts normally began with official inaction, with the withholding of stored food from the local market, with obvious profiteering and, especially, with the effort to remove sorely needed grain from the locality. The latter was the case, for example, at Vernon in 1699, when the citizens roughed up the merchants who came to the local market to buy grain for Paris

(Boislisle, 1874—1896; 1: 512). During that crisis, as well as those of 1693—94 and 1709—10, military demand was only one of several attractions drawing grain away from local consumption with the sanction of the state. In all five of our regions, the three crises brought out popular resistance to the diversion of food from local markets.

By-Products of the Military Presence. At one time or another, all five of our regions also produced conflicts which were essentially by-products of the presence of troops: soldier-civilian brawls, clashes over military smuggling or poaching, and the like. In the seventeenth century, whoever said soldier also said trouble. In times of open war, foraging and conflicts over booty made the trouble worse than ever. An incident on the Flemish frontier in 1693 gives the flavor. The Sieur de Beauregard, acting captain of the free company of the Governor of the city of Condé, was sent out on his own on 24 June; he had seventy men, and a warrant to bring back booty. His force met a loaded wagon on the road from Brussels to Mons. Etienne Gorant, the driver, showed a passport covering far fewer goods than his wagonload. Beauregard seized the wagon and the driver. He sent them off to Condé with twenty men and a sergeant. "But that sergeant," he reported, "was pursued by a military detachment from Mons which, being larger, took away the loaded wagon without listening to his objections. The violent manner of the chief of the Mons detachment made it clear that he was in league with the merchants. Your petitioner has been to Mons, but has been unable to obtain justice" (*AN*, G[7] 287, letter of 7 July 1693).

Military commanders remained ambivalent about the struggle for booty. It could distract soldiers from conquest or defense, and stir up the civilian population inconveniently. But in an age in which piracy, privateering, and regular naval warfare overlapped considerably, land forces did not make neat distinctions between legal and illegal acquisiton of property either. When the pay of soldiers was meager, irregular, and a tempting source of income for greedy commanders, military chiefs often found it expedient to let the troops supplement their pay with pillage.

Another tactic was to wink at smuggling. Now the civilian population did not necessarily suffer—if soldiers could bring salt or coffee into the region duty free, they could easily sell it at a profit below the official price. But the tax farmer, always sensitive to attacks on his pocketbook, felt the pinch at once. Thus on 8 January 1633, as so often before and after, the king issued an edict against military salt smuggling. Its preamble stated the remonstrance of Philippe Harnel, the general contractor for France's salt tax:

> That soldiers garrisoned for his Majesty's service in the kingdom's frontier cities smuggle salt publicly every day, & go about in bands of twenty, thirty, forty or fifty soldiers armed with muskets and other offensive weapons, recruiting civilian salt-smugglers & many others whom they lead and escort to the borders of foreign lands & lead them back to their hiding-places with their wagons, carts and horses loaded with said illegal salt . . .(*AHA*, A[1] 14).

Since those same soldiers were the chief force the crown had at its disposal for the tracking down of smugglers, royal edicts tended to be ignored, and salt farmers developed a strong interest in organizing their own paramilitary forces.

In the frontier areas of Burgundy, for example, both civilians and soldiers made money by bringing in contraband salt. An interesting cycle developed. Civilians who were agile enough to speed salt across the border were also attractive prospects for military service. If the salt-tax guards caught civilian smugglers with the goods, the tax farmer sought to have the smugglers convicted with fanfare and shipped off for long terms in the galleys, far from Burgundy. While they were being held in jail pending the royal ratification of their sentences, however, Burgundy's military commanders, as short of recruits as ever, frequently pled for the convicts to be given the choice between enlistment and the galleys. The military commanders often prevailed over the remonstrances of the tax farmers. The local army units then gained recruits who were of dubious reliability as men of war, but who certainly knew how to smuggle salt.

Resistance to Officeholders' Exactions. Our next step out from war concerns resistance to attempts of officeholders to exact new or larger returns from their privileges and official duties. Its connection with war is indirect but real; most of the new offices and privileges in question came into being as part of the crown's effort to raise more money for warmaking. In May 1691, the intendant of Languedoc announced a schedule of fees for the newly established administrators of public sales. (They were the *jurés-crieurs publics*, parallel to the registrars of burials whose establishment in Dijon about the same time caused a great deal of trouble.) Instead of merely collecting fees at public sales, the agent of the officeholders tried to set up a tollgate at the Entrance to Nîmes, and collect the fees on all goods entering the city. The intendant stopped him but neglected to forbid him to do the same thing elsewhere.

The persistent agent tried the same game in Toulouse. The clerks, "who come from the dregs of the common people," reported the intendant, "asked 10 sous at the city gate for each wagonload of wood that came in, and a certain sum for each basket of peas, salads and fruits." Several women beat up a clerk. The intendant decided to punish both the women and the agent. In the case of the women, he said, "it seems important to me to get people out of the habit of making justice for themselves in such cases." As for the agent, his offense was a "genuine swindle" which could not be tolerated in such difficult times (*A N*, G[7] 300, letter of 2 June 1691). Yet the intendant faced a dilemma: people bought the new offices for their financial return, and expected the government to guarantee the perquisites of office. If the offices were not attractive, they would not sell—and the government would lack the ready cash it needed for its incessant wars.

As a result, the intendants usually took the side of the officeholders. When the "young people" of Toulouse attacked the city's "clerk for marriage banns" in January 1698, and gave sword wounds to the clerk and his would-be rescuer, the same intendant of Languedoc despaired of getting action through the local courts. He proposed a royal prosecution "so that the people of Toulouse will understand that it is a major crime to attack and insult without reason those who are responsible for royal business" (*A N*, G[7] 303, letter of 5 January 1698). The business of venal office-holders readily became "royal business."

Vengeance Against Violators of Everyday Morality. The title is portentous, the contents are heterogeneous. Let us include here all those conflicts in which the rights and obligations at issue had a shadowy basis in law, but a strong grounding in popular belief. Some of the forms of contention examined under previous headings qualify here as well. The food riot is a notable example; one of the chief reasons for its rise at the end of the seventeenth century was, precisely, the declining legal support for the old system of local controls over food, in a time when popular beliefs in the priority of local needs continued strong. But there were others we have not yet encountered in descending the scale of proximity to war: the *rixe*, or local brawl, pitting two groups of artisans or the young men of neighboring communities against each other in a struggle over honor and precedence; popular retribution against an actor, an executioner or another public performer who failed to meet the public's standards; the charivari/serenade; the rescue of prisoners from their captors.

In the Dijon of 1625, for example, the executioner set up to decapitate Mlle. Gillet, who had been convicted of infanticide. When the nervous hangman failed to kill the young woman with two sword blows, his wife took her turn and likewise botched the job. At that, the spectators stoned the executioner and his wife (*AMD*, 1 116). In the Nîmes of 1645, the friends of imprisoned paper cutter Cabiac snatched him out of jail. One of the two rival intendants of Languedoc,[1] Baltazar, treated the jailbreak as a sedition. The other intendant, Bosquet, pooh-poohed his colleague's alarm: "At bottom, whether the son of Cabiac is guilty or innocent, we know that what's at issue is the revenge of a certain Cassague, collector of the paper-cutters' fees, on said Cabiac's family. In this case, justice is really serving to hide the guilty parties, and as a pretext for revenge of one side's private wrongs" (Liublinskaya, 1966: 133; letter of 1 May 1645). If it had not been for the irritating presence of his rival Baltazar, intendant Bosquet would probably have handled the affair on his own, without divulging the details to the *contrôleur-general* in Paris. Except when they grew too big for the local forces of order, these jailbreaks, brawls, feuds, charivaris, and similar events were contained and settled by the officials on the spot.

Religious Conflicts. That was not true, however, of most religious conflicts. The balance of power between Protestants and Catholics remained an affair of state throughout the seventeenth century. Whether the initiative for a conflict came from local religious groups or from actions of the government, royal officials had to pay close attention to its outcome.

Often, members of one religious group attacked individuals belonging to the other. In 1611, in Paris:

the Protestants went to bury a small child in their Trinity Cemetery, near the rue Saint-Denis; they went in the evening, but before sunset. Two members of the watch officially led the procession. A vinegar-maker's helper began to throw stones at them, and was imitated by his master and by several others. One of the watchmen was wounded. The *lieutenant criminel* of the Châtelet had them arrested and, on the first of July, the helper was whipped outside of Trinity Cemetery. But on Sunday the 21st of August, Protestants coming back from Charenton were insulted (Mousnier, 1978: 75; Charenton was the location of the one church the Protestants of Paris were then allowed).

In Paris, the Sunday trips of the Protestants to Charenton were frequent occasions for abuse from Catholics, and sometime occasions for violence. When the news of the death of the [Catholic] Duc de la Mayenne at the 1621 siege of [Protestant] Montauban arrived in the city, crowds attacked the carriages of the Protestants, battled with the watchmen stationed at the St. Antoine Gate to protect them, and rushed out to burn down the church. Later "the other clerics and common people who had busied themselves with setting the fire and burning the Temple and drinking 8 or 10 kegs of wine that were in the concierge's cellar, and eating the provisions, after making a flag of a white sheet, came back to Paris through the St. Antoine Gate, 400 strong, shouting *Vive le Roy*" (*Mercure*, 1621: 854). That "Vive le Roy" should remind us of the connection between popular hostility and official policy. In this instance the sanctioning of armed guards to prevent an attack on the Protestants makes it dubious that royal officials directly instigated the violence. Yet from early in his reign Louis XIII sought to cow the Protestants, to demilitarize them, and to circumscribe their activities.

Local groups of Protestants and Catholics also fought intermittently. Where the Protestants were relatively strong, as in Nîmes, Montpellier and much of urban Languedoc, we find a series of struggles over control of public offices. In the mainly Protestant city of Pamiers, the Consuls sought to exclude all Catholics from the Consulate. In March 1623, the Catholics demanded representation; they persuaded the Parlement to decree equal representation of the two religious groups. The Consuls closed the city gates to the Parlement's emissary, and then to the emissary who carried confirmation of the decree by the king's council. Only when the king sent troops did the Consuls give in (*Mercure*, 1624: 381–385). Later the same year, the emboldened Catholics complained against the stay in the planned destruction of local Protestant churches, and demanded a division of the city keys—two per gate—between Protestants and Catholics. By that time, Pamiers actually had three competing factions: the Protestants, the Catholics who had stayed in town during the Protestant/Catholic wars of Languedoc in the previous years, and the bishop, priests, and (presumably wealthier) Catholics who had fled Pamiers when the wars came too close (*Mercure*, 1624: 871-877). In 1625, the Pamiers Protestants joined those of a number of other cities of Languedoc in a new rebellion against the crown. In this case, as in most, the national conflict and the local one reinforced each other. Louis XIV continued the effort. Then, in the 1680s, he began the drive to rid France entirely of the Huguenot scourge.

The striving of kings and intendants to weaken the Protestants produced the largest-scale religious conflicts of the seventeenth century. We have already seen Louis XIII marching out his armies to besiege La Rochelle, Montauban, Nîmes and other Protestant strongholds. Those campaigns against the Protestants were veritable civil wars. They continued through the 1620s. By the time France reentered the world of international war after 1630, the autonomous military strength of the Protestants had cracked. Even during the Fronde Protestants did not appear as a distinct national bloc, or as a major threat to the monarchy.

From the 1630s to the 1680s, the government ground away at the so-called Reformed Religion intermittently and without drama. Local battles continued. A case in point occurred in the Protestant stronghold of le Mas-d'Azil, near Pamiers, in October 1671: a day laborer who had recently converted to Catholicism

> was attacked in the middle of the fair by François and David Cave, former Huguenots . . . and many others armed with swords and staves. They wounded him so badly that he was left for dead . . . . The Brother Prior and the Benedictine monk who happened by complained to them . . . and they shouted against [the day-laborer], *Get the Rebel, Get the Rebel, for taking a religion that is worthless to its supporters* and other words forbidden by law on pain of death (Wemyss, 1961: 36, quoting interrogations of witnesses).

But no sustained, large-scale conflict developed at le Mas-d'Azil or elsewhere until after 1680, when the government of Louis XIV began the campaign to squeeze out the Protestants. In le Mas-d'Azil the campaign started in earnest with the decree of 29 April 1680, which forbade Protestants to sit on a city council they had previously divided equally with the Catholic minority. In 1685, after the revocation of the Edict of Nantes, local people went through the mechanics of conversion to Catholicism en masse and without open resistance. A trickle of emigration began. The new converts of le Mas-d'Azil survived by stratagem and subterfuge. The first serious confrontations there began after the Peace of Ryswick (1697), when word spread that royal policy toward Protestantism was going to relax. The local Protestants—not nearly so converted as it had seemed—began holding secret assemblies, or church services, in the countryside. Royal prosecution drove Protestant religious practice back underground very quickly that time. But whenever the royal authorities and the Catholic clergy turned their attention elsewhere, the hidden organization of the local Protestants started to reemerge (Wemyss, 1961: 96-107).

Elsewhere in Languedoc the struggle between Protestants and royal authorities turned to open rebellion, to civil war. The cockpits were the mountain regions of the Vivarais and the Cevennes. As early as 1653 "a band of seven or eight thousand Protestants tried to establish by force of arms the right to hold services at Vals in the Vivarais" (Bonney, 1978: 398). That became the standard pattern: Protestants assembled to hold forbidden services in the countryside, royal officials sent troops to stop them, the "assemblies in the desert" evolved into armed rebellions. By August 1683, the intendant of Languedoc was reporting that the Huguenots of the Vivarais are continuing not only to preach in forbidden places, but also to prepare for war. It is true that they have no leaders, not even some moderately-qualified gentry, as a result of the effort we have made to take away all those who came into view or whom we suspected. Nonetheless those who remain have set up a sort of encampment. They are organized by companies under designated leaders. They have taken various castles, have dug in, have ammunition and weapons and, in a word, show every sign of intending to resist the king's troops, aroused as they are by ministers who preach nothing but sedition and rebellion (*AN*, G⁷ 296).

Within two years, the intendant was sending armies into the hills to search out and exterminate the Protestant guerrilla forces, who eventually became known as the Camisards. The outlawing of Protestantism in 1685 started a brutal civil war. With many interruptions and changes of fortune, the War of the Camisards lasted twenty-five years.

War and Rural Contention in Counterpoint

Our scale of distance from war, it seems, bends back on itself. As we move away from the forms of contention that occurred as the most immediate consequences of royal warmaking, we approach another sort of war. No contradiction there: early in the seventeenth century the distinction between international war and domestic rebellion barely existed. Later, every new surge of warmaking stimulated popular rebellion, and every popular rebellion posed a threat to the state's ability to wage war. In a state so strongly oriented to war, it could hardly have gone otherwise.

A new wave of conflicts followed each acceleration of French warmaking. The seventeenth century's most impressive examples were the dozen years of war against Spain and the Empire beginning in the late 1630s and ending in the Fronde, and the 1690s, dominated by the War of the League of Augsburg. In 1643, for example, the child-king Louis XIV and his mother Anne of Austria took power after the death of Louis XIII, Cardinal Mazarin took over the prime ministry from the recently decreased Richelieu, the resourceful Particelli d'Emery became finance minister, the war with the Habsburgs continued, and the new team squeezed the country for revenues as never before. Conflicts and rebellions multiplied. Here is a partial list of 1643's larger affairs:

1. Multiple armed rebellions against the *taille* in Guyenne and Rouergue.
2. An uprising against the *taille* in Alençon.
3. Armed rebellions against the *taille* in Tours and its region.
4. Multiple local revolts against the *taille* in Gascony.
5. Armed resistance to the collection of the *taille* in villages around Clermont.
6. Attacks on tax collectors in the Elections of Conches and Bernay.
7. "Seditious" crowds complaining about the lack of cheap bread in Bordeaux.
8. Attacks on tax collectors in Caen, Bayeux, Vire, Mortagne and elsewhere in Normandy.

9. Insurrections in Tours and vicinity, beginning with the mobbing of wine-tax collectors.
10. Rebellious assemblies of notables in Saintonge and Angoumois.

In Anjou, 1643 brought an unauthorized assembly of Angers' parishes against the military-inspired *subsistances*. In Languedoc, the people of Valence chased out the tax collectors with the declaration that the Parlement of Toulouse had forbidden the payment of the *taille*, while in Toulouse itself a crowd killed a tax collector. At the edge of the Ile de France, an assembly of "five or six hundred peasants" attacked the company of soldiers sent to enforce the collection of taxes. Most of these conflicts centered on the royal effort to raise money for the war.

A full analysis of seventeenth-century rebellion would include a presentation of the century's major risings: the several rebellions of the Croquants (southwestern France, 1636 and after), the Nu-Pieds (Normandy, 1639), the Tardanizats (Guyenne, 1655–1656), the Sabotiers (Sologne, 1658), the Lustucru rebellion (Boulonnais, 1662), the revolt of Audijos (Gascony, 1663), that of Roure (Vivarais, 1670), the Bonnets Rouges (also known as the Torrében: Brittany, 1675) and the Camisards (from 1685 onward). Many others could easily find their way onto the list. All of these risings involved significant numbers of peasants, or at least of rural people. Their frequency, and the relative unimportance of land and landlords as direct objects of peasant contention within them, require some rethinking of peasant rebellion. The universal orientation of these rebellions to agents of the state, and their nearly universal inception with reactions to the efforts of authorities to assemble the means of warmaking, underscore the impact of statemaking on the interests of peasants. Not that landlords and capitalists had no impact on the fate of the peasantry; that was to come, with a vengeance. But in the seventeenth century the dominant influences driving French peasants into revolt were the efforts of authorities to seize peasant labor, commodities, and capital. Those efforts violated peasant rights, jeopardized the interests of other parties in peasant production, and threatened the ability of the peasants to survive as peasants. Behind those incessant efforts lay the attempt of the national government to build a giant warmaking machine.

From the perspective of peasant rebellion in general, did the peasants of seventeenth-century France behave oddly? At the start of this essay, I pretended as much. After a review of the evidence, the impression remains: those peasants took part in rebellions, but their rebellions did not conform to widely held sociological models of peasant rebellion. Perhaps, however, we should blame the models rather than the peasants. To the extent that models of peasant rebellion concentrate on struggles between peasants and landlords for control of the land, they neglect crucial features of the situations of seventeenth-century French peasants, and of peasants in most times and places: a) the delicate, risky balance they have typically worked out with *all* factors of production—labor, land, and capital—and not just the land; b) the presence of multiple claimants—kinsmen, heirs, other community members, religious officials, merchants, and various governmental authorities, as well as landlords—to all factors of production; c) the tendency of increased pressure from any of the claimants to threaten the interests of the other claimants, to incite peasant resistance and, where successful, to force a reallocation of wealth, income, and social commitments—for example, by requiring the increased marketing of crops previously relied upon for subsistence; d) the fact that, in predominantly peasant countries, the bulk of the alienable resources are embedded in peasant enterprises, and therefore that any large effort to increase governmental resources in such countries almost inevitably attacks peasant interests, and the interests of others who have claims on peasant enterprises.

Where peasant communities have a measure of solidarity and some means of collective defense, where new or increased claims clearly violate publicly known agreements or principles, where some visible person or group that is close at hand stands to gain by the new demands on the peasants, and where effective coalition partners are available to the peasants, collective resistance becomes likely. When that resistance is sustained, and involves organized attacks on the enemy, we have peasant rebellion. In a mainly peasant world, both statemaking and the expansion of capitalism promote most of these conditions at one moment or another. When the conditions combine, the resulting rebellion need not lock peasants and landlords in a struggle for control of land. It will sometimes produce a coalition of landlords and peasants against state officials, or capitalists, or both at once. Thus the experience of seventeenth-century French peasants moves from being a troubling exception to serving as a standard instance of rural rebellion.

Acknowledgements

This is a revised version of chapter five in Charles Tilly, *As Sociology Meets History* (New York: Academic Press, 1981). I am grateful to Academic Press for permission to reprint the material taken from that chapter. The National Science Foundation supported the research reported in the paper. My thanks to Nels Christianson, Mary Jo Peer, and Danièle Rodamer for research assistance, to Cecilia Brown and Joan Skowronski for help with bibliography, and to Rose Siri and Debby Snovak for aid in producing the paper.

3. Indian Uprisings under Spanish Colonialism: Southern Mexico in 1712

Robert Wasserstrom

Although the subject of peasant rebellions has received much scholarly attention in recent years, Indian uprisings in colonial Spanish America have by and large escaped the notice of specialists in Europe and the United States. The reasons for this oversight are not hard to find: for one thing, documents on such movements are generally scattered among a number of different archives on two or more continents; for another thing, our vision of the events at hand must be gleaned from trial records and official reports which frequently present a highly distorted picture of what may or may not have actually taken place. Consider, for example, the case of Tupac Amaru II, who in 1780 organized a revolt against Spanish administration in highland Peru which precipitated a crisis in the entire edifice of imperial rule. Despite the fact that this revolt preceded by more than fifty years such well-known affairs as the Sepoy rebellion in British India, it has only now become the subject of full-scale study and examination (Flores Galindo, 1976; Golte, 1980). Much the same situation has prevailed among scholars of colonial Mexico, where in 1712 a sizable group of Maya Indians, rejecting the authority of both crown and mitre, established their own kingdom and created their own native church. What drove these men and women to rebel, what prompted them to question a social order which had already survived for almost two full centuries, must surely modify our understanding both of peasant movements in general and of colonialism itself.

In the following pages, I shall examine the origins of one such movement, the so-called Tzeltal rebellion, which took place in the central highlands of Chiapas (then part of Guatemala, subsequently annexed to Mexico). Like native people elsewhere in Spanish America, Indians in Chiapas had suffered the twin catastrophes of conquest and demographic collapse, had converted to Christianity long before English settlers arrived at Jamestown, and had slowly rebuilt their devastated communities under the watchful eyes of both Dominican friars and royal functionaries. By 1620, they had grown accustomed to an economic system which reduced their livelihoods to the barest minimum—and sometimes to less than that. At the same time, they had accepted the ever-increasing burden of ecclesiastical taxes, fees, and other gratuities. Within these narrow limits, they had elaborated their own "moral economy," a vision of communal salvation derived primarily from their Christian faith and their collective traditions. Throughout the seventeenth century, as provincial officials and local priests raised their demands for native labor, they drew heavily upon this vision to sustain and console them. In fact, I would suggest, it was only after 1690, when religious authorities recklessly embarked upon a full-scale effort to undermine native religious belief, that existence for Indians in central Chiapas became intolerable. And predictably, the reaction to such meddling took the form of a holy crusade. Not economic exploitation alone, but rather the destruction of their way of life itself prompted these people to reject colonial rule and to try their hand at a desperate throw of the dice.

Money-Lenders in the Temple: Spanish Rule in Chiapas

Almost two centuries after Spanish conquistadores first arrived in Chiapas (1524), a young Tzeltal girl—inspired, she claimed, by the Holy Virgin—informed her followers in the remote highland town of Cancuc that both God and the king had died. The time had come, she declared, for *naturales* in the province to rise up against their Spanish overlords, to avenge their past sufferings and reestablish true religion. Within a week, word had spread to native pueblos as far away as Zinacantan, Simojovel and San Bartolomé. According to the *alcalde mayor* (governor) of Tabasco (which borders Chiapas to the north), for example, a band of Indians "showing signs of rebelliousness" arrived three days later in the Chol town of Tila to take possession of the community's religious ornaments. Then, he continued, these men—who appeared to be acting as public heralds—stated their message: "it was God's will that [the Virgin] should come only for His native children to free them from the Spaniards and the ministers of the Church, and that the Angels would plant and tend their *milpas*, and that the sun and the moon had given signs that the King of Spain was dead, and that they must choose another" (López Sánchez, 1960, 2: 714).

In order to understand these events, which took place between early August and mid-December 1712, when the revolt was crushed by Spanish troops from Guatemala and Tabasco, we must consider carefully the transformation which, since 1590, colonial society had undergone. Surely the greed and rapaciousness of Spanish authorities, as important as such elements may have been, had not by themselves brought highland Indians to the brink of despair. Nor can it be said, as Herbert Klein maintains, that such "rude exploitation" coincided with "a temporary relaxation of provincial government control" (Klein, 1970: 153). Between 1685 and 1790, Spanish authority increased steadily and without relaxation, in spite of royal efforts to limit and contain it. Not diminished but unbearable authority— corrupt, self-serving, and ultimately lawless—it was that prompted the Indians to rebel. Then, too, like most indigenous uprisings in America, the 1712 movement did not represent an isolated case of seditiousness or discontent. On the contrary, it was preceded by similar events elsewhere in the region. In 1660, native people in Tehuantepec revolted against the provincial authorities of Oaxaca; within a few weeks, Indians throughout that jurisdiction had risen in arms (López Sánchez, 1960: 704). Thirty-three years later, in Tuxtla, Zoque people, disgusted by the onerous *repartimientos* to which they had been subjected, killed Chiapas' *alcalde mayor*, Manuel de Maisterra, in the public plaza (*AGCh*, 1955: 25–52).[1] Similarly, in 1722, ten years after the Cancuc uprising, still other Zoques (in Ocozocuautla) forced their overzealous parish priest to flee for his life (*AGCh*, 1955: 53–66). And finally, in 1761, Yucatecan Indians attempted once again to end Spanish rule in southern Mexico.

How did this situation, a situation of endemic revolt and internal ferment, come about? We know that after 1600 high provincial officials, taking advantage of the power and perquisites of their offices, embarked upon a course of self-enrichment. Although they were occasionally reprimanded by the *audiencia* (royal court) in Guatemala, their activities took place with the implicit (and often explicit) conniv- ance of the crown.[2] In 1714, the *audiencia* convicted Chiapas' *sargento mayor*, Pedro de Zabaleta, of having inflicted numerous "excesses, vexations and ill treat- ment" upon the area's Indians. But eight years later, the Council of Indies in Spain declared that "we hereby exonerate said Don Pedro de Zabaleta of all that he has been charged with . . . and that as a result . . . he shall recover all of his possessions, as well as the use and exercise of his office of *sargento mayor*" (López Sánchez, 1960: 690). Similarly, as Manuel Trens observes, Spanish authorities carefully filled native *ayuntamientos* (town councils) only with those Indians whose person- al fortunes might be confiscated to pay uncollected or overdue tribute. As a result, indigenous officials who could not meet such imposts often found themselves im- prisoned in Ciudad Real, to be released only when their families and friends had delivered a sizable bribe to the *justicias* of that city (Trens, 1957; Klein, 1970: 154). For much the same reasons, according to the Dominican chronicler Francisco Ximénez, provincial authorities early in 1712 reduced to a state of poverty and bitterness the native officials of Yajalón. And it was precisely these men, he added, who several months later led their townsmen against the royal forces that besieged Cancuc (Ximénez, 1929, 3: 261–2).

Like Chiapas' civil authorities, ecclesiastics such as Bishop Juan Bautista Alvarez de Toledo (1710–1713) dedicated themselves to the pursuit of wealth and riches. Ximénez himself has provided us with an extensive and highly disparaging portrait of Alvarez de Toledo, upon whom he places much of the blame for the 1712 revolt (Ximénez, 1929: 257). In the same vein, Klein has written that "it was especially the Church . . . which intensified the normal patterns of taxation and of tithing in the years before 1712, which set the stage for revolution" (Klein, 1970: 153–4). Long before Alvarez de Toledo arrived in Chiapas, however, the province's missionaries had ceased to regard their principal task—the preparation of Ameri- ca's natives for the Day of Judgement—with a sense of urgency and expectation. On the contrary, thanks to cheap Indian labor, ecclesiastical haciendas and cattle *estancias* had prospered and grown—surely sufficient reason for priestly *finqueros* to postpone the Second Coming. Furthermore, New World missionaries in general had begun to preach a message which taught that salvation could be earned only through loyal service to Spanish masters, through countless repetitions of the Rosary, through endless patience. "Have you paid your dues to the Church, as all faithful Christians must?" asked one Tzotzil confessional, echoing a theme com- mon to virtually all Catholic teaching at the time. And on the subject of redemption, this manual continued "where you go at the world's end depends upon whether you do penance . . . for this reason you must be good, you must pray . . . in front of Our Holy Mother St. Mary, so that she will play upon your hearts . . . so that you will leave off sinning" (Hidalgo, 1735).

If Alvarez de Toledo cannot be held responsible for this "change in the direction of the Church," it is equally senseless to blame him for the general rise in ecclesiastical taxes which occurred after 1630. On the contrary, between that year and 1720, the number of highland parishes increased from seven to twelve—an event which added four new Dominican parishes (complete with tithes and other charges) to the Tzeltal region alone. As for the manner in which these monks fulfilled their duties, at least one bishop, Marcos Bravo de la Serna y Manrique (who preceded Núñez de la Vega) asked the king for permission to suspend seven Dominican missionaries. His request was granted in 1680 (Ximénez, 1929, 2: 454). Curiously, too, despite the unabated decline in Chiapas' Indian population, episcopal emoluments increased. After dropping from 8000 pesos per year to 5000 pesos, income climbed in 1668 to the extraordinary level of 9000 pesos. Fortunately, Thomas Gage (an English monk who travelled throughout the area) has revealed to us how such an apparently mysterious phenomenon occurred:

> the Bishop's place . . . is worth at least eight thousand ducats [pesos] a year. . . . Most of this bishop's revenues consisteth in great offerings which he yearly receiveth from the great Indian towns, going out to them once a year to confirm their children. Confirmation is such a means to confirm and strengthen the Bishop's revenues, that none must be confirmed by him who offer not a fair white wax-candle, with a ribbon and at least four reals. I have seen the richer sort offer him a candle of at least six-pound weight with two yards of twelve-penny broad ribbon, and the candle stuck from the top to the bottom with single reals round about (Thompson, 1958: 142–3).

Ignoring Chiapas' declining birthrate, a series of entrepreneurial churchmen—among whom Alvarez de Toledo distinguished himself only for his shamelessness—inflated to confiscatory proportions these "voluntary" contributions. In 1649, for example, native *mayordomos* in San Andrés (a Tzotzil community which later joined the rebellion), unable to pay the cost of episcopal *visitas*, found themselves compelled to spend their own money and to borrow still more—just as civil authorities in highland towns often paid tribute with their own funds. After 1650, however, when poverty among indigenous people reached a point of desperation, church authorities recognized that new measures of tax collection were in order. In 1677, therefore, after attempting unsuccessfully to raise ecclesiastical fees, Bishop de la Serna decided to collect his revenues entirely in the form of alms—which in a highly detailed and widely circulated pastoral letter he regulated with great care. So confident was he in this method of taxation, in fact, that he inscribed the following message—extraordinary for its naiveté—in native parish registers: "In the General Ecclesiastical Visit undertaken by his Holiness Sr. Doctor Don Marcos

Bravo de la Serna, Bishop of this Diocese, in this town of [name of community], he did not wish to cause the Community, nor the Indians within it, any expense whatsoever on his account . . . seeing with his eyes how poor they are" (Bravo, 1679).

How did Indians react to this steady and unabated deterioration in their material circumstances, to this attack not only upon their way of life, but upon their very physical survival? Given their position in colonial society, the future itself promised little relief: each year, fewer children were born to replace those men who had died. Each year, too, there were more monks and priests to support, more festivals to celebrate. Indeed, in 1690, one royal *visitador*, José Descals, ordered Chiapas' clerics to limit these severely (López Sánchez, 1960: 684n). If God had survived so much sinfulness, so many excesses in His name, then surely He listened to Indian prayers with a special ear. One day, they knew, perhaps tomorrow, perhaps in a century's time, He would answer their lamentations, He would inflict His terrible justice upon that band of merry monks and centurion-like governors—at once so mindful and so heedless of their Roman heritage—who week by week grew fat upon the toil of red men. In preparation for that fateful day, they cleansed their souls, they danced "in His sight," and in the sight of His emissaries, the saints. They sang, they rejoiced. In the dark hours of early dawn, they called upon their ancestors, Indian saints whose great sufferings Christ had surely rewarded with eternal life. In the privacy of their houses, in the seclusion of the forests, on mountaintops, they offered their rum and candles—sacramental wine and wafer—to Our Lord, while in village churches, Spanish priests defiled these holy sacraments at the altar. "If you only knew how Christ suffers when you celebrate unworthily," wrote Bravo de la Serna to his priests in a rare moment of vision, "and the ways in which you crucify Him, how you would weep with pain and sorrow for your misdeeds! . . . For more priests will be damned at the altar than ever common rogues and highwaymen were hung on the gallows" (Bravo, 1679).

But of course, most priests did not weep with contrition, nor did they leave off their profligate exploitation of Indian lives and labor. On the contrary, they became increasingly alarmed at native ceremony and ritual, which, they claimed, was inspired by superstitions and charms. In this vein, the same Bravo de la Serna, in his pastoral regulations of 1677, ordered parish priests to "attend the dances which Indians celebrate . . . such as the dance of Bobat, when they jump and shiver as if from the cold, but at midday, and around their fires, through which they pass without the slightest injury" (Bravo, 1679). Such observances, he continued, were prohibited. Equally reprehensible, he declared, was the custom of "removing [effigies] from churches to private houses, in order to continue their festivals with the profanation of food, drink, dances and other operations, which are the effective causes of greater evils" (Bravo, 1679). Finally, ten years later, Núñez de la Vega expressed his horror that "a painting of the nahual Tzihuitzín or Poxlóm" had been discovered inside the church in Oxchuc. In order to remedy this situation, he not only conducted a public auto de fe there, but he also repeated and reaffirmed these prohibitions (Trens, 1957: 181).

Naturally, ecclesiastical attacks on native "superstition" were not limited to autos de fe and other demonstrations of civic piety. By 1670, the insouciance with which local clerics had treated their pastoral responsibilities had created far greater doctrinal problems, problems which called for direct and decisive action on the part of church authorities. Not content to celebrate their strange and distasteful rituals in the shadow of Spanish liturgical practices, Chiapas' natives had carried such activities directly into village churches and public ceremonial life.[3] In response, therefore, Bravo de la Serna initiated a full-scale campaign to deprive indigenous ministers of their offices and functions, a campaign which Núñez de la Vega continued until his own death in 1710. "It is hereby ordered," Bravo wrote, "that no priest may permit Flags and Penants to be unfurled as the Host and Chalice are raised, both because those who hold such Flags irreverently turn their backs upon the Divine Sacrament, and cover themselves, and because of the disturbance which they cause, diverting attention from the Sovereign Mystery" (Bravo, 1679).

In similar fashion, he declared, church ornaments and banners were not to be employed by "private persons or even legitimate officials of inferior grade, since no distinction is made regarding the position or rank of His Majesty's officers." And finally, he added, "out of reverence for the Divine Mysteries," only "consecrated priests, lords or nobles of Castile, Presidents and Judges and Governors, and *alcaldes mayores*" might remain seated in church during Mass. However corrupt and unworthy these officials might be, he seemed to say, however many of them might one day be "condemned at the altar" like common thieves on the gallows, Indian vassals must respect and revere them—even as they revered the sacraments themselves.

Behind these regulations, we vaguely perceive the outlines of an indigenous religious experience that sought both to understand and to transcend the tragedy of colonialism. Out of the spiritual disorder which sixteenth-century evangelization had inflicted upon Indian communities, native *alcaldes* and *regidores*, *mayordomos*, and *alféreces*, labored to create an orderly and coherent ceremonial life of their own. Individual salvation, far too precarious an idea in those years of early death and sudden flight, remained in their minds strictly a Spanish notion. Among Indians, men and women might attain salvation only if their villages outlived individual members, and if their descendents lit candles for them and wept over their graves on the Day of the Dead. As for their souls, these became absorbed into that collective soul commonly called "our ancestors." To the memory of these righteous forebears—who, as Christ had promised, would one day rise again and live for a thousand years—to their memory and to the village saints, native men and women addressed their prayers and their lamentations. For had not the Fathers told them that the souls of good Christians live forever at God's right hand? Inspired by the ideal of communal solidarity, then, they surrounded their pueblos with shrines and crosses. Beyond these limits, they seemed to say, lies a hostile world, a world of ladinos and untamed beasts, of human savagery and unbridled nature. Inside, they declared, our ancestors watch and wait, ready to speak on our behalf when the Day of Judgement arrives. And periodically, as if to reaffirm their faith, native *mayor-*

domos and *alféreces* carried their saints, flags flying, trumpets sounding, to the far corners of this animate landscape—there to recall the past and to contemplate their future deliverance.

In large measure, Chiapas' clerics themselves contributed unwittingly to such practices, or at least aided and abetted the movement toward native liturgical independence. Throughout Central America, as Murdo MacLeod has pointed out, monks and priests, avoiding the rigors of rural life, withdrew from Indian towns to urban convents and monasteries. Between 1637 and 1776, according to baptismal records from Zinacantán, this curate received only about seventeen pastoral visits each year. In their stead, Spanish priests often left a group of *fiscales de doctrina*, men who aided in the tasks of instructing other Indians in the faith. Chosen for their youth and intelligence, many of these *fiscales* succeeded in becoming both partially bilingual and semi-literate. Moreover, they possessed an elemental knowledge of Christian doctrine and ritual, knowledge of which most native people were customarily deprived. Indeed, during those long years when parish priests kept to their convents, many *fiscales* participated in liturgical functions which in theory at least were reserved only to consecrated ministers. Predictably, it was Bravo de la Serna again who tried—unsuccessfully it would seem—to put a stop to such practices.

"Ya no hay Dios ni Rey": Holy Mother and Native Children

> Arriving one day at my milpa, I found on a fallen branch this Lady who, calling to me, asked if I had a father and a mother, and when I answered no, she told me that she was a poor woman named Mary, who had come down from Heaven to give aid to the Indians, and she ordered me to inform my *Justicias* that they should build their chapel at the entrance to the town (Ximénez, 1929, 3: 266).

So testified a young girl to Fr. José Monroy when in March 1711, he interrogated her in the Tzotzil village of Santa Marta. Like other missionaries in that region, Fr. Monroy had become alarmed at the growing signs of restiveness which, three years earlier, had appeared among highland Indians. Early signs of discontent had caused only mild ripples to form on the apparent placid surface of Chiapas' spiritual waters, ripples which ecclesiastical authorities hoped would disappear as suddenly as they had arisen. Several years later, Fr. Monroy would recall that one day in 1708, "about two o'clock in the afternoon, some Indians from the town of Santo Domingo Zinacantán arrived . . . and told me that on the road to that town, inside a tree-trunk, an inspired hermit was exhorting them to repent and that inside that same tree-trunk one could make out a statue of the Holy Virgin which, having descended from Heaven, emitted beams of light giving them to believe that She had come to offer Her favor and aid" (Ximénez, 1929: 263). Upon being questioned by Bishop Núñez de la Vega, this hermit (who proved to be a mestizo from New Spain) explained simply that he was "a poor sinner whom they will not allow to love God." Judging him to be insane, the bishop locked him away in the Franciscan monastery in Ciudad Real.

For two years, the matter was forgotten. Then, in 1710, Church officials discovered this man once again in Zinacantán, where he had built a chapel. By that time, word of the hermit's activities had reached native people as far away as Totolapa. In order to visit him, these men and women, like other Indians throughout the area, ceased to attend Mass in their parish churches. After burning his chapel, therefore, Alvarez de Toledo banished him permanently from Chiapas. All to no avail: within a few months, the Virgin had reappeared in Santa Marta, where for half a year indigenous authorities hid her effigy from prying clerical eyes. And no sooner had Monroy confiscated this statue than he learned of still another and more impressive miracle: "The inhabitants of San Pedro Chenalhó . . . arrived to give notice that several days before they had constructed a chapel for Señor San Sebastián in their town because his image had sweated on two occasions . . . and that one Sunday they had seen beams of light coming from the Image of San Pedro and from his face, and that the next Sunday the same thing had occurred again" (Ximénez, 1929: 268).

Despite Monroy's sangfroid, however, native people refused to be calmed. In June, 1712, a group of Indians from the Tzeltal town of Cancuc informed Alvarez that a miraculous cross, descended from heaven, had appeared in their pueblo. To celebrate this event, Cancuc's civil authorities had constructed a chapel there, a chapel to which Indians from the surrounding communities daily brought offerings and gifts. The town's pastor, Fr. Simón de Lara, immediately went to investigate. To his horror, he found that such a chapel had indeed been built—not, as had been suspected, to honor the cross, but rather to house the image of yet another Virgin. Like the effigy in Santa Marta, he learned, this image had been discovered in the forest by a young Indian girl. His horror was increased when he learned that this girl, surrounded by a group of *mayordomos* and other religious officials, remained continuously in the Virgin's company and interpreted aloud her otherwise silent will. Infuriated by such sacrilege and nonsense, de Lara arrested the town's *alcaldes* and *regidores*, whom he sent to Ciudad Real. After replacing them with Indians he trusted, he attempted to destroy the chapel—an act which almost cost him his life. To make matters worse, at that moment the *regidores* whom he had jailed returned to Cancuc, where they declared "that they alone were true friars and that only those whom they elected were *alcaldes*. . . . [they ordered] that the chapel, which was the work of their hands be maintained, that other *pueblos* be called to defend it, and that the Indians count not their trials, for soon they would be relieved of all toil" (Ximénez, 1929: 270).

By July, 1712, when Alvarez de Toledo notified indigenous *ayuntamientos* of his impending visit, native people had already rejected the spiritual authority of Spanish clerics and had taken steps to free themselves from ecclesiastical domination. Although Alvarez did not create this situation he undoubtedly provided the catalyst—the spark which ignited the powder, as one important Dominican official later wrote—which brought highland Indians to the point of open rebellion.

Responding to his letter, the Virgin summoned native *justicias* from throughout the highlands to Cancuc (now renamed Ciudad Real) where, She proclaimed, they were to celebrate a grand festival in her honor: "I the Virgin who have descended to this Sinful World call upon you in the name of Our Lady of the Rosary and command you to come to this town of Cancuc and bring with you all the silver of your churches and the ornaments and bells, together with the communal funds and drums and all the books of the *cofradías*, because now neither God nor King exist; and for this reason you must come immediately, for if you do not you will be punished for not coming when I and God called you" (Ximénez, 1929: 271).[4] The Spanish God, she declared, that leering caricature of Our Lord, draped in episcopal finery—that God had died. In His place, a true Redeemer had appeared, an Indian king of kings who had come to reward native people for their sufferings and trials. And finally, she proclaimed, Indians must arm themselves, they must rise up against the "Jews in Ciudad Real" who even at that moment were preparing to kill her and reestablish once again their unholy rule over Christendom.

On August 10, five days after Alvarez departed from the city to begin his visit, civil and religious officials representing nearly twenty-five Tzeltal, Tzotzil and Chol towns gathered in Cancuc to venerate the Virgin. Under the leadership of a Tzotzil prophet, Sebastián Gómez, they and their townsmen were divided into military divisions and placed under the command of native captains. These *capitanes generales*, who in previous years had frequently served as assistants and *mayordomos* to parish priests, seem especially to have despised the Dominican Order. For Gómez instructed indigenous *alcaldes* "that no one was to give food to the Fathers, under pain of death, an order which was punctually fulfilled" (Ximénez, 1929: 280). Within a few days, Indian leaders took even more militant steps. First, they attacked the Spanish settlement in Chilon and killed all the town's adult non-Indian men. Spanish women and children were taken to Cancuc where they were called "Indians" and compelled to serve native authorities as domestics. A short time later, indigenous armies stormed Ocosingo, where they destroyed the Dominican haciendas and suger *ingenio*. Thereafter they proceeded systematically to capture whatever hapless friars fell into their grasp. By late November, they had wrought havoc upon the Church in central Chiapas.

One naturally wonders about the form of worship which these men and women preferred instead of Spanish religion. And in pursuing this question, we must examine in detail the attitudes and activities of Sebastián Gómez. Arriving in Cancuc in July 1712, from Chenalhó (where he led the unsuccessful movement to build a new chapel for San Sebastián), Gómez proceeded to organize an indigenous Church which, he hoped, would replace the Church of the Jews: "he brought a small image of San Pedro wrapped in cloth which he placed in the chapel, and said that this saint had chosen him to be his Vicar, and had granted him the power to ordain and appoint other Vicars and Priests who would minister to the towns" (López Sánchez, 1960: 720; Ximénez, 1929: 281). One month later, following the execution of Spanish clergymen, Gómez summoned Indian *fiscales* from seventeen Tzeltal towns to appear in Cancuc. After ascertaining which among them could read and write, he ordained several of them into the new priesthood: "The method of ordination was to compel each *Fiscal* to remain on his knees for 24 hours with a candle in his hand repeating the Rosary, and then in view of the whole town Don Sebastián de la Gloria (as he called himself) sprinkled him with water which, they claimed, had been blessed. . . . Having been ordained and assigned to their parishes, they began to exercise their office like very correct pastors, preaching, confessing, and administering [the sacraments]" (Ximénez, 1929: 281–2).

At first, Gómez seemed content to dispense with the elaborate hierarchies which characterized the Spanish Church. In establishing a system of authority, he appointed one of his priests, Gerónimo Saraes, to the office of vicar general—a common enough post in colonial dioceses. At the same time, Saraes and another priest, Lucas Pérez, became secretaries to the Virgin. And in the true spirit of Christ, who as we recall washed His apostles' feet, Gómez named to the "See of Sibacá" an old man who "had spent his life making tortillas for the Fathers" (Ximénex, 1929: 284). Soon, however, he expanded this primitive hierarchy until it had assumed alarming (and familiar) proportions. Thus, Saraes, too, was granted an episcopal throne, while two Indian friars—both of whom enjoyed the title of *predicadores generales*—became vicars general. Little by little, divine justice became obscured behind a battery of new prelates and patriarchs.

Meanwhile Gómez turned his attention to the difficulties and problems of civil administration. For in his vision of a theocratic state, he regarded Chiapas' *república de indios* as a New Spain, a second empire in which Indians had become Spaniards and Spaniards had become Indians (Ximénez, 1929: 287). But if God and king were dead, if native people no longer owed their obedience and loyalty to the *audiencia* in Guatemala, who would rule the republic in San Pedro's name and in the name of his earthly vicar? Within Indian pueblos, of course, native *cabildos*—appointed by the movement's leaders—continued to govern in local matters. But such elementary and primitive forms of government, he felt, were ill suited to an Indian empire—especially an empire that was at war. In order to rectify these problems, as Ximénez tells us, "in order to dispense justice to those who require it, and reward those who merited it, [they decided] that they would found an *audiencia* and that this should be in Huitiupán. With this in mind they styled the Town Guatemala with its President and Judges" (Ximénez, 1929: 287). And finally, Gómez and other leaders promised at least one military commander, Juan García, that if the rebellion succeeded he would be crowned king of Cancuc (López Sánchez, 1960: 716).

To be sure, Gómez's state was not universally admired. There were many Indians who refused to accept these measures, who even lost their lives in defense of the colonial order. The *fiscal* of Tenango, for example, Nicolas Pérez, who remained loyal to Fr. de Lara, was whipped to death in front of the chapel in Cancuc. Similarly, the inhabitants of Simojovel and Palenque chose to abandon their homes and hide in the mountains rather than join the rebellion (Orozco y Jiménez, 1911: 152). In the same fashion, Indian pueblos along the periphery of highland Chiapas (San Bartolomé, Amatenango, Aguacatenango, Teopisca, and Comitán), and

Zoque towns to the northeast of Ciudad Real refused to support the Virgin. More important, however, Gómez's empire building, his careful imitation of Spanish administrative and ecclesiastical forms, soon provoked disenchantment even among many Indians who had at first followed the movement with enthusiasm. In particular, they demanded an end to tribute, to tithes and—above all—to the Order of Saint Dominic. Instead, as one witness wrote, Gómez reprimanded them sharply:

> because there have been complaints among the subjects to the effect that [the Virgin's] word has not been fulfilled with respect to the abolition of tribute, of the Order of Santo Domingo, of the king and of the rule of the Jews, let it be known that Señor San Pedro told his chosen emissary Señor Don Sebastián Gómez de la Gloria that he could not preserve the world without earthly bondsmen. Our Father Señor San Pedro has offered himself as our bondsman, before God and thus, according to the heavenly word which is not of the earth there must be in each town a priest who will serve as bondsman before God by means of the Mass, because without them, as the world is filled with sin, the World will end, and for this reason the Masses which these Fathers celebrate will calm God's anger (Ximénez, 1929: 282–3).

In the end, it may well have been this theocratic bent which brought the Cancuc rebellion to a quick end. To be sure, Spanish authorities possessed sufficient military power to vanquish the Virgin's poorly armed and ill-disciplined legions. But colonial forces had been taken by surprise, and had found themselves completely unprepared to defend Spanish settlers. During those weeks when Ciudad Real's meager militia, entrenched in Huistán, stalled for time, Indians in Zinacantan and Chamula, sympathetic to the Virgin, enjoyed ample opportunity to attack and subdue the city. Why did they not do so? Certainly, their love of Spanish bishops and governors was no more intense than that of other Indians elsewhere in the highlands. On the contrary, because of their talents as porters and their proximity to Ciudad Real, Zinacantecos had suffered even more acutely than many Indians at the hands of colonial authorities. Did they then fear the punishment which these officials would surely inflict upon them? Apparently not, for they prepared and organized themselves to march against the city. No: their reluctance to pursue this venture does not appear to have been inspired by fear or timorousness. Instead, they allowed themselves to be dissuaded by Fr. Monroy who, we must presume, convinced them that the Virgin was in reality a fraud. And in the days that followed, such key towns as Chenalhó and Chalchihuitán also defected from Her cause. Why, they seem to have asked, should we exchange one earthly kingdom for another?

Indeed, Gómez himself, it would seem, anticipated such opposition. In his order to disgruntled tributaries, he declared that even in the New Age, Indians would continue to sin and would therefore require the services of their priesthood. Otherwise, he wrote, the world would end. This vision of the Day of Judgement, however well it served his purposes, must in the end have inspired little enthusiasm among men and women who yearned for justice and for an end to exploitation. On the contrary, it undoubtedly offended them. For it violated that sense of community, that sense of promise which since the days of Bishop Bartolomé de Las Casas, the famous *defensor de los Indios*, had become the cornerstone of their own spiritual and political lives. The feelings of discontent and expectation which swept Chiapas between 1708 and 1712 had reflected a desire to realize those old ideals in modern form, to transform the multitude of isolated pueblos into a single native community founded upon faith, equality, and divine law. For this reason, according to Klein, the movement's leaders declared at one point that their Spanish captives must marry Indians. From such a union, they proclaimed, there would spring a new race—neither Spanish nor Indian—which would truly merit salvation. And despite the movement's failure, these feelings continued to stir native imaginations, to hang in the air like incense—while colonial authorities, jubilant at their victory over the forces of darkness, took up the unfinished business of capricious law and systematic graft.

Given these motives, it is not difficult to understand the Church's response to this cry for moral regeneration. As might be expected, the rebellion only confirmed those opinions, common among clerics of the day, which held that Indians suffered from a special variety of original sin. "The points upon which our sermons concentrated," wrote Ximénez, who preached to the subdued defenders of Cancuc, "were, first, the hardness of their hearts, because in 200 years of instruction God's law had not taken hold in their hearts . . . second, how much better they lived under the rule of the King of Spain than in pagan times under Moctezuma. . . . fourth, their origins, descended from the Jews whom God had punished for their idolatry and who later came to these lands by unknown routes" (Ximénez, 1929: 333–4). Moved by such convictions, Spanish priests intensified their efforts to suppress native religiosity and ritual. In his Tzotzil catechism, for example, F. Hidalgo took great pains to impress upon his listeners that their own earthly travails—however great and painful these might be—paled to insignificance beside the agonies which Christ had suffered on their behalf. "Your price is a great one," Hidalgo wrote, "and for this reason He suffered terribly while here on earth" (Hidalgo, 1735). Furthermore, in order to assure that Indians heard and understood this message, the number of priests and parishes doubled, then tripled. By 1780, most of these *prebendados* had installed themselves in their curates, where they hoped they might maintain a closer and more vigilant watch over native religious life.

At this point, it is perhaps of interest to compare and contrast our view of the 1712 rebellion with that presented by Herbert Klein. Like other scholars, Klein has claimed that in large measure local "civil-religious hierarchies," composed primarily of older and wealthier Indians, organized and led the movement (Klein, 1970: 150–2). And yet, as we have seen, Gómez and his confederates did not allow local councils of this sort to assume more than a minor role in the uprising. Instead, they took great pains to organize civil and religious institutions, unknown in Indian pueblos, in unequivocal and direct copy of Spanish models. Kings, vicars general, bishops, *predicadores generales*, military governors—these were the men upon whom they conferred political and spiritual powers. Like their non-Indian counterparts, these officials, who commanded the obedience of local *cabildos*, ruled within well-defined jurisdictions and territories. And in contrast to Klein's belief, many of these officials, being quite young, had played only minor roles in municipal government before the rebellion: Juan García, *capitán general* and king-designate of Cancuc, had served previously as the town's chief constable and as servant to Fr. de Lara. Similarly, native *fiscales* like Lucas Pérez and Gerónimo Saraes, who became bishops and secretaries to the Virgin, were neither particularly aged nor particularly wealthy.[5]

No: the 1712 rebellion traced its origins not to a sudden "tearing open" of an otherwise durable colonial social order, but in a more fundamental sense to the corrupt and dissolute nature of colonial society itself. Certainly, such afflictions as tribute, the *repartimientos*, and peonage (combined with frightening mortality rates and starvation) set the stage for revolt. But as the case of Zinacantan indicates, hardship and exploitation—the common condition of highland Indians—did not by themselves provoke native people to rebel. Instead, these men and women, like other colonial subjects, took up arms only when their very humanity itself—that is, the way of life which they had devised as a defense against cultural annihilation— was called into question. In the end, it was not simply economic exploitation but the relentless ideological repression exercised by priests such as Núñez de la Vega and Simón de Lara which drove them to insurrection.

Conclusions

Unlike the Indians of Oaxaca who, according to William Taylor, "were still self-sufficient farmers on the eve of . . . independence," indigenous people in central Chiapas had long before abandoned their traditional economic and agricultural occupations (Taylor, 1972). Here and there, individual families or family groups managed to eke out a living from their small milpas. Indeed, throughout the highlands, land was not a major cause of concern in the seventeenth and eighteenth centuries among Indians. Only in a few highland valleys did they find themselves deprived of their ancestral patrimonies. In contrast, taxes, tribute and the system of *repartimientos* to which these gave rise brought about profound transformations in Indian communities. By means of such devices, provincial governors organized and mobilized a vast native labor force, a labor force which produced cacao, cochineal, sugar, and cotton cloth. Even as late as 1819, thirty years after such *repartimientos* had been abolished, native people in Chiapas still paid an exhorbitant amount of tribute in comparison to the Indians in New Spain (Semo, 1973: 88). In the absence of serious competition from private landowners, Chiapas' *alcaldes mayores* created a highly sophisticated network of plantations, markets, and manufacturers. And incredibly, they devised this network without purchasing either a single vara of land or beast of burden. Both land and animals remained in Indian hands: they formed the capital which each year native people themselves husbanded and regenerated.

Contrary perhaps to our expectations, the wholesale reform of civil government in Chiapas after 1790 did not in general permit highland Indians to return to subsistence farming. Instead, large-scale smuggling in Central America created new demands for the region's hides, dyes, and other products. In order to augment their production, local landowners expanded their existing plantations and, in the area near Ciudad Real, founded new ones. Freed from the restraints which jealous *alcaldes mayores* had imposed upon them, they nonetheless required more labor. As a result, they began to recruit Tzotzil and Tzeltal Indians from the southern highlands to work their properties as peones and tenant farmers. Because tribute requirements remained extremely high, many of these Indians acceded to their new fate with resignation. Others (primarily Zinacantecos) accepted merchandise on consignment from merchants in Ciudad Real. Using their wits and their mules, these Indians travelled as far afield as Oaxaca and Tabasco in search of customers for their wares. In both cases, such arrangements persisted and indeed predominated among native people until the end of the nineteenth century.

How did indigenous communities react to their new and ever-changing position in colonial society? First, as MacLeod has written, by creating barrier institutions, they attempted to protect themselves as best they could from the depredations of Spanish governors and prelates. Among these institutions, colonial *ayuntamientos* and *cofradías* functioned primarily to assuage and pacify rapacious ladino authorities. But these *ayuntamientos* alone—controlled and regulated by Spaniards—could not effectively reconstruct an indigenous way of life. As we might expect, this most urgent task fell to native *fiscales* and religious officials, men and women who had kept faith with the militant and combative Christianity of an earlier age. Despite clerical efforts to substitute a banal and self-demeaning religiosity in place of Christ's promise of eternal life, these native *ministros* integrated Christian teaching into the very soul of Indian identity. For if native people, uniquely among the area's inhabitants, had been elected to suffer at the hands of the mighty, they reasoned, then would they not also be chosen to live forever in God's sight? And if they alone would rise and rejoice on the Day of Judgement, as they firmly believed, then surely their race inhabited that true Church, that community at whose head, as earlier friars had told them, stood the Redeemer Himself. And so, with these ideas in mind, they joyfully and willingly developed their own amalgam of doctrine and liturgy. Far better to honor Him on the hilltops than to obey those corrupt and unworthy men who celebrated in village churches.

It was this combination of sentiments—at once worldly and messianic—which by 1700 permeated native life in Chiapas. And as native communities in general began to recover and grow after 1720, so also did the notion of communal solidarity—often in the form of collective ritual—acquire new significance and urgency. By means of such ritual, indigenous people kept alive that spirit of resistance, that insistance upon their collective distinctiveness and dignity, which mitigated the daily outrages of colonial life. For it must be remembered that colonial society brought Spaniards and Indians together not simply as distinct ethnic groups, but as members of antagonistic social classes—that ethnic relations quickly became a pretense for perpetuating inequities and injustices of a much more familiar sort. Then, too, the options of emigration and transculturation—of *mestizaje*, which many chose to pursue—remained open to Indians in most parts of Mexico and Central America. Despite such options, however, in Chiapas at least a significant number of these men and women chose instead to modify their beliefs and customs and traditions in every way possible so as to avoid the one fate which they evidently feared most: the loss of their right to be *naturales*. After all, as Stéfano Varese has so eloquently argued, ethnic diversity did not emerge with the appearance of class society, much less with the advent of colonialism (Varese, 1978). Under these circumstances, native people quite reasonably rejected transculturation as a solution to those problems of inequality and exploitation which plagued them: why, they asked, should we forsake what little we have salvaged to enter the lowest levels of ladino society? And to this question—a question which remains as perplexing to modern scholars as it was to colonial churchmen—we might add, how much would such a sacrifice today alter the economic and political relations upon which society in Mexico is presently based?

Acknowledgements

Much of this essay was published under the title of "Ethnic Violence and Indigenous Protest: The Tzeltal (Maya) Rebellion of 1712," *Journal of Latin American Studies*, 12, 1 (May 1980). The author wishes to thank JLAS and its editors for permission to reprint it here.

4. Capitalist Penetration in the Nineteenth Century: Creating Conditions for New Patterns of Social Control

Joel S. Migdal

Peasant rebellions have been rare occurrences. Through all or most of their days, practically all peasants have led rather docile, one might even say humdrum, lives. Lack of rebellion by peasants is not due to happenstance. Nor is it the result of some defining peasant characteristic, such as contentedness or fatalism. Rather, peasants' failure to rebel can be understood in the context of the way their lives have been organized.

The formal and informal social organizations peasants have been part of—families, clans, castes, villages, states, and the like—have prescribed peasant behavior. A careful weighing of the incentives that these social organizations use in order to gain peasant conformance has been necessary for peasants in order to insure sheer survival. Such incentives have included rewards (e.g., a way to make a living, protection from marauders, security in old age). They also have included sanctions (e.g., physical violence, denial of access to land and water, withdrawal of status, ostracism). Together, the various arrays of rewards and sanctions have determined the characteristic forms of social control in peasant society. In addition, the social organizations usually have offered symbolic configurations which, together with the rewards and sanctions, make up the strategies of survival peasants have employed in a world that has frequently been seen as threatening and hostile.

When does peasant rebellion occur? Although certainly no single factor can answer such a question, a necessary condition is the failure of peasants' strategies of survival. Changing circumstances may weaken the force of certain sanctions or make given rewards insufficient to meet the needs of peasants. Such changing circumstances may be as limited as escalating demands by a rapacious landlord or much more widespread such as an extensive drought or famine. Failure of strategies of survival, reduced effectiveness of rewards and sanctions, make the prescriptions and proscriptions of the groups organizing peasant life less relevant to peasants' situations and more difficult to enforce. The inadequacy of existing strategies of survival may precipitate strangulation of the peasantry, or it may lead to widespread peasant avoidance of demands upon them, peasant flight from a locale, or active peasant resistance and rebellion.

The struggles for social control associated with peasant rebellions and revolutions—struggles over which social and political organizations will provide viable strategies for peasant survival—are, then, products of unusual circumstances. The relationship between the spread of capitalism from northwestern Europe to the far reaches of the globe and the occurrence of peasant rebellion may be understood in the context of a sudden and severe weakening of the social organizations that had exercised social control among peasants. In the wake of such a weakening, fierce struggles for resources and new forms of social control ensued. This essay analyzes a specific set of state policies that facilitated the spread of the world market deep into peasant societies and led to a sudden disruption of existing patterns of social control. The combination of state policies and the spread of capitalism had their impact in the latter half of the nineteenth century. While they alone certainly were not sufficient causes for peasant rebellion, they did greatly weaken old forms of social control in a relatively short period across an area of previously unimagined scope. The state policies and the market forces those policies promoted, created the necessary conditions for the development of a great variety of political and social struggles that blanketed Latin America, Asia, and Africa down to the lowest levels of their societies—struggles that in some cases included the great peasant revolutions of our time.

The New Penetration of the World Economy

With the gain of the capitalist mode of production in Europe from the sixteenth century on, the relationship of European states and entrepreneurs to those outside Europe increasingly was characterized by trade vital to the maintenance and growth of that production. For some areas, the absorption into the new world market, even in the sixteenth century, was as sudden and intense as being drawn into a vacuum. The results were frequently disastrous. While the *encomienda* system of forced labor took hold as a typical form of enterprise in New Spain (Mexico), for example, the country's population fell from about eleven million at the beginning of the sixteenth century to as low as one and one-half million by the middle of the seventeenth century. The disruption of the existing society and its strategies for survival was practically total as the Indians rarely survived their mobilization to extract silver from the land and to engage in other tasks important to the European-centered economy.

For many areas in Asia and Africa, however, the results of an expanding, avaricious world economy in the sixteenth century were not nearly as immediately disruptive to old forms of social organization and social control. This is not to argue that there was not terrible human suffering because of the slave trade or other forms of forced labor that accompanied the spread of capitalism. Indeed there was! At the same time it can still be said that the penetration of the world market was quite limited in scope in many areas until well into the nineteenth century. Intense penetration in most parts of Asia, Africa, and Latin America during much of the sixteenth through eighteenth centuries was usually in coastal enclaves. For the majority of the population in the hinterlands of many areas, there was only a mediated and sporadic tie to the world economy. European companies often established themselves in the ports and then relied on indigenous middlemen for any trade with the interior. Producers, particularly peasants in these inland areas, were affected intermittently and selectively by the new forces emanating from Europe. Even in New Spain where the indigenous Indian societies had been decimated by the Spanish conquerors, by the seventeenth century there was economic contraction and decline. In fact, one can speak of a partial disengagement of those in New Spain (and in much of the rest of Latin America) from world capitalism at that time.

All that changed in a relatively short period. The socially explosive effects of the spreading world market were felt in country after country by all members of the society in the span of only a few critical decades beginning in the latter part of the nineteenth century. It was then that the intermittent, tenuous, and selective connections of most producers to the world economy were totally transformed. Peasant economic crises and the crumbling of existing social organizations and social control ensued. The reasons for the suddenness and depth of the world market's penetration to all segments of society are related to a number of technological and administrative breakthroughs and new needs that came out of Europe's industrial revolution.[1] These changes have been dealt with extensively by historians and others.

What has been less carefully examined is the means by which two primary goals of European traders, industrialists, and investors were achieved: (a) guaranteed access to distant markets and suppliers providing raw materials vital for European food needs and for industry and (b) a change in foreign production assuring that the commodities most in need in Europe would be produced in sufficient quantity (rather than produced simply for local consumption). Despite the nineteenth-century liberal credo of free trade and the invisible hand that apparently minimized the economic role of the state, states in fact played an integral role in achieving these two goals so critical to the success of the international economic order of the time. While important questions of production and allocation of goods, wealth, and opportunities did remain in the private sector, out of the hands of public officials, public policies did play active and critical roles in helping gain access to peasant producers in Asia, Africa, and Latin America and in assuring that those peasants produced for the needs of the international market.

Hegemonic Western states, epitomized by Britain, adopted a series of policies in areas they ruled directly that facilitated deeper, rapid, and near-universal penetration of world markets deep into those areas and precipitated the emergence of new forms of production. Indigenously ruled regimes, such as that in Mexico, often ended up employing much the same set of policies as the Western powers did either as an attempt to emulate the West, hoping to unlock the secret of concentrating vast wealth and power, in order to ward off the threats Western powers posed internationally or, in bleaker circumstances, as a means of compliance with the wishes of the Western powers. Three types of state policies underlay the rapid and widespread weakening of old social and political arrangements among the world's peasantry. These policies were: (1) effecting important changes in land tenure patterns; (2) changing tax collection: greatly increasing collected, individual taxes and switching from taxes in kind to taxes in cash; and (3) opening the hinterlands, particularly through railway construction.

Land Tenure Laws

In disparate parts of the world ruled by different states and empires, small free-holding peasants almost simultaneously faced catastrophic changes in the rules of land tenure in their societies. It is most striking that these land tenure changes came in a number of countries almost at the same moment in history. In 1856, Mexico passed its *Ley de desamortización*, also known as *Ley* Lerdo; in 1858, the Ottoman Empire enacted the *Tapu* Law; in 1858, the British rulers issued the Proclamation of 1858 for the province of Oudh in North India; and, also in 1858, Said Pasha issued a law strengthening private landowning rights in Egypt. And that is not all. Legislation and administrative decrees changing proprietary and social relationships to the land could be found from South America to East Asia in the single generation following the mid-1850s. Bolivia's *Ley de Exvinculación de Tierras* in 1874, for example, capped an eight-year process of abolishing communal holdings. In Guatemala the legal onslaught against communal Indian lands began around 1870; and, in Venezuela, a series of policies culminated in 1882 (International Labour Office, 1953: 296–99). The Dutch enacted the Agrarian Land Law in Indonesia in 1870. There were cases in which major areas escaped the effects of induced transformation of land tenure, such as major parts of sub-Saharan Africa, but in the areas that did experience these changes the results were often momentous.

The purposes of these changes in land tenure, whether effected by indigenous states or outside rulers, were complex. In many areas, they were linked to the establishment and maintenance of as secure a hegemonic rule as possible. Wherever enacted, however, one prime purpose of such laws was to facilitate changes in agricultural production that would increase yields and that would lead to the planting of crops suitable for export. Simultaneous changes in land tenure in seemingly unrelated parts of the globe came in large part because of increased demand in Europe and the United States for cotton, sugar, coffee, jute, indigo, and a number of other select crops. The cotton industry, which was Britain's biggest exporter, for example, increased its imports of raw cotton by more than 100 percent between the early 1850s and the early 1880s (Clapham, 1952: 225; Bodey, 1975: 156; Usher, 1920: 305).[2] The heightened demand for raw materials frequently precipitated an uneasy alliance in Asian, African, and Latin American countries. That alliance was between state leaders or governors of colonies hoping to garner huge additional revenues for their coffers by taking advantage of demand for the country's exports and powerful rural or urban entrepreneurs aiming to exploit the new commercial opportunities by laying their hands on vast tracts of cultivatable land. New production techniques for specific crops that were developed at this time also increased the pressure for consolidating land so as to gain greater economies of scale. It is essential to note that frequently the intended effects were not gained, but land tenure rules are such sensitive instruments that even when goals were not achieved the unintended effects could be monumental on peasant societies.

Rationalization for the new laws came cloaked in the rhetoric of nineteenth-century liberal ideology. This was the period, after all, of the Emancipation Proclamation and the emancipation of Russian serfs. In Mexico, the *Ley de desamortización* was tied to the termination of differentiations based on race and of the special status of the church's holdings. Also, in Mexico as well as in almost every other area where land tenure changes were introduced, the new regulations were presented as a step against the mortmain, the inalienable right of communal organizations to hold land. Modeled after the antifeudal and antiecclesiastic Statutes of Mortmain, the new laws made for individual ownership and registration of plots rather than the various types of communal church, village, or clan land rights that had been found so characteristically in Mexico, India, and elsewhere.

Whatever the precise purposes and rationalizations for the changes in land tenure, they precipitated eruptive, universal dislocations wherever enacted. They signaled changes in agricultural production and class relations that entered so deeply into the fabric of societies that their effects are often still readily discernible today. In Mexico, the 1856 *Ley de desamortización* stated that all landed property held by civil or religious corporations should be divided in ownership among those who actually worked the plots. A clause was included in the law exempting land, such as the *ejidos*, held in common for the use of the people actually working it. Once the measure was incorporated into the 1857 constitution, however, this exemption was dropped. The Indians now became individual proprietors of the plots they had farmed and of their formerly common-held land in their villages and towns. The new legislation did not achieve the aims of state leaders, particularly President Benito Pablo Juárez, of insuring the existence of a landed peasantry with firm title to individual holdings, but instead the law had catastrophic consequences for the campesinos (McBride, 1971: 133, 69–70; López Rosado, 1968, 1: 191–193). Speculators, corrupt officials, hacendados, and others exploited the new right of the campesino to dispose of this land freely by freely disposing him of his land.

The result was a rapid consolidation of former communal lands into haciendas and other big farms and ranches in a country already characterized by the big hacienda. The primary effects of the legislation were felt in the last quarter of the nineteenth century. Additional legislation reinvigorated the process alienating campesinos from their land during this period. Several presidential decrees were followed by the Act of 1876 and then the so-called Law of Colonization in 1894. All these made it easier to seize properties that lacked properly registered titles. The need to parcel out any remaining communal land and grant individual title through the *Gran Registro de la Propriedad* was reiterated. Hacendados, in particular, took advantage of the provision of the law allowing them to denounce imperfect titles—through neglect, fear, or ignorance many Indian titles were imperfect—and acquire the plots attached to such titles (McBride, 1971: 74–81).

The former members of inward-oriented, corporate villages were absorbed into the haciendas as peons or lived precariously as landless laborers.

Wherever laws or decrees, such as the *Ley de desamortización*, were enacted, they helped induce new rural class relations—relations more suited for export-oriented production.[3] The precise nature of those relations was greatly influenced by sector, different crops having different sorts of economies, so that questions such as tenancy versus labor tended to be answered according to the suitability of local areas for specific sorts of export-oriented production. As in a number of other countries, production of Mexican campesinos on their own plots did not change immediately and totally from its subsistence orientation, but the proportion of campesinos able to maintain their own holdings was low indeed (estimates range from 80 to 95.5 percent landless) (International Labour Office, 1953: 298; Nash, 1970: 174; López Rosado, 1968, 1: 103; McBride, 1971: 3; Katz, 1974: 1–47). The law resulted in a landgrab of stupendous proportions. The figures are truly dramatic. At the start of the Revolution, 300 haciendas contained at least 25,000 acres each, and 11 haciendas had more than 250,000 acres apiece. More than 2.25 million acres of communally held property were acquired by estate owners.[4] "By 1910," wrote Robert A. White, "less than 1 percent of the families of Mexico controlled 85 percent of the land, and 90 percent of the villages and towns on the central plateau had almost no communal land" (White, 1969: 115).[5]

Where communal land was not an immediate barrier to land consolidation in the second half of the nineteenth century, no single law had so overwhelming an effect as in Mexico. This was especially true in countries such as India, where even earlier than the mid-nineteenth century the road had been paved for making land a freely exchanged commodity and thus opening the way for rapid land consolidation. India had had a series of acts, laws, and proclamations that allowed for the same market-oriented production and growing peasant landlessness as elsewhere.

Abrogation of peasant land rights had already occurred prior to the mid-nineteenth century in parts of India. British land policies in India had affected different parts of the country at different times. The most notable, the Permanent Settlement of Bengal in 1793, had established zamindars, mostly Calcutta businessmen, as the proprietors of the land—a sharp departure from previous Indian history (Bhatia, 1965; Campbell, n.d.; Driver, 1949).[6] In 1858, the British reconfirmed this method of land consolidation for a part of India by issuing a proclamation that enabled the *taluqdars* (zamindars) of Oudh to gain large tracts of land following the outbreak of a peasant revolt there (Raj, 1965).

Even in cases, such as that of India, where a series of land tenure changes was enacted over a number of decades rather than a single major law, some of the most decisive effects of these changes came in the few decades following mid-century. Social control changed irrevocably as landowners consolidated holdings and integrated themselves (and, along with them, their workers and tenants) much more fully into the world market economy. The rural poor throughout Asia, North Africa, and Latin America found that the land tenure changes, whether effected in the middle of the nineteenth century, or in a series of decrees that began even earlier, now meant they could no longer produce as they had earlier. As tenants, laborers, or small landholders, their efforts were increasingly related to the tastes, needs, and demands of people in far-flung places on the globe.

Taxes: Increases in Revenues and the Change from Kind to Cash

Land tenure laws were hoes preparing the ground for the deep and broad sowing of the expanding world economy. The harvest of land grabs, export-oriented plantations, and vast increases in tenancy and landless laborers meant new rural class relations and whole new sets of needs for the producers—the peasants. Rather suddenly and almost universally, existing forms of social control were rocked to their foundations in country after country. In both countries enacting major land tenure laws and those with no land tenure changes, or with only a series of smaller, legal and administrative changes, two other factors often reinforced the trend towards land consolidation. Those factors were the increases in revenues collected from the peasants by the ruling state and the switch to taxes collected in cash rather than in kind. These same two factors also had a major impact even when land consolidation was not achieved—on those fortunate enough to hold onto a cherished plot of land or to secure a viable tenancy.

High taxes were certainly not new experiences for peasants. Indian and other cultivators had been known to have abandoned their land in certain periods on account of high exactions by lords and tax-farmers even prior to the nineteenth century. The increases in taxes that came in the latter half of the nineteenth century often differed from those in the past in that they were relentlessly administered by the state throughout the country rather than by local tax farmers or other intermediaries down to the level of the individual. Like Cain after the slaying of Abel, cultivators found it impossible to flee or hide, particularly in the face of new administrative revenue-collection techniques copied or imported from Europe. Not only were taxes now higher and more efficiently collected, but often the taxes were fixed and did not vary with peasants' ability to pay in a given year. "Nothing about the colonial order," wrote James C. Scott on Southeast Asia, "seemed to infuriate the peasantry more than its taxes" (Scott, 1976: 91).

Higher taxes and the resulting rural indebtedness had a devastating impact on small holders in India. Here, peasants paid for the grand technological schemes of Europe. Even though the Indian railroads, as we shall see momentarily, were financed primarily with British capital, a quick return on investments to the numerous British investors was only possible by increasing taxes on the Indian peasant. The increased peasant indebtedness that resulted from the new taxes had an unprecedented effect, for the new British land codes allowed land to be held as security against loans by the moneylender. "Once an agriculturist fell into his clutches," wrote Bhatia, "he (the agriculturist) rarely got out before his land was sold in satisfaction of his creditor's debt" (Bhatia, 1965: 147). Even where the zamindari system of large owners was not instituted by the British and they opted instead for the *ryotwari* system of small peasant holders, the new rigidity of land revenue collection still led to peasants' losing their land through debt collection. Also, the new civil courts introduced by the colonialists made it much more likely that creditors could actually expropriate the land from the cultivator.

British perplexity about the causes of the new severity of rural debt in India (as seen in their numerous inquiries into the subject) came as their collected land revenue grew by 50 percent and their gross revenues by 200 percent in the second half of the nineteenth century. British policymakers had hoped that the surveys and assessments of land begun in 1855 together with the more systematic collection of *ryotwari* taxes would prod small farmers towards wider cultivation. Increased cultivation, they reckoned, would lead to greater revenues without increasing the burden on the individual peasant household. In fact, the peasant's burden grew from the 1860s until about 1890. As Dharma Kumar wrote of South India, "The assessment policy of late *raiyatwari* had nominally been meant to scale it down. But, as we have seen, actual collections were often raised. . . . It remains true that the burdens of British revenue administration were inordinately heavy, and had serious social consequences" (Kumar, 1965: 95, 97–98).

Blame was more apt to be placed on the poor peasant than on the pressures generated by high taxes, as seen in the following statement by P. J. Thomas: "If the ignorant pariah does not mind selling his labour for life for having the pleasure of seeing his kith and kin get drunk on his wedding eve—a common occurrence among the labourers in several parts—many a brahmin will encumber his whole property and exhaust even his personal credit for celebrating marriages and paying dowries" (Thomas, 1934: 2).

Peasants in India (and elsewhere) found the costs of existing forms of social control—such as having a festive wedding—depleted the resources needed for survival in their new environment marked by the world economy. The pressure of high taxes did not generally have the effect in India of creating large surplus-producing estates. Nevertheless, it did displace the peasantry as landowners and led to a deteriorating or stagnating standard of living for the majority of India's population through the end of the nineteenth century and into the twentieth.[7]

Indebtedness for cultivators was further assured in many countries through laws and administrative decrees that demanded taxes be paid in cash rather than simply as a percentage of one's yield. The British considered one of their main achievements in India to have been "the systematic commutation of the share of produce into a money tax" (Meek, 1949: xvii).

A major purpose in the change to cash taxes during the latter part of the nineteenth century was to force the peasant more and more into market relations and to stimulate production for export: peasants, it was assumed, would produce the higher paying export crops in order to gain sorely needed cash so that they could pay their taxes. Almost universally, however, the new rigid tax systems and the vagaries of production and of the money economy simply overwhelmed small peasants living on the margin of survival. The result was the growth of moneylending elements who frequently used the change to cash taxes as yet another basis for land consolidation. In India and elsewhere, the land itself became the security upon which lenders advanced their credits.

Lenders came from different elements of the population in various countries. At times, they were men of the village, usually either shopkeepers or larger land-owners; in other instances, they were urban entrepreneurs or big landowners from outside the village. Members of ethnic or religious minorities played the money-lending role in numerous countries. Frequently, colonial rulers were able to influ-ence who would and could be in a position to lend money, where cash was still scarce but evermore essential.

The change to cash taxes was a major condition for the broad and deep penetra-tion of the world economy. It allowed for a much freer exchange and movement of goods, as almost all cultivators came to gear larger shares of their production ac-cording to market dictates. The change just as importantly promoted the mobility of labor so critical to the operation of a capitalist market economy. Along with the added pressure of land tenure changes and increases in state revenue collection, the switch to taxes paid in cash led to galloping increases in rural debt and subsequent sequestration of peasant lands. Growing numbers of landless laborers or under-employed peasants were thus "freed" to constitute the new urban and rural work-force. Alienation from the land further aided the establishment of the world mar-ket in a number of areas by precipitating land consolidation where conditions were suitable for the highly demanded crops amenable to new technologies and greater economies of scale. The timing of the eruptive penetration of the world market in each case depended on one final factor that guaranteed the freer exchange of goods and peoples—but especially of goods. That factor—the railroad—was the symbol of the new technological age that fittingly paved the way for the total penetration of the world economy.

Railroads

Important changes in the relationship of Western societies, particularly Great Britain, to societies in Asia, Africa, and Latin America, came in the wake of the large increases in investments abroad by Western private entrepreneurs and states. At the same time that British total domestic investment increased only 13 percent (from 1841–50 to 1851–60), net investment abroad grew by more than 200 percent (Clapham and Power, 1978, 7, pt. 2: 69, 91).[8] From 1870 on, much of this foreign investment capital was directed away from the United States and Europe and to-wards other regions of the world. This growth in exportable capital, the increased demand for raw materials (both crops and mineral resources), and the technologi-cal changes associated with the whole development of railroads were the chief fac-tors in Europe that precipitated a revolution in transport in Asia, Africa, and Latin America. The laying of railway track from the mid-nineteenth century on was the great trailblazer of the expanding world economy. Isolation and inaccessibility were broken down. The new market economy became an everyday reality as the giant freight cars forged through forests, mountains, and deserts to move manufactured goods, people, and most strikingly, the raw commodities produced in Asia, Africa, and Latin America. Expansion of the railroads continued through the century and into the twentieth century, but the tremendous surge of growth that opened up the most populated and rich areas came for many countries in a relatively short period. In India in 1853, Governor-General Lord Dalhousie expressed the frustration and motivation that were to cause the 1860s to be the beginning of explosive social and economic changes in India:

> Great tracts are teeming with produce they cannot dispose of; others are scantily bearing what they would carry in abundance if only it could be conveyed whither it is needed. England is calling aloud for the cotton which India does already produce in some degrees [sic] and would produce sufficient in quality and plentiful in quantity if only there were provided the fitting means of conveyance for it from distant places to the several ports adapted for its shipment . . . Ships from every part of the world crowd over ports in search of produce which we have, or could obtain in the interior, but which at present we cannot profitably fetch to them . . . It needs but little reflection on such facts to lead us to the conclusion that the establishment of a system of railways in India judiciously selected and formed, would surely and rapidly give rise within this empire to the same encouragement of enterprise, the same multiplication of produce, the same discovery of latent resources, to the same increase of national wealth, and the same similar progress in social improvement, that have marked the introduction of improved and extended communication in various Kingdoms of the Western World (Banerjee, 1966: 83–84).

With the new methods of machine production of textiles in Europe, the demand for cotton grew tremendously. Along with the increased demand was the need to build means to transport that cotton. And build they did! Transport under Dalhousie's guidance in India was transformed from the enormously costly means of buffaloes, camels, and pack bullocks to the faster, far-less-costly trains. After four days of transport, an oxen consumed more grain than it carried. Such impediments alone prevented deep penetration of international markets (McAlpin, 1974: 682). In 1858, about 430 miles of track were open, only about 1 percent of India's eventual railway lines. The increases thereafter were phenomenal: five years later, there was already a 400 percent increase with considerably more than 2,000 miles open for transport. Growth in cotton exports reflected the greatly expanded rail system. With the disruption caused by the American Civil War, Indian cotton exports rose from Rs. 5.6 crores in 1859–60 to Rs. 37.5 crores in 1864–65. In the next five years from 1863 to 1868, there was another approximately 100 percent growth in rail lines, and then about *another* 100 percent increase over the next 15 years. By 1882, the trains were transporting about 5,000 times more freight tonnage than they had in 1858, much of that the raw cotton so important to British manufacture (McAlpin, 1974: 334–35; Sanyal, 1930: diagram 1 and p. 35; Dubey, 1965: 336; Dutt, 1969, 2: 548). Between 1882 and 1912, there was a sixfold increase in net ton-miles carried which came with a threefold increase in the miles of track.

Although the railroads were the most striking part of the opening of village India to the full force of the European world economy, roads too played an important role in procuring raw materials easily at a low cost from peasants. A. S. Finlay stated before the Select Committee on Indian Territories, 1852–1853, "I consider that at present there are no roads in India suitable for commercial purposes of any extent" (Banerjee, 1966: 63).[9] Dalhousie was important in remedying this situation as well, creating public works departments that vastly expanded the road network from the 1850s on. British capital and administrative skills were important elements in the pace and the scope of the construction of India's railway system and road network. Before the completion of the conquest of India in 1857, there had been a net outflow of capital from India to Britain. After that, however, the situation was reversed, and British export capital to India played a major role in several sectors of the economy (Bose, 1965).[10] Railways accounted for more than three-quarters of total British investments in India from 1865–1894. Initially, private British capital was attracted to railroad enterprises by a guaranteed 5 percent return. Many investors were middle class—by 1868 there were almost 50,000 share and debenture holders. Eager to gain as much profit as possible, they pressured the British government to accelerate railway construction in India, forcing a parliamentary inquiry and a new regime in India ". . . which promised to be more directly responsive to the wants and interests of the people of the British Isles" (Jenks, 1927: 215). Within a short period, however, state rather than private capital became most important. Up to the end of 1891, for example, almost 60 percent of all expenditures on railroads were by the British state (Dutt, 1969, 1: 549; see also Macpherson, 1955–56: 177–86).

In Mexico, problems beset initial efforts at constructing a railway system until the emergence of a reinvigorated Mexican state during the last quarter of the nineteenth century. During that period, there was a very rapid expansion of the system based largely on foreign investments. In 1876, only approximately 640 kilometers of track had been laid, but by 1884 this had increased 800 percent, in large part because of the construction of the Mexico City-Paso del Norte line to the border with the United States. The tremendous construction campaign was promoted through government subsidies as a means to lure foreign investment. The Mexican railway was designed to reach the most productive areas of the country, unlike some others in Latin America, which were used to stimulate settlement (McBride, 1971). There was another 100 percent increase by the end of the century, and by the eve of the Revolution all of Mexico was laced by a complex railroad grid (Cosío Villegas, 1965, 7, pt. 4).[11]

Social Change and Social Control

Effective social control depends on manipulating resources and services and on devising strategies that are relevant to people's life situations—their mundane needs as well as their material and spiritual aspirations. Changes in land tenure laws, tax procedures, and transportation laid the way for a rapid, near-universal transformation in these life situations. The basic life conditions that had supported particular forms of social control—where people lived, how they were employed, the nature of agricultural life—were no longer; they had been substantially transformed in an eruptive change that affected all parts of peasant society in one way or another within the brief span of only a couple of decades (often in even less time).

Large numbers of people changed their places of residence; mining towns often mushroomed almost overnight; villages and towns became cities, beginning a process of urbanization in the Third World that has still not abated. City populations today are often growing three percent annually due to net migration alone. Rapid urbanization began during those critical decades of the late nineteenth century. Indian cities and towns were already growing by about one percent a year in the 1880s (Weber, 1963: 126).

Even for those who did not shift their place of residence permanently, there were important new changes in occupation for many. Villagers often became daily commuters or seasonal migrants to coal mimes, cocoa plantations, sugar mills, or other types of enterprises geared to provide goods for the world market. Land consolidation and new manufactured products were making the old forms of survival through subsistence agriculture and handicraft production impossible. The lack of fit between the numbers displaced from old types of employment and available positions in new types of enterprise often complicated the search for new means of survival. As Clark Reynolds wrote of Mexico in the period immediately prior to the Revolution of 1910, "The growth of machine manufacturing . . . tended to displace artisans at a greater rate than workers were absorbed into the new plants and mills" (Reynolds, 1970: 25). The momentous increase in the population growth rate that followed the colonial powers' pacification efforts and the introduction of the West's new public health measures also contributed to a worsening employment situation in many areas. Even those fortunate enough to find jobs frequently faced severe economic crises. ". . . increased income associated with rapid growth of the economy, attributable particularly to extractive industries, cash crops, and manufacturing," wrote Reynolds on Mexico, "did not transmit itself to the labor force in terms of proportional increases in wages and salaries. Instead, income growth in the leading sectors was being captured by the owners of capital, land, and subsoil resources"(Reynolds, 1970: 24). Many of these owners, as in Mexico, India, and elsewhere, were foreigners.

Life situations and the types of social control relevant to them were altered rapidly and irreparably during those critical decades even for those—the clear majority—who changed neither their places of residence nor their occupations. Agriculture remained the way that most people made a living. Even after Mexico's two-decade spurt of social and economic changes beginning about 1870, for example, more than 80 percent of the population were still supported by agriculture. What changed during those years, as we have seen, was people's agricultural production, their relationship to the land, and their position with respect to those in other social classes. Production shifted clearly toward cash crops, especially those in high demand for export. Although production for export was most pronounced on estates and plantations, clear changes away from growing overwhelmingly for subsistence needs only were evident among small landowners and peasants, even in the most noncommercialized parts of Mexico. Only the fortunate few, however, retained ownership to their land. Life situations changed most drastically as land was consolidated into haciendas, estates, and the like. In areas where new economies of scale were being introduced into agricultural production, peasants often became day laborers in large commercial enterprises, while in other areas they became tenants or joined the growing world ranks of wandering landless laborers.

The position of peasants with respect to those in other social classes changed in varying ways. At times, for example, the landlord and moneylender were one and the same, while in other instances moneylenders made up a distinct (often an ethnically distinct) group. Almost everywhere, however, peasants found growing gaps between them, and those who controlled resources crucial for their survival. Peasants' relationships to landowners did vary from place to place, of course, especially according to the degree that an area became commercialized.[12] In general, widening income gaps, different places of residence, and varying styles of dress and speech increasingly separated peasants from those in the classes above them. Many found supervisors and overseers now mediating between them and their landlords or creditors.

There has been a growing debate of late over how destructive the state policies discussed in this paper and the capitalist penetration these policies facilitated really were. Morris, for example, has argued against prevailing opinion concerning nineteenth century India, "On the whole, then, I would argue that there is a strong likelihood that the traditional sector, generally speaking, did not decline absolutely in economic significance and therefore did not constitute a depressing element in the performance of the nineteenth century economy. It is even possible that absolute growth occurred" (Morris, 1968: 9). Similarly, McAlpin challenges the notion that Indian increases in cotton production came as a result of a switch in land-use away from food crops. The increase, she argues, came from an extension of land under cultivation, a process far less disruptive (McAlpin, 1974: 665). Kuman demonstrates that landlessness and debt existed even before British rule in India and were not simply a result of the colonial era (Kumar, 1965: 34, 45, 190).

Such works raise important questions about the mythical, idyllic past in the precapitalist era and the distribution of effects of capitalism in the late nineteenth century. There certainly were those able to insulate themselves better than others from changes in life situations. Many peasants, McAlpin's findings indicate, simply did not become very price responsive for much of the nineteenth century. Nevertheless, the pressure on existing social arrangements was immense during this period, precipitating rapid and universal change in social arrangements, as even the very evidence of these authors intimates.

Kumar found, for example, that for seven districts in Tanjore surveyed, all but one had falling wages in the last quarter of the century. The decline was substantial, between 13 and 42 percent. He writes that ". . . the beginning of a trend towards the payment of money wages can be discerned, particularly for casual labourers and cash crops, but the pace of monetization was both slow and uneven" (Kumar, 1965: 146). Yet the numbers of landless agricultural laborers were rising substantially (indicating also, Kumar asserts, a decline in handicraft industry). Peasant debt also was growing quickly. Morris too points to the sorts of changes producing transformations in life situations: the growth of factories for the production of cotton and jute, the expansion of coal mining, and the like (Morris, 1968: 9). Rao takes McAlpin to task for minimizing the effects of railways but not looking at the increase in area of cultivation and the persistent proportion of food grains grown in a disaggregated manner. He argues that increases in cultivated areas came as those dislocated by the penetration of capitalism that the railroads precipitated were thrown back on agriculture, reabsorbed as poor agricultural workers facilitating agricultural expansion. The area under cash crops increased significantly in the second half of the nineteenth century, while the area under food grains increased as well, especially where railways had not penetrated (Rao, 1978). The effect is much more disruptive on the lives of peasants than McAlpin's undisaggregated figures might indicate.

Even in many of the sanguine interpretations of the spread of capitalism to peasant societies, then, there is still an image of substantial, rapid demographic, occupational, and productive changes. For those interpretations that attempt to build a rather stable picture of the late nineteenth century, there is little evidence. With all the changes in life situations—place of residence, type of job, what one produced, relationship to land, and ties to other classes—people's needs changed drastically. The result was an overall weakening of the ways peasants' lives had been organized, as old means of social control throughout the society crumbled simultaneously. Old sanctions, such as community ostracism or gossip, became less powerful as many commuted from the village, finding new reference groups, or moved from the village altogether. Old rewards, such as the benefits of mutual work teams to harvest specific crops, became meaningless in environments where many became landless or production shifted to new cash crops. Old strategies, such as settling disputes through the mediation of the village headman, became more and more irrelevant as interactions grew with those who neither knew nor respected the headman.

The environment the peasant faced changed drastically in only a short period, beginning sometime in the latter part of the nineteenth century. Land tenure changes, higher taxes, demands for taxes in cash, and railroad construction laid the way for changes in the environment that made old strategies of survival irrelevant to the new problems. True, there were important variations in the rates of change and the degree to which old forms of social control were debilitated. Such differences from community to community were especially evident in countries with varying topographical and climatic areas. Various areas differed significantly in the degree to which they were readily accessible and attractive to penetration by world market forces. The ability to maintain viable social organizations and the extent to which those organizations could shield individuals, depended on such factors as the suitability of the soil and climate to cash cropping and economies of scale, the proximity of the peasant produce to adequate transport, and other factors linked to the penetration of the world market.

In Mexico, for example, those Indians on the coast experienced the most severe change as social control by local community organizations disintegrated rapidly in the face of expanding plantations and estates, while those Indians in the more remote highlands were able, at times, to maintain some semblance of what Nash called "defensive corporate communities" (Nash, 1970: 183). In the poor and isolated state of Oaxaca, it was not until well into the twentieth century that the limited peasant marketing system was overwhelmed altogether by the market system stretching from Mexico City and beyond (Beals, 1975: 11–12).

It must be stressed, nevertheless, that in all but the most remote areas of Asia, Africa, and Latin America, old forms of social organization and social control were weakened substantially to one degree or another in the years following the new land laws, tax procedures, and railway construction.[13] In some cases, these old forms of social organization and control had survived for centuries, and in others they had been the products of other recent changes, such as peasants' settling on frontier lands. Whatever the case, the expansion of the world economy had a sudden and momentous impact on the basis of people's social relations. Whether thrust into a growing rural or urban proletariat or able to maintain a foothold in a still viable village community, people universally found themselves parts of enterprises linked directly or indirectly to the expanding market economy. In each country, the environment changed drastically for individuals as the society as a whole transformed its place and role in that world economy.

India was among the first non-Western areas to experience the shockwaves of a rapidly changing environment due to the society's new role in the world market. Its eruptive social and economic transformations began in the early 1860s, spurred on by the demand for cotton production caused by the disruptions in trade resulting from the American Civil War. The total value of exports from India grew about 140 percent in the twenty year period after 1860 and increased another 140 percent in the next twenty-seven years (Bhatia, 1965: 124).[14] In fact, India's absolute growth in trade was second in the world only to that of the United States in the last quarter of the nineteenth century. Certainly, the opening of the Suez Canal in 1869, reducing the sea voyage to India from Europe by thousands of miles, was a great impetus to the changes in India's economic environment. Overall growth in trade, including flourishing exports, however, did not assure those displaced from their old occupations or those who remained in agriculture a share of the new wealth. While India's exports were growing in value by 280 percent, its real industrial wages at constant prices fell.[15] Agricultural workers fared no better. True, European demand for the products of rural India was considerable. Even though cotton exports declined somewhat after the American Civil War, the level of demand for foodgrains, oil seeds, jute, tea, opium, indigo, and animal hides and skins was unprecedented. At the same time, the pressure brought to bear on Indian cultivators as a result of the changing economic environment was tremendous. By the year of India's independence, ". . . at least one-fifth of the total area under cultivation even in Ryotwari tracts could be said to have passed under open tenancy while an unknown, though substantial proportion of area was worked under forms of crop-sharing, in essence no different from tenancy" (Khurso, 1965: 183).

Typically, in other parts of Asia and in Latin America, eruptive changes in the economic environment began to occur a decade or so later than in India. For most of Asia and Latin America, the tremendous confluence of changes precipitated by the administrative changes in land tenure and tax regulations and by the building of new transport systems, began around 1870 and permeated each society by the early 1890s. In Mexico, the renewed relationship with the world economy had a devastating effect on peasant land ownership (by the time of the Revolution, there were over 8,000 haciendas) as well as a great impact on raw materials production, whether in the form of goods for import-substituting industries or for export. Production increased on an average of only 0.65 percent annually from 1877 to 1907 in the troubled agricultural sector, but, in that sector, raw materials for export grew during the same period by a hefty average of 7.45 percent annually (Cosío Villegas, 1965: 3, 107). Among the major select export crops of Mexico, growth was even more dramatic. From 1877 to 1880, for example, the value of coffee exports increased 55 percent; henequen exports, 80 percent; and vanilla exports, 58 percent. For the years 1881 and 1882 to 1891 and 1892, the increases were 128 percent for coffee, 138 percent for henequen, and 398 percent for tobacco (López Rosado, 1968, 1: 66–71, 95–100). The overall result of changes in agriculture was that most Mexicans were eating less while some were exporting more.[16] Though there were important regional differences in Mexico, estimates of the decline in real wages for agricultural laborers in the period 1876–1910 range between 20 and 30 percent (Katz, 1974: 1).

Conclusion

Penetration of the world economy to all levels of society, in a period of two decades or less, radically altered the environment in which all society's members sought survival and other crucial life goals. Leaders of existing social organizations in each society frequently found the strategies they offered irrelevant to the needs and problems of their constituencies. There was a sudden and rapid weakening of the ways social and political life of peasants were organized throughout Asia, Africa, and Latin America as levels of social control declined substantially to one degree or another.

Social organizations and their corresponding forms of social control differed considerably from one society to another, but in each, one finds a similar lament about the onslaught against these organizations during this period of increased world market penetration. In India, for example, T. N. Madan complained of the decline of the Hindu joint family (Madan, 1965). Eric Wolf wrote of the demise of Mexico's self-governing landholding *pueblos* (Wolf, 1969a: 17).

Certainly the weakening of these old forms of social control and many others did not signal an end to a romantic and harmonious precapitalist era.[17] The old forms of social control could be demeaning, exploitative, and personally debilitating. Also, the new deeper and wider penetration of the world economy did not always precipitate a quick end to old social organizations. What did happen was a distinct weakening of these societies as the old forms of social control became suddenly less suited to the daily exigencies of most people's lives. The old rewards, sanctions, and strategies were no longer providing the same compelling dictates to behave and believe one way rather than another.

Capitalism was not some inexorable force that simply swept away existing institutions through the very force of the market mechanism. In many societies, social organization had been a means to insulate peasants from direct or sustained contact with the international market. For peasants to produce what the market demanded they produce, there had to be an additional force insuring compliance with the market's demands. That force was the state. Backed by the coercion of armies and police, the state adopted a set of policies—on land, taxation, transportation—that greatly enhanced the force of the new market. Along with its violent forces, the state brought an array of techniques capable of undoing the existing ways of organizing peasants. These techniques included tax rolls, land registers, land surveys, accounting procedures, standardized currencies, guaranteed state bonds for railroad investment, and much more.

State officials and capitalist entrepreneurs often worked at cross-purposes, especially as the nineteenth century progressed. States, for example, often wanted railroads as a means to move troops quickly to quell rebellion and were not as interested as the entrepreneurs in building the tracks to areas best suited for growing or mining export commodities. There was sufficient overlap in means, however, as states sought an increase in the mobilization of resources to use for political purposes, and entrepreneurs sought increased wealth, to lead to state policies promoting the penetration of capitalism and creating a crisis in existing peasant social organizations.

The crisis of the peasantry was the demise of its strategies for survival and for achieving other aspirations. The need was to find new institutional means to achieve goals. In the case of Mexico, the struggles to establish new social control and new strategies of survival included a major peasant revolution. In India, those struggles included a variety of modes, ranging from peasant avoidance to peasant mobilization into national or ethnic political movements, but they did not involve major peasant rebellion. While the penetration of capitalism and the state policies that promoted capitalism were critical elements weakening old ways of organizing social and political life among peasants, they alone did not account for the form or outcome of struggles to reorganize social and political life. An analysis of those factors that have influenced such reorganization are beyond the scope of this paper

(I hope to deal with that subject elsewhere), but it can be said that success in such struggles depended on two factors. It depended on the relationship of peasant societies to political and economic resources injected into them at the time of the international market's great surge, and on the ability to use those resources to establish relevant strategies of survival for those so deeply affected by the force of the international market.

5. Bandits, Monks, and Pretender Kings: Patterns of Peasant Resistance and Protest in Colonial Burma, 1826-1941

Michael Adas

One of the greatest advances in our understanding of the meaning of the era of European imperialist dominance for the peoples of Africa and Asia has resulted from recent studies which have forced a blurring of the distinction between the precolonial and colonial periods. Battle dates charting campaigns of European conquest, the overthrow of indigenous dynasties, or official proclamations of new modes of administrative organization have diminished in importance as numerous studies, focused on conditions at the local level, have documented the persistence of precolonial institutions, the tenacity of entrenched elite groups, and the limitations of the European colonizers in manpower, material resources, and knowledge of the areas and peoples that came under their control. The combination of these factors greatly restricted the colonizers' ability to exert effective political control, particularly over local elite groups and beneath them the mass of the cultivators at the village level. This meant in turn that European policies and initiatives from revenue collection to public works and social reforms were considerably transformed, steadily undermined, and at times completely ignored by the colonized peoples for whom they were intended (Washbrook, 1976; Baker, 1976; Ranger, 1969; van Velsen, 1964). Indigenous elite groups learned to turn the military might and legal apparatus of the alien colonizers to their own advantage, thereby establishing or enhancing their own power over the mass of the cultivators. In areas like South India, which has been the focus of extensive research in recent years, after decades of European rule, indigenous factions and local leaders were in some ways more autonomous and influential, and indigenous institutions, especially caste, more entrenched than they had been in the precolonial era. Ambitious British schemes for remaking the Indian sociopolitical order had been frustrated by the surprising resilience and strength of institutions and arrangements that had once appeared vulnerable and in need of reform.

Although our growing awareness of the limited usefulness of chronological compartmentalization, the checks on European power, and the persistence of indigenous elites and institutions has forced reassessments of many aspects of the colonial experience, perhaps none merits reexamination more than our approach to resistance and protest on the part of colonized peoples. Clearcut distinctions between primary resistance, postconquest risings, "archaic" or primitive protest, and "real" nationalist movements that were never very convincing, have been blurred, if not obliterated, by recent research. Writers like T. O. Ranger (1968), Sartono Kartodirdjo (1973), and Reyaldo Ileto (1979) have amply demonstrated that there are not only fundamental ideological and organizational links between movements grouped in each of these categories, but that forms of protest like millenarianism or banditry, once associated with primary resistance or the archaic phase, persist in the so-called nationalistic era and beyond into the independence period. As the studies of Washbrook and Baker cited above also reveal, an understanding of precolonial social and political institutions and the ways in which these persisted, despite European conquest and rule, is essential to any attempt to explain outbursts of social protest or, as important, the absence of them in the colonial era. Nationalist leaders, for example, did not suddenly appear, but emerged gradually as the result of shifts in the orientation and organization of longstanding elite groups and factions. Thus, the large-scale rebellions and nationalist party struggles that hitherto have been the focus of most research cannot be isolated from modes of thinking and organization or from broader traditions of protest whose roots lay in the precolonial past.

The historiography of the area that presently makes up the nation of Burma provides a striking illustration of the distortions that result from placing too much emphasis on discontinuity and differences between phases of anticolonial resistance and protest. It is difficult to think of an example of imperialist expansion where the contrast between pre- and postconquest conditions has been more sharply drawn. In the established view, shared even by the critics of British expansion in Burma (Furnivall, 1957; Adas, 1972), a poor, backward and isolated enclave ruled by despotic, often cruel monarchs was, as the result of British conquest, abruptly opened to the forces of the world economy and brought under the administration of one of the most effective bureaucracies of the nineteenth century, the Indian Civil Service. Though Burma was conquered in stages between 1824 and 1886 and most writers clearly recognized that the colonial impact was greater in some regions than in others, the rapid expansion of cultivated acreage, steadily rising revenue and export figures, the ready participation of the Burmese in the market economy, and their addiction to the consumer rewards that resulted, all appeared to confirm the official assessment—at least until the late 1920s—that Burma was a model province, a superb example of the good government and economic benefits that could result from colonial rule.[1] This view also appeared to be supported by the long periods of internal peace and stability that followed each colonial conquest. According to this interpretation, after the xenophobic and misguided defenders of inept rulers had been defeated and criminal elements put down in the 1850s and 1880s, the province enjoyed decades of prosperity and tranquility until nationalist agitators, often posing as Buddhist monks, sought to stir up the peasant masses in the years after World War I.

Though some writers, most notably J. S. Furnivall, dissented from the view that change benefitted the great majority of the Burmese, all stressed the depth and abruptness of the transformations resulting from European conquest and rule. Both defenders and critics of colonization have seen discontinuity—political, economic, social, and intellectual—and the decline of "traditional" ideas and institutions as the central features of the British period in Burmese history. In fact, discontinuity and the decline of tradition came to be viewed as the underlying causes of the succession of popular upheavals that shattered the facade of colonial peace and prosperity in the 1920s and 1930s, and they have also been considered responsible for Burma's return to a position of isolation and limited development in the postindependence era.

It cannot be disputed that colonialism brought fundamental changes to Burma. These changes, however, were neither as abrupt nor often as pervasive and lasting as they have generally been pictured. Even in Lower Burma, where the spread of the market economy and the introduction of new land tenure systems were concentrated, precolonial attitudes, institutions, and modes of organization and interaction persisted decades after the formal British takeover, and in some cases outlasted the colonizers into the independence era. A close examination of the responses of Burmese peasants and local elite groups in both Upper and Lower Burma to British conquest and rule reveals much continuity with the precolonial period amid the far reaching changes that have been emphasized in most works on British Burma. Despite grand British schemes for administrative reorganization and claims of centralized bureaucratic control, large portions of conquered areas remained beyond the effective control of the colonizers for decades after they were formally annexed, and some regions were never governed by the British at all in any meaningful way. Even in the more accessible riverine and coastal lowland areas where the British most actively pursued their political and economic designs for the province, the peasants' centuries-old hostility toward government officials and their struggle to retain the maximum degree of local autonomy continued. Local elite groups, who had succeeded in attaching themselves to the new rulers and in winning administrative posts on the lower rungs of the colonial hierarchy, employed the same techniques of concealment, deception, and tactics of bribery and embezzlement that their ancestors had used to blunt the revenue demands of Burmese monarchs.

Despite the deep involvement of large numbers of peasants, especially in Lower Burma, in the export economy that developed in the late nineteenth century, my investigation through revenue records, police reports, and special enquiries into economic conditions and incidents of social unrest, reveals that large numbers of the cultivating classes were never reconciled to British rule. They retained a deep longing for the return of their own monarchs and a fierce attachment to the beliefs, rituals, and symbols—both religious *and* political—of Theravada Buddhism as it was practiced in Burma. The British tendency to link rising crime rates and other social disorders to the breakdown of Buddhist education and to the weakening hold of Buddhist ethics on an increasingly market-oriented and consumer-minded peasant population not only diverts attention from causes of unrest rooted in the disruptions and injustices of the colonial political economy, but also seriously distorts the relationship between the peasantry and Buddhism. Despite decreases in the proportion of youths receiving a formal Buddhist education, especially in areas like Lower Burma, and a decline in discipline within the Buddhist Sangha, Buddhism remained central to the identity of the vast majority of lowland Burmese. As in precolonial times, Buddhist ethics played a vital role in the regulation of social and economic relations and in judging the performance of those who governed. From the earliest risings against the British colonizers in the 1820s, through the rebellions and communal clashes of the 1930s, and the final struggles for independence, the defense of Buddhism was used by princely pretenders, prophets, and nationalist leaders alike to rally peasant supporters to their cause.

The persistence of this theme was paralleled by a broader continuity of ideological appeals, leadership styles, and symbols employed by all Burmese leaders who were able to build a popular base for their movements, with the partial exception of the *Thakins* who emerged in the late 1920s. In addition, the main modes of popular protest—banditry, cult withdrawal, risings led by princely pretenders, flight, and communal clashes—remained constant throughout the colonial era, though the causes that gave rise to individual outbreaks or movements varied somewhat as new grievances were spawned by political and economic change. For example, economic hardship and nationalism, in the European sense of the term, contributed to the depression rebellions of the 1930s, usually associated with the prophet-pretender, Saya San. The causes for which most cultivators rose in these rebellions, however, and especially the forms their dissidence took were strikingly similar to those of the local lords, *pongyis* (Buddhist monks), and peasants who so stubbornly resisted the advance of the British conquerors in the 1850s or in the 1880s and 1890s.

Relying primarily on the abundant archival and published evidence available for British Burma, I will attempt in this essay to demonstrate the persistence of traditions of peasant resistance and protest. I will also seek to show why and how these traditions changed in response to broader political and socioeconomic transformations. Central to my approach is the assumption that individual instances of collective protest are shaped not just by the conditions and specific causes that consciously motivate their participants, but also by longstanding and well-tested traditions of protest, which shape the ways in which aggrieved groups respond to those whom they view as their oppressors. According to this approach, movements that are normally treated as single "great rebellions," such as the Saya San risings of the 1930s, can often be found upon examination to be loosely-linked conglomerations of local risings and disturbances involving very different modes of collective protest. This approach results in an emphasis on the continuity between protest movements of different types and widely varying sizes, and the ways in which these movements are rooted in traditions of resistance and protest that predated the period of colonization and that persist into the independence era.

Excepting the temporary setbacks which the British suffered at the hands of the able Burman commander,[2] Maha Bandula, in the First Anglo-Burmese War, the resistance offered by the Konbaung rulers to the advance of British armies in the wars of 1824—1826, 1852, and 1885, was at best feeble, and increasingly so in each encounter (Hall, 1964; Woodman, 1962; Htin Aung, 1965). This poor showing on the part of the Burman defenders was surprising to contemporaries given the Burmans' reputation for military prowess and bellicosity, and their impressive victories in the late eighteenth century over their bitter rivals, the Siamese, and invaders from Ch'ing China. The ease of the British conquest has normally been attributed to the inept leadership of the later Konbaung rulers and their officials and military commanders (excepting Bandula), and especially to the overwhelming technological and organizational superiority which the British possessed in armed conflict with a backward and inward-looking kingdom. As the century progressed, the weaknesses of the Burman rulers became more and more apparent and the British military edge ever more awesome.

Whatever the merits of these arguments, they obscure more fundamental reasons for the failure of Burman resistance, reasons centered on the monarch and state. Resistance at this level was ineffectual not only because conventional armies and battles played to the strengths of the British, who could draw upon the technology and resources of an industrializing society and a global empire, but also because the center of the Konbaung state was perhaps its most fragile and vulnerable component. This was especially true by the first decades of the nineteenth century when that state was clearly in decline. Thus, the British confronted a dynasty whose court was riven by the struggles of rival claimants to the throne, factional intrigues, and the plots of disgruntled princes and nobles (Koenig, 1978; Htin Aung, 1967). The debilitating effects of these struggles, which were characteristic of the contest-state (Adas, 1981) form of polity found in precolonial Burma, were exacerbated by the steady increase in the degree of autonomy enjoyed by regional lords and local leaders that was both a consequence and a symptom of dynastic decline (Lieberman, 1976: 39, 45, 105—6, 220, 227ff).

As the court's control of areas beyond the capital decreased, its ability to marshal the manpower and supplies needed to meet the British challenge diminished. In the first Anglo-Burman confrontation, the Konbaung state could still muster substantial armies and support these for fairly extended periods of time. Even in this phase, however, Burman forces were made up mainly of ill-trained, poorly armed, and unwilling conscripts recruited by the retainers of regional lords. These troops repeatedly failed to hold, and often to man at all, superb defensive positions, and only stood their ground when led by able and charismatic commanders like Bandula. The feebleness of state-led resistance at its strongest in the first war is most strikingly revealed by British and Indian casualty figures. Deaths by disease (malaria, cholera, dysentery) greatly exceeded those due to battle wounds (Majumdar, 1963: 110). At the time of the second war in 1852, the control of the court had grown so weak that Burman armies offered only token resistance to the rapid advance of the British up the deltas of the Irrawaddy and Sittang rivers. In the final clash in 1885, the capital and the dynasty itself fell with virtually no armed struggle whatsoever.

The importance of the vulnerability of the Burman state structure in the failure of resistance to British conquest is evidenced by the greater success achieved by risings which broke out in the months just after different areas of the Konbaung kingdom had been formally annexed by the British. Though fugitive nobles and officials from the Konbaung court played some role in these risings, they were led for the most part by regional lords and local notables, or in some instances by *pongyis* and bandit chiefs. As the capacity of the Konbaung state to check the British advance declined with each successive confrontation, local resistance grew in scale and duration. After the annexation of Arakan and Tenasserim in 1826, only minor disturbances occurred (Furnivall, 1939: 15; *Akyab*: 36). By contrast, the annexation of the Irrawaddy delta region in 1852 was followed by nearly a decade of local risings and "bandit" attacks. After the 1886 annexation of the remaining portions of the Konbaung kingdom to the Indian Empire, British occupation forces struggled for over five years to put down widespread resistance, again spearheaded by local leaders, in both Upper and Lower Burma. Though the last Konbaung monarch, Thibaw, was easily toppled, the British were forced to call in reinforcements from India and expend considerable resources to put down repeated challenges to their rule at the regional and village level. Despite soaring exports in the following decades and frequent references on the part of British writers to the peace and good government that colonial rule had brought to Burma, rising crime rates—which were regularly the highest in Burma of any province in the Indian Empire (*Rangoon Gazette*, 1929: 22; RPAB, 1920: 12)—sporadic local risings, and communal clashes sustained a tradition of anticolonial resistance and peasant protest which peaked in the antitax campaigns, rebellions, and communal riots of the 1920s and 1930s.

The greater effectiveness of postconquest resistance was in part due to the fact that the gap between the British and local Burmese forces in manpower and armaments was so great that conventional assaults were suicidal. Therefore, regional lords or bandit chiefs resorted to hit-and-run attacks, ambushes, and raids that were characteristic of centuries-old techniques of guerrilla-style warfare. The British ignorance of the local terrain, which rebel bands exploited fully, and the dense forest cover that in many areas prevented the British from making effective use of their overwhelming advantage in firepower, rendered guerrilla resistance by far the most difficult for the British to suppress (Crosthwaite, 1912; Geary, 1886; Tha Aung and Mya Din, 1941). The more effective resistance provided by localized risings was also due to the greater strength of the ties that bound regional lords, village headmen, and bandit chiefs to their supporters—ties that were usually based on personalist and reciprocal patron-client exchanges. In contrast to the rather fragile and often short-lived power of the state center, the dominance of local elite groups was frequently maintained for generations and, in some instances, centuries (Tha Aung and Mya Din, 1941: 131; Lieberman, 1976: 202). In the precolonial era the authority and influence of headmen and regional lords peaked in periods of dynastic decline and breakdown as the already limited control of the state was more and more constricted, and these local leaders became the upholders of law and order in the locality. With each defeat and finally the collapse of the Konbaung dynasty in the face of foreign invasion, local notables rallied their followers to resist the imposition of British control over their lands and villages. If their proclamations to their followers are to be believed, some of these leaders themselves hoped to establish a new dynasty in place of the vanquished Konbaung overlords. These aspirations were by no means without foundation, for on a number of occasions in Burmese history local leaders had succeeded in winning the throne—in fact, Alaungpaya, the founder of the Konbaung dynasty had begun his rise to power as a village headman in the Shwebo district who had organized resistance against Mon invaders from Lower Burma (Htin Aung, 1967: 157ff).

Local Konbaung officials, especially *thugyis* (heads of clusters of tiny hamlets) and *myothugyis* (township heads), who were displaced by the British conquest and annexation, were the main leaders of the resistance struggles that followed the 1852 war. Resistance in a number of areas was led by *pongyis*, but they tended to support *thugyi*-led bands rather than assume control themselves. According to British accounts, the other major source of resistance in the post-1852 period came from bandit gangs that roamed the wilderness of the lower and western Irrawaddy delta region for decades after the formal conquest. As some British officials admitted (*Tharrawaddy*: 26), however, the bandit or *dacoit* label was applied rather indiscriminately to resisting ex-Konbaung officials and professional criminals alike. This meant that men like the ex-*thugyi*, Gaung Gyi, who fought to drive out the alien invaders and restore the rule of his Konbaung overlords, were hunted down like common criminals.

Whether ex-officials, *pongyis*, or professional bandits, all resistance leaders claimed to be commissioned by the Konbaung court, which in 1852 still ruled in Upper Burma, to carry on the struggle against the British. Leaders of the larger risings, like Gaung Gyi, wielded the ancient symbols of Burmese political authority: gilt umbrellas, royal elephants, and sacred gongs. Some rebel leaders claimed to be princes of the royal house. Widespread popular support for resistance groups, particularly in the form of food and shelter, demonstrates the strong hold these symbols and appeals continued to exercise over peasant communities despite the dynasty's setbacks. Some of this support was admittedly given out of fear of reprisal raids, but many villagers willingly allowed themselves to be treated as subjects by rebel leaders and refused information and supplies to British forces in pursuit of rebel bands. Any Burmese who cooperated with the invaders became targets of rebel assaults. Headmen and cultivators were slain and on a number of occasions whole villages were put to the torch, such as several settlements along the Irrawaddy that had supplied fuel for British steamboats moving up or down the river. Though robberies were carried out and a number of ambushes against British columns and raids on occupied towns were attempted, most rebel bands spent much of their time eluding British patrols or simply struggling to survive. When the hopelessness of their cause became apparent following the new king, Mindon's, refusal to continue the struggle, many rebels resorted to the time-tested peasant defense of flight and slipped into Upper Burma.[3]

After the overthrow of the Konbaung dynasty and the annexation to the Indian Empire of the remaining portions of the Burman kingdom in 1885–1886, the British were confronted by resistance in both Upper and Lower Burma that far exceeded in scale and ferocity that which had appeared so troublesome at mid-century. The modes of resistance adopted after 1886 were much the same as those employed earlier, but rebel bands were much larger and better organized, and rebel leaders made much more elaborate use of kingly rituals and royal symbols in their efforts to give legitimacy to their cause. Some forms of resistance were also more in evidence in this phase. Of these, an increase in flight or mass migration is the most notable. As British columns advanced into the Dry Zone, they found many villages deserted. Though in many cases the British argued that the inhabitants of these villages had fled to avoid dacoit depredations, they were also forced to admit that peasants had abandoned their homes in an effort to avoid submission to alien invaders. Most villagers sought at first to hide in nearby forests or distant hills, but many eventually joined the rebel bands and dacoit gangs that spearheaded resistance to the imposition of British rule (Geary, 1886: 49, 51; Crosthwaite, 1912: 34; Mya Khan, 1969: 68).

Because the court center itself was overthrown in 1885, Konbaung officials, princes, and princely pretenders played a much greater role in the disturbances following the third Anglo-Burman war than they had in earlier resistance efforts. In December of 1886, two princes, Teiktin Hmat and Teiktin Thein, raised the standard of revolt in Shwebo, the home district of the Konbaung dynasty's founder, Alaungpaya. Several "dacoit" leaders, their followers, and thousands of peasants armed with *dahs* (long knives), spears, and muskets rallied to the princes' cause, but after a series of defeats in skirmishes with British and Indian troops, in which one of the princes was killed, resistance in the district soon dissipated (Geary: 276–78; *Shwebo*: 34ff).

One of the exiled King Thibaw's stewards also left the palace to arouse the people to resist the British and he was joined by one of King Mindon's surviving sons,[4] who left his monastery refuge to fight against the British conquerors. In addition to genuine scions of the royal house, numerous pretenders appeared who claimed to be of royal blood and urged their followers to aid them in their efforts to restore Konbaung rule. Perhaps the most interesting of the would-be princes was a former actor who took the title of the Kyimyindaing Prince. His great skill at assuming the style and manipulating the symbols of Burman kingship in order to attract peasant followers is explained by the fact that he had often played the role of a senior prince in *pwe* (theatrical) performances at the palace. The pretender claimed that he had been carried away as an infant into the wilderness by one of the queens who feared for his life. Indigenous accounts also relate that he had led a rather feeble rebellion against King Thibaw and was on his way to the court in chains when war with the British broke out. Other royal pretenders—some claiming to be *Minlaungs* or imminent kings—emerged in areas as widely separated as the Myingyan district in the heart of the Dry Zone and the Ye–U township in Lower Burma (Tha Aung and Mya Din, 1941: 81–4, 93, 97, 103, 121–4; *Yamethin*: 37).

Both genuine princes and pretenders sought to rally support for their resistance efforts by building palace centers that were essential symbols of kingly authority in Burmese culture, and recreating, insofar as possible given their limited resources and constant challenges from British forces, the administrative hierarchy and procedures associated with the Burman monarchy (Heine-Geldern, 1942: 17, 19–26; Yi Yi, 1961; Ireland, 1907, 49). Mindon's son, who came to be known as the Myinzaing Prince, bestowed military commissions and official titles on the *Bohs* or commanders of the forces that fought in his name. He appointed counsellors and a "prime minister," and mobilized thousands of peasants in his struggle to restore the dynasty. After being driven from the Dry Zone, the Myinzaing Prince took refuge in the rugged Shan hills where he found time to direct the construction of a royal city and palace which was given the auspicious title of the "City of the White Elephant." Though he was later to die of malaria, a fugitive abandoned by his followers, in the weeks after his palace center was established his armies swelled to over twenty thousand men and proved a major challenge to the British conquerors (Tha Aung and Mya Din, 1941: 85–6, 107, 124).

As was the case with the post-1852 resistance in Lower Burma, most of the support for princely rebels—genuine or pretender—after the 1886 annexation in Upper Burma was recruited from the dependents and retainers of local lords and village notables. Though some court officials, like the steward mentioned above and the commander of the king's cavalry, threw in their lot with the rebels, township heads (*myothugyis*) and village headmen (*thugyis*) made up the great majority of the secondary leaders of the resistance (Tha Aung and Mya Din, 1941: 83–4, 91–6; 101, 105, 114, 117, 121; *Pakokku*: 18) with the exception of the so-called *dacoit* chiefs who will be discussed in greater detail below. As British observers pointed out, the decision of headmen or township leaders to resist normally meant that large numbers of villagers rallied to the rebel side. Thus, rebel forces were made up of uneasy alliances of distinct, and sometimes hostile, bands of untrained peasants, rather than well-integrated and drilled soldiers. When confronted by the well-armed and disciplined troops of the colonizers, rebel forces usually broke down into small groups whose continued resistance was dependent on the strength of the personalist, patron-client bonds that were the backbone of social and political relations in precolonial Burma. However cohesive and steadfast these bands proved to be, the British were able to hunt them down and defeat them piecemeal.

Other than pressures applied by local men of power, the main motives for joining rebel bands in Upper Burma were hostility towards the British invaders and a desire to restore rule by indigenous overlords. The British, who had long regarded Burman monarchs as cruel tyrants, were surprised by the extent and intensity of resistance to foreign conquest, particularly that on the part of ordinary villagers. As Grattan Geary, who wrote one of the most vivid and honest accounts of the campaigns in Upper Burma, admitted, the conquerors were amazed to find good roads and a population that was well fed and housed, and generally content with their rulers. He noted that most of the former subjects of the Konbaung monarch, " . . . made no complaint of oppression and gave no evidence of rejoicing at our (the British) coming; on the contrary they took kindly to dacoity against us" (Geary, 1886: 292–3).

The resistance offered by regional lords and village leaders in Upper Burma in the name of the defeated Konbaung dynasty was also inspired by a less "patriotic", but perhaps more deeply felt desire to preserve the high degree of autonomy that regional and local elites and village dwellers generally had enjoyed in the precolonial era. The ancient struggle of these groups against state intervention into and control over their affairs, and especially their efforts to limit state tax and manpower demands, was now directed against the new British rulers. Some sense of the transformations that had occurred in Lower Burma since 1852, must have heightened fears for the erosion of local control and the patron-client exchanges on which it was based. More immediately threatening was the impressive display of mobility and military strength by which the British had so easily toppled the enfeebled Konbaung dynasty and moved to establish their control over the village population. Our post-World War II obsession with anticolonial resistance has often led us to lose sight of the importance of this age-old struggle for local autonomy against *any* overlord, whether European or indigenous.

Although some *pongyis* or Buddhist monks had joined in the resistance after the 1852 annexation of Lower Burma, in the late 1880s for the first time they assumed a major role in the struggle against the British. Their leadership of rebel bands was most apparent in Lower Burma which had been ruled by non-Buddhist foreigners for over three decades. It was also in this area, especially in the delta districts around Rangoon, that the challenges to Buddhism posed by the influx of a market, consumer-oriented economy, Christian missionaries, and Western courts and legal procedures had been felt the most strongly. *Pongyis*, most of whom claimed to be acting on orders from the king, led risings in Tenasserim, Toungoo, and Tharrawaddy in Lower Burma and in the Minbu district in the Dry Zone (Geary, 1886: 7, 225; Crosthwaite, 1912: 107ff; Sarkisyanz, 1965: 104–5; Plant, 1886: 1, 4–6). The most serious of these risings was that begun by a monk named U Thuriya in the Tharrawaddy district in July of 1888. This outbreak warrants detailed examination both because it exhibited patterns that were strikingly similar to the majority of postconquest rebellions that followed and because it illustrates some of the major differences between the causes that gave rise to resistance in Upper Burma, which had just been annexed, and Lower Burma, which had been under colonial rule for over thirty years.

The British advance into Upper Burma in 1885–86 touched off disturbances throughout the Tharrawaddy district in the upper delta region. Policemen and village leaders in many areas refused to continue to serve the colonial authorities and joined or formed rebel bands or dacoit gangs that roamed the district with impunity for several years. Tax collectors, loyal headmen, and police posts were the major targets of rebel assaults. Most leaders claimed to have been commissioned by the deposed king, but some like Nga Aung adopted regalia, including gilt umbrellas, that suggest that they themselves had dynastic ambitions. The causes of these disturbances were similar to those focusing on the defense of the monarchy and hostility to foreign conquest that motivated those who resisted in Upper Burma. The causes of U Thuriya's rebellion, however, which was by far the largest rising in Lower Burma in this period, went beyond patriotism and involved disaffection caused in part by changes that had occurred as a result of colonial rule.

A severe cholera epidemic, poor rainfall, and crop shortages fueled the discontent that gave rise to U Thuriya's rebellion. These conditions may also have lent credence to widespread rumors concerning dynastic decline that had long been associated with bad weather and that were now directed against the foreign overlords. Special taxes on peasant households, that the British levied to pay for extra manpower to police the troubled district, also contributed to widespread disaffection. Discontent was heightened by further rumors that an income tax would soon be imposed on all town dwellers in the district. These cesses—actual and imagined—were doubly resented because the policemen they supported were mainly recruited from the ethnic minority Karens, who were said to demand food and labor from the peasant population without payment. The recent confiscation of firearms held by villagers in the district also angered the peasants since it left them at the mercy of wandering gangs of dacoits for which the heavily forested district had been notorious for centuries. Crop shortages in conjunction with the gradual abandonment of communal village granaries in the face of the market-oriented, competitive political economy that had developed under colonial rule resulted in sharp increases in local food prices that the government did little or nothing to bring under control. The sale of children by peasant families to rich merchants and landowners for adoption was perhaps the most dramatic sign of the desperate condition of the poorest cultivators in the district.

The rising had apparently been prepared well in advance of the actual outbreak on 2 July 1888. Its leader, U Thuriya, a *pongyi* from a monastery near the town of Gyobingauk, administered an oath of loyalty to those who agreed to join him in rebellion. Many of his followers were also tattooed with magic letters that were intended to identify them as the *pongyi's* supporters and make them invulnerable to British bullets. Recruits were also given palm-leaf enlistment tickets, of which over seventeen hundred were prepared, and read proclamations that U Thuriya claimed had been issued by the Myingun prince. According to British accounts, all of the dacoit gangs in the district pledged their support for the rising. On the night of 2 July, which had been chosen by an astrologer as auspicious, attacks were launched on several towns, telegraph lines were cut, and the railway line between Gyobingauk and Zigon was badly damaged. After threatening a village records-keeper, the rebels headed south to attack the Prome mail train, or at least the British believed that this was what they intended to do. Before they reached their target, however, the special police and military had been alerted. No major clashes between government forces and the rebels occurred, but by the end of the following day the rising had been put down without any loss of life and eighty-four arrests. Once again resistance in the district reverted to sporadic raids by dacoit gangs (*Tharrawaddy*, 1920: 35–7; Dunn, 1920: 17–19).

Although the nature of resistance in Upper and Lower Burma differed in important ways, one mode of response was, according to British accounts, pervasive in both areas—dacoity or gang robbery. Most of the *Bohs*, whose followers swelled the ranks of the forces of princes and pretenders in Upper Burma and *pongyi* agitators in Lower Burma, were classified as bandits or common criminals by the British. In part the label represented an attempt, whether conscious or unconscious, on the part of the British to allay doubts about policies that had evoked such widespread and determined resistance by the Burmans. As it is used in official accounts of the disturbances after the 1852 and 1886 annexations, the term is meaningless. To begin with, though some leaders whom the British branded as dacoits had in fact been bandits in the precolonial period (Tha Aung and Mya Din, 1941: 129; *Pakokku*: 18), the label was also applied to resistance leaders whose prior occupations ranged from courtiers and Konbaung administrators to betel-leaf sellers, messengers, cultivators, and disbanded soldiers. So-called bandit gangs sometimes numbered in the thousands. They were often well armed and organized into regular fighting units with battle standards and battle orders which called for conventional encounters with advancing British forces (*Thayetmyo*: 13–14; Tha Aung and Mya Din, 1941: 119–20, 122; *Shwebo*: 35, 37, 41). As Grattan Geary candidly observed, it was usually difficult to distinguish between ordinary villagers and professional dacoits, especially in times of economic or political breakdown when community survival could depend on alliances with dacoit gangs and the forcible seizure of scarce food supplies (Geary, 1886: 46–7, 71, 232, 276).

It cannot be doubted that some dacoits were in fact professional criminals, but many of those whom the British routinely referred to as dacoits opposed the colonizers for political reasons and received widespread support, often long after their cause was clearly lost. So-called dacoit chiefs or *Bohs* often claimed control over specific areas, from which they collected revenue on a fairly regular basis, and respected the territory of allied rebel leaders. In some cases *Bohs* brandished gilt umbrellas or other royal regalia and one leader in Shwebo used some of the revenue he collected to build a pagoda that he managed to complete before he died (Crosthwaite, 1912: 14, 23, 27, 31, 53, 103–5; *Yamethin*: 38; *Shwebo*: 40). The *Bohs*' own sense of their genuine patriotism and the righteousness of their cause is perhaps best indicated by the papers found on a dacoit leader from the Minbu district who was killed in action in October 1877. In addition to oaths swearing loyalty to the throne and orders that all *Bohs* and their followers shall, "Obey (their) superiors as the cow obeys the cowherd," the papers contain repeated references to the British as "foreign rebels." It appears that both sides were capable of employing ad hominem labels to discredit their opponents (White, ms. IOR).

Though the degree to which villagers in different areas willingly submitted to the demands of rebel *Bohs* is difficult to determine, British writers reported widespread collusion between village leaders and alleged dacoit chiefs. British commanders complained that the peasants in areas where dacoit bands were active refused to provide supplies for government troops or information concerning the whereabouts of bandit gangs. The British also had great difficulty recruiting informers or scouts from peasant communities in the disturbed tracts. The British practice of supplying arms to villages in these areas to enable their inhabitants to defend themselves had to be abandoned because these arms soon found their way into rebel or (in official parlance) dacoit hands. Even the British commander, Sir Charles Crosthwaite, was forced to concede the widespread support which the so-called dacoits received from the village populace when he concluded that: "If the people would have given us information, the dacoit system could have been broken in a very short time. As they would not, the only course open was to make them fear us more than the dacoits (1912: 104)."

Two additional patterns emerge from accounts of the post-1886 disturbances that, though they are mentioned only in passing, ought to be noted because they take on great importance in later protest movements. Necromancers and charm sellers are for the first time mentioned as leaders of local risings, and though direct references to talismans are rare, Burmese cultural traditions and the evidence we have suggest that magic was a potent means by which rebel leaders attracted and held peasant support. U Thuriya used cabalistic tattooes. Bo Shwe, the dacoit leader from Minbu, was found with numerous charms on his body, including one designed to prevent bullet wounds, one to induce bouyancy and great speed, another to make one's enemies sleepy (*Tharrawaddy*: 36; White ms., 10R). Though millenarian ideas that would play a prominent role in many later rebellions are rarely mentioned in accounts of the postconquest resistance struggles, a pretender in the Kyaukse district in Upper Burma is referred to as a *Sektya* or embryo Buddha in a British police report (RPAB, 1888: 11). Little more is said about the use of the title by this rebel leader, but the term and its millenarian associations would come to be closely identified by the British with protest and sedition.

Though stubborn and costly, Burman resistance to conquest and colonial rule was ultimately crushed. British organizational and military superiority played critical roles, particularly since the forces which opposed them were generally poorly trained and coordinated. British success, however, often depended heavily on a number of age-old techniques of empire builders. They recruited police and special military forces from minority ethnic groups, like the Karens and Shans. The British also bought elite allies and Burman informers, one of whom played a critical role in the quick suppression of U Thuriya's rising (*Tharrawaddy*: 37). The British bribed rebel chiefs, including some whom they considered dacoits, into submission with the promise of positions under the new regime. The colonizers exploited rivalries between Burman nobles and local lords, between village headmen, and between neighboring villages whose inhabitants sometimes saw the breakdown of political order as an opportunity to settle old grudges. As the indigenous accounts of the post-1886 disturbances in Upper Burma amply illustrate, Burman officials who collaborated with the British played vital roles in defeating those who resisted and in enabling the colonizers to establish lasting control (Tha Aung and Mya Din, 1941: 81, 85–6, 88, 98, 102, 120, 123, 130). When these more subtle techniques failed to put an end to local resistance, the British resorted to more brutal measures, including village burning, and in at least one instance the destruction of forest cover within fifty feet of a roadway where British forces had been ambushed (Geary, 1886, 49, 52, 75–7; *Thayetmyo*: 13; *Shwebo*: 41).

In the standard accounts of Burmese history and according to the accepted categories for the analysis of resistance and protest, the risings described thus far can be grouped under the heading of primary resistance. Closer examination, however, reveals important differences, particularly between resistance in Upper and Lower Burma in the period after the 1886 annexation. Though the late nineteenth century is normally viewed as a time of prosperity and rapid economic growth in the delta regions of Lower Burma, some groups and whole areas were either left behind or adversely affected by the great transformations that accompanied British rule and Burma's integration into the global economy. Natural setbacks—drought and crop shortages—combined with adverse market conditions and colonial taxation to threaten considerable numbers of peasant households with starvation, at least in limited areas in the upper delta. Some peasants chose to barter their children for the means to survive; others followed leaders like the *pongyi*, U Thuriya, into rebellion. Like those who resisted the British throughout Upper Burma, the rebels in Tharrawaddy also fought to save the Konbaung dynasty and protect Buddhism. In Upper Burma, however, patriotism and the defense of religion were largely unrivalled motives for resistance because the market economy had only marginally affected the Burman rump state that survived after 1852, and colonial bureaucracy and taxes were as yet only a future menace.

Both of these issues—the restoration of the monarchy and the protection of Buddhism—were to remain central to protest movements throughout the colonial period. As Grattan Geary perceptively noted in his account of the conquest, the British made a major error when they deposed King Thibaw and put an end to the Konbaung dynasty. After describing how grown men and women wept when the king and his queen were taken down the Irrawaddy river to be exiled, Geary argued that the conquerors might better have left a puppet Burman ruler on the throne, for in removing the king the British created among their Burman subjects a deep sense of injury and humiliation and a rallying cause for anticolonial protest that would cost the British dearly in subsequent decades (1886: 294). In overthrowing the dynasty and failing to preserve at least a facade of religious and political legitimacy, which had centered upon the king in precolonial Burma, the British forfeited any possibility that they might have had of gaining widespread acceptance of their rule and of mollifying Burman fears for their religion and distinctive cultural identity. These fears would fuel protest movements throughout the colonial era, just as they had motivated those who supported the postannexation resistance efforts.

The post-1886 resistance temporarily slowed the rapid expansion of rice cultivation for export, which was concentrated in the delta regions of Lower Burma. Rice exports, which had recovered from a fairly severe slump in 1884–85 and risen in 1885–86 to near record totals, dropped steadily from late 1886 until the end of 1889, when they again began to increase as the colonial economy entered a period of sustained growth that was to continue for nearly two decades. The amount of acreage under rice cultivation also declined in the troubled Pegu division of Lower Burma between late 1886 and 1889, though offsetting increases in less disturbed areas in Lower Burma sustained steady growth in rice production in the province as a whole (Cheng, 1968: 244, 257). Beginning in the 1890s, however, Burma entered a period of rapid growth that soon transformed it into the world's leading rice-exporting area. This growth was paralleled by dramatic increases in the population of the rice-producing districts; fed by a rising stream of migration from India and Upper Burma, and to a lesser extent by natural increase. It also meant deeper and deeper involvement in the market economy, as the British intended, by large numbers of Burman cultivators. In addition, the extension in the 1890s of export production into Upper Burma, on a more limited scale, and into crops like peanuts and sesame rather than rice, exposed the cultivators of large tracts who had formerly been subsistence-oriented to the opportunities and perils of involvement in an unstable world market system (Adas, 1974: chs. 2, 3, 4, 7).

The peasants' eagerness to claim new lands and cultivate cash crops and their avid pursuit of the consumer rewards—from kerosene lamps and watches to bicycles and Western furniture—that could be gained through the sale of surplus rice, concealed from all but the most perceptive observers the underlying weaknesses of the economy and the society that had developed under British rule. Ancient rivalries between ethnic groups within Burma itself were greatly intensified by competition in the laissez faire market arena and by the collaboration of minority groups like the Kachins and Chins with the colonizers. The Karens, who had once been concentrated in the highland areas to the west and east of the Irrawaddy delta region and who were largely isolated from contacts with the predominately Burman-Mon population of the lowlands, migrated in large numbers into the Sittang and Irrawaddy deltas to take up rice production for the export market. Large Karen villages that were established throughout Lower Burma were known for their prosperity and for their avoidance of contact with nearby Mon or Burman settlements. Burman suspicion of and antipathy toward Karen settlers, as well as toward Chin and Shan migrants, was also aroused by the willingness of these groups to serve in the colonial police and military forces where their numbers far exceeded the number of Burman-Mon recruits in proportion to the percentage each group made up in the indigenous population as a whole (Marshall, 1922; Tadaw, 1959; Furnivall, 1956: 178–84).

The great influx of Indian migrants into Burma, especially after 1852, added a new dimension to preexisting communal tensions and rivalries. Indian laborers, merchants, moneylenders, and civil servants were drawn primarily to Lower

Burma like internal migrants by the economic opportunities which the rapid development of the rice export economy provided. From several thousand in the early 1800s, the Indian population in Burma rose to nearly 300,000 by 1900. Indian administrators, soldiers, and policemen had been essential in the campaigns to conquer and to establish British rule in Burma. By the end of the nineteenth century, Indian landlords controlled large estates throughout the districts of the Irrawaddy delta region; Indian merchants, millers, and money-lenders played pivotal roles in the marketing and processing of rice for export; and a surfeit of Indian laborers vied with a growing class of Burmese landless cultivators for positions as tenants, rural laborers, and mill workers, and for jobs on the wharves of Rangoon and in other urban centers (Cheng, 1968: chs. 4–7; Adas, 1974: chs. 4, 5, 7).

As long as the export economy expanded steadily in step with rising overseas demand for Burma rice at ever higher prices, and cultivable but unclaimed land was available in the delta frontier area, inter-ethnic tensions and the discontent of the colonized remained at manageable levels. Resistance continued, however, and protest movements erupted even in the boom decades of the 1890s and early 1900s. Much of this resistance was led, as earlier, by local leaders and dacoit gangs struggling to maintain their autonomy in the face of British determination to extend effective control to the village level. In response to the poor showing of local leaders and the indigenous constabulary during the post-1886 disturbances, the British carried out far reaching changes in the nature of village and local administration in Lower Burma. They abolished the indigenous hamlet circle and replaced it with the forced creation of nucleated village settlements patterned after those the British had long known in India and had recently encountered in Upper Burma. Circle *thugyis*, whose authority had depended mainly upon their standing among the hamlet populations under their jurisdiction, were replaced with village headmen. The British strove to orient the headmen to the demands and needs of the colonial administration rather than to those of the village populace and to strengthen their position within the village community. Only headmen were allowed to keep firearms, and they were provided with recordskeepers and policemen to help them keep order, at least in the larger villages. Most critically, the headmen were placed in charge of revenue collection in the areas assigned to them—a move that simultaneously enhanced their power and ability to profit from the posts they occupied and transformed them into the most prominent, and often the most disliked, agents of the colonial regime (Mya Sein, 1938).[5]

Although intended to strengthen the position of the village headmen, the changes introduced by the British actually weakened their hold over the peasants in their charge, for the latter came to regard the headmen, often quite rightly, as mere pawns of the alien overlords. The severing of the paternalist and reciprocal patron-client ties that had linked village notables and ordinary villagers in the precolonial era was a major blow to the system of social control that had evolved over centuries at the local level. The disintegration of the *athin* and *ahmudan* systems of regimental organization that had been central to manpower control in precolonial Burman kingdoms,[6] but were discarded by the British conquerors, also undercut the webs of dependency that had traditionally bound together elite groups and the peasantry.

In Lower Burma in particular, the open land frontier and its concomitant high rates of geographical and social mobility among the cultivating classes meant that patron-client ties were generally weak and short-lived. The absence of a well-entrenched landlord class in Burma, similar to those which the British had encountered in most areas of India, was a key factor in the success of British efforts to encourage the growth of a peasant-proprietor-dominated economy. This initial advantage, however, ultimately proved a liability for the colonial rulers as market reverses, land shortages, indebtedness, and land alienation produced growing numbers of displaced landowners and disgruntled tenants and laborers whose ties to an emerging landlord class—a class that in many areas was made up of a large percentage of immigrant Indians—were transient and purely contractual, rather than long-term, personalist, patron-client bonds. This meant that in contrast to most areas in India (Low, 1977: 2–3), the British could not base their strategy of rural social control on landlords and well-to-do peasants who were able to dominate a large portion of the cultivating classes through dependencies rooted in patron-client exchanges. Also in contrast to India,[7] landlord groups in Burma, though active in different nationalist organizations, were able to do little to check the mounting unrest in rural Burma in the 1920s and 1930s. Violent protest was rarely led by rural notables. It was, on the other hand, often directed against landlord groups, especially Indian estate owners and moneylenders who were so prominent in many areas of Lower Burma. The communal rather than class thrust of most rural protest tended to shield Burmese landlords and moneylenders who strove to deflect the dissatisfaction of the cultivating classes against the British overlords.

In addition to village reorganization and administrative reform, the British sought to gain effective control over the rural populace through an acceleration of the land-revenue inquests and settlements that had begun in the late 1870s. New areas brought under cultivation were quickly surveyed, mapped, and recorded with a thoroughness that was inconceivable in the precolonial era. Periodic revisions were carried out in areas where settlement operations had previously been conducted, and settlement operations were extended to the Dry Zone districts of Upper Burma. As a consequence of these efforts and related census work, the British knew a good deal more about the numbers and composition of the cultivating classes under their control, and the quality and productivity of the land they worked, than had even the strongest of Burman monarchs.

British control, however, was not gained without a struggle and was never fully complete, even in those areas that appeared to be the most secure. The rapid expansion of cultivated acreage and the highly mobile character of the peasant population, especially in Lower Burma, had posed great difficulties for census takers and revenue collectors from the first years after the 1826 and 1852 annexations (*RAP*, 1854–55: para. 26). As long as large tracts of open land remained, cultivators could and did evade taxes or debts they could not pay by migrating—just as they had migrated to escape what they considered to be intolerable demands by indigenous overlords in the precolonial era (*R & A Proc.*, 1904: 84; Bridges, 1881: 10; Nisbet, 1901: 1, 296–7). The existence of unclaimed, but arable land, provided opportunities for landless peasants and laborers to become small landholders; it also offered a second chance for peasants to succeed who had once held land and lost it through debts in the unfamiliar and unstable market arena. Until the late 1890s, opportunities for horizontal and, in many instances, vertical mobility deflected confrontations and potential clashes between the cultivators and the moneylenders, merchants and large landowners, Indian and Burmese. Peasant mobility and sustained economic growth also reduced tension between different ethnic groups which, like the British rulers themselves, continued to believe that there were enough places for all long after this was in fact the case.

Though losses in the post-1886 risings and systematic removals in the years of reform that followed did much to deplete the ranks of heriditary *thugyis*, there is evidence of continued resistance to colonial control at the village level. As in the years after the 1852 annexation (*RAB*, 1865-6: 10), remnants of rebel bands, which often turned to crime to survive and thus truly merited the title of dacoits applied by the British, were sheltered by or in collusion with local headmen. In the Akyab district, which had been relatively quiet in the years after 1886, a peasant named Paw Aung proclaimed himself the Minlaung, or imminent prince, and joined with his father, who had been a *thugyi* under the British, in forming a gang that attacked other headmen and military police stations. Paw Aung's band refrained from attacking local villages and was in turn supported by them in the belief that the gang was fighting to free Burma from foreign rule. Similar support given by villagers in other areas and the widespread refusal of peasants to assist the British in their efforts to hunt down dacoit bands suggests continued local resistance to the imposition of British control (*RPAB*, 1891: 10; 1894: 64; 1899: 4–5; 1900: v; 1901: iv, 10). In some instances popular support for dacoit gangs was so great that bandit leaders had the audacity to offer large rewards for the heads of the British officers charged with hunting the outlaws down (*Amherst*: 56). Despite heavy fines levied on uncooperative villages and sustained military and police campaigns, some bandit groups survived due to peasant support and protection, for over a decade after 1886. The fragmentary evidence we have suggests that many of these gangs were social bandits in Eric Hobsbawm's sense, viz. disgruntled peasants who resort to crime to strike back at the state and its allies when other avenues of protest fail and who are perceived by other agriculturists as avengers or proponents of causes they deem themselves helpless to advance.

In addition to collusion with dacoit bands, village headmen and lower level Burman officials sought to thwart British efforts to gain control at the local level through time-tested techniques of corruption and evasion that had served them so well in the precolonial era. In the years after the 1852 annexation, underreporting on census rolls and revenue inquests was rampant, and as late as 1889 investigations by British settlement officers revealed that the *thugyis* in some districts had reported as little as 25 percent of the area actually cultivated in the villages placed in their charge (Mya Sein, 1938: 111; *SPC*, 1856: para. 179; Matthews, 1890: 23). Local officials also supported the efforts of large landowners to amass great estates, often at the expense of peasant settlers and in direct opposition to the government's policy of fostering a smallholder-based market economy. One of the key signs of the power and quasi-autonomy enjoyed by local land magnates and their administrative allies was the presence of what amounted to private armies in many areas on the delta frontier. Bands of retainers, sometimes numbering in the hundreds, were used to collect the landowner's or moneylender's full due from recalcitrant tenants, to bully smallholders into abandoning their holdings so they could be claimed by large landlords, and even at times to do battle with the forces of rival landlord families (Adas, 1974: 73, 142, 172–3).

Even though the resistance of local notables to effective British control was mainly self-serving rather than patriotic, its widespread and sustained occurrence indicates that the social and economic changes brought about by colonization may not have been as pervasive and radical at the grass roots level as the British believed and as subsequent historians have argued. It also suggests that there were ample opportunities for disaffected cultivators to protest against specific grievances or even to plot the overthrow of the colonial regime.

From 1886 until the 1920s, protest in British Burma took three main forms: localized and usually short-lived rebellions; violent assaults on government officials and men of property, which the British viewed as common crimes; and communal rioting. Between the 1890s and the late 1920s, the tradition of resistance established in the post-1852 and 1886 annexation disturbances periodically burst forth in small-scale risings that, though they were easily suppressed, kept alive challenges to the legitimacy of British rule and the dream of restoring the Burman monarchy. Little is reported in the available sources about the social or economic conditions that gave rise to these disturbances, but, unlike the other major forms of protest in this period, their timing, location, and goals appear to have been little influenced by market fluctuations or the social conflicts that developed as the export economy began to unravel in the first decades of the twentieth century.[8] The risings in Pakkoku (1894), Mandalay (1897), Toungoo (1906), Shwebo and Sagaing (1910), and Henzada (1912), as well as risings in Meiktila, Pegu, and Tavoy which broke out in the early and mid-1920s, all occurred in periods of growth and prosperity in Burma as a whole and in areas that were not economically distressed at that time. In fact, the rising in Toungoo came just a year *before* the post-1907 slump that was touched off by a worldwide credit squeeze; the Myoka rebellion in Henzada broke out on the eve of the period of economic contraction and hardship brought on by shipping shortages in World War I, and perhaps the largest of these rebellions, U Bandaka's in Shwebo in 1928, occurred just before the Great Depression began to ravage the export-oriented economy of the province. A survey of the followers of U Bandaka, one of the few such enquiries extant, found that though many were laborers whose families existed barely above subsistence, many others were well-to-do landowners and local leaders (Langham-Carter, 1939: 28).

Rather than economic grievances, political and religious concerns appear to have motivated those who supported these risings. Like U Oktama, who led the 1906 Toungoo rebellion, and Maung Tun Hla (alias U Bandalaka), who instigated the Shwebo outbreak nearly two decades later, the leaders of these movements claimed to be Konbaung princes, Minlaungs, or in some cases *Sekhya Mins* or embryo Buddhas. Some leaders like Tun Hla and Nga Po Mya, who organized the 1912 rising in Henzada, were *se sayas* or practitioners of traditional Burmese medicine; others like U Oktama and Nga Hmun, the leader of the Pakokku rising in 1894, were *pongyis*. In all of the rebellions where detailed information is available, *pongyis* played key roles as advisors and organizers, reflecting an early and sustained concern for the decline of Buddhist influence under colonial rule. Whether *pongyis* or healers, rebel leaders proclaimed themselves invulnerable to the weapons of the colonizers and distributed protective talismans to their followers. Many leaders attempted to bolster their claims to royal descent by establishing court centers and assuming the trappings of Burman monarchs. U Bandalaka made the fullest use of these key symbols of Burman rulers in the decade after he established his pilgrimage center at Bishu in the Shwebo district. He issued a biography in which he claimed to be invulnerable, built a palace patterned after those found in Ava and Mandalay, erected a victory pagoda, contributed to the repair of existing shrines in the vicinity of his capitol, and claimed to be a Minlaung with great magical powers.

In virtually all respects—including its outcome—U Bandalaka's movement and rebellion closely resembled U Thuriya's nearly a half century earlier. After the failure of police attempts to arrest Bandalaka and assaults by his followers on local headmen and police posts in retribution, Bandalaka's adherents were routed by a large police expedition in February 1927. Similar patterns can be discerned in all of the risings in the decades between U Thuriya's and U Bandalaka's which appear to have transcended causes associated with the great economic and social changes brought about by colonization. As in the post-1852 and 1886 resistance, the risings that periodically erupted in the 1890s and the first decades of the twentieth century arose mainly from a desire to put an end to foreign rule and to restore the Burman monarchy and the vital roles of the Buddhist *Sangha* in the Burman polity.

Because it took the form of acts which were regarded as common crimes by the colonial authorities, the second major form of protest in the post-1886 period is also the most difficult to identify clearly and to analyze in detail. The highly biased and often abbreviated summaries of dacoit raids, petty thefts, or violent assaults recorded in the police records or special government enquiries into crime, make it extremely difficult to distinguish between acts that were genuine expressions of protest and those that were in fact common crimes. The predisposition of many contemporary scholars to turn virtually all evidence of social unrest in colonial societies into patriotic outbursts of resistance compounds this difficulty and underscores the need for even greater caution. It is probable that the great majority of criminal acts dutifully recorded by colonial officials, and perhaps an even larger number that did not come to their attention, were in fact crimes pure and simple perpetrated out of the desire for illegal, personal gain at the expense of others. In some instances, however, what the colonizers labelled criminal acts were something more than that; they were expressions of anger, retribution, or desperation by dispossessed smallholders or laborers without work.

Though some administrators and government reports insisted that Burma's excessive crime rates relative to other provinces in the Indian empire were due to the greater number of wealthy targets in Burma, to the declining morality which was linked to problems in the Buddhist *Sangha*, or to Burmese personality traits such as a love for adventure or a need to prove manly virtue (*BCR*, 1926: 7–10; *RPAB*, 1904: 12; 1918: 8, 10; 1921: 16ff.), numerous government observers admitted that criminal acts were often tied to economic distress and tensions between well-to-do landowners and moneylenders and hard-pressed tenants and landless laborers. Criminal acts that were linked to adverse social and economic conditions were in fact much better gauges of the magnitude of the disruptions and inequities associated with the market economy and property-oriented legal system established under the British than the sporadic risings led by *pongyis* and pretenders aimed at restoring an imagined golden age of the past.

Assaults by large dacoit gangs, which had been one of the main forms of postconquest resistance, remained a major problem for government officials throughout the British period. As late as the 1920s, British officials admitted that the major obstacles to the suppression of dacoit bands operating in many areas remained the support and protection they received from local headmen and villagers generally, despite heavy fines that the British levied on all communities suspected of aiding the gangs. Headmen not only enjoyed a sizable cut of the earnings of bandit gangs, whose members often resided in their villages, they sometimes organized and led the gangs themselves. The fact that village communities as a whole gained from *dacoit* raids is suggested by the lavish, community-wide *ahlus* (feasts) that were reported to be held periodically even in villages of modest means—feasts that were financed, or so the British suspected but could not prove, by bandit operations. Popular support for at least some dacoit groups may also have been reflected in the encouragement and active support they were given by Buddhist *pongyis*.[9]

The targets of dacoit raids and violent crimes in general reflect the social tensions and economic distress that were generated by the uneven impact of the market economy. Rich landlords, merchants, and moneylenders—Burmese, Chinese and especially Indian—were the most frequently cited targets due to their wealth, but the available sources suggest a protest dimension to many of the recorded assaults, namely, laborers and tenants squaring accounts with exploitative landowners and indebted smallholders seeking to forcibly break the hold of local and foreign moneylenders. The struggle of marketing middlemen and landlords with the cultivating classes is also indicated by widespread efforts by tenants and laborers to conceal part of the rice they harvested, thus depriving the landlords of the large and growing share they claimed as their due. Concealment became so pervasive after 1900, expecially on the tenant-cultivated estates that developed in many areas in the lower Irrawaddy delta region, that landlords were forced to hire *durwans* or watchmen to oversee cultivation, to guard warehouses, and to monitor the transportation of harvested paddy to the landlord's granaries. Watchmen also proved necessary in many areas to guard large landlords' holdings against poaching by the landlord's laborers or against arson and vandalism by disgruntled ex-owners or tenants, or mistreated workers seeking revenge (Adas, 1974: 149–50; Thein Pe, 1973: 25, 28).

Because of considerable variations between and within different regions in market and cropping conditions, it is difficult to plot clear connections between overall indices of provincial prosperity or economic crisis—rice prices, export totals, etc.—and the rise or fall of crime rates. Many British officials, however, argued that there was a direct connection between socioeconomic conditions and fluctuations in crime rates.[10] As early as 1895, a sharp increase in crime in the districts of the lower Irrawaddy Delta was attributed to general poverty resulting from a sharp fall in the price of rice. In subsequent police reports, British administrators repeatedly cited poor harvests and high rice prices, which made it difficult for the families of landless laborers to make ends meet, or market slumps, which hit tenants and smallholders especially hard, as the root causes of increases in criminal activities. More than any other, these contrasting effects of market shifts illustrate a fundamental contradiction in the Delta economy that grew in importance as open land ran out and competition for employment grew. In a situation where a sizable proportion of the cultivating classes were smallholders dependent on stable or rising rice prices for their well being, while a large and growing number of cultivators were landless laborers who had to purchase their staple foods, whichever way the market turned some group was bound to be adversely affected.

The crimes which were linked in police reports to economic shifts ranged from cattle thefts to gang raids on the homes of moneylenders and rich landlords. Government observers frequently noted that the highest crime rates were found in the most progressive districts, that is, in those where the market economy was most firmly entrenched. In these areas greater discrepancies in incomes, the large sums of money amassed by moneylenders and large landlords, and the weakness or a complete absence of paternal patron-client links between the landowning classes and landless cultivators all contributed to the tendency on the part of the poor and displaced to turn to crime in times of economic need. The weaker hold of Buddhist institutions and ethical standards on the heterogeneous and consumer-oriented populations of these districts was also frequently cited as a major source of higher crime rates.

As time passed, the connection between increasing criminality and socioeconomic distress was more and more explicitly admitted by police and revenue officials. After the failure of a handful of insightful government officials to win approval in the 1890s and early 1900s for legislation regulating agricultural loans and land alienation (Adas, 1977: 112ff.), the smallholder-based economy which the British had painstakingly fashioned in the late nineteenth century began to break down. Market reverses and the closing of the land frontier greatly accelerated the agrarian indebtedness, land alienation, and spread of landlordism that had been confined to limited areas through most of the late nineteenth century. As officials like H. L. Eales, the Commissioner of Pegu, had warned as early as 1911, these trends were bound to stir up social unrest and eventually political challenges to the British overlords (*R & A Proc.*, 1911: 403). Though widespread political disturbances were still over a decade in the future, the immediate impact of the decline of the smallholder-based economy can be seen in the sharply rising incidence of crime in the first decades of the twentieth century. In districts in both Upper and Lower Burma, administrators reported that in addition to poor harvests and market fluctuations, unemployment and the loss of opportunities for social and economic mobility for the laboring classes were responsible for increases in crime rates (*RPAB*, 1918: 11).

The most detailed discussion of the relationship between worsening economic conditions and increased crime is provided by Thomas Couper, who carried out a special enquiry into the living standards and working patterns of tenants and agricultural laborers in Burma in 1924. Couper argued that there was a direct connection between the soaring increase in crime and the steady empoverishment of the laboring classes. He dated the marked rise in dacoity, theft, and other crimes against property in Burma from the 1905–1910 period, when a credit crisis forced widespread mortgage foreclosures, thus depriving many cultivators of land that they had transformed from wilderness into productive paddy fields after years of arduous labor. Reduced to the status of landless laborers at a time when the available cultivable land had all but run out, large numbers of cultivators found steady employment difficult to obtain and only at low wages when it was available. Couper argued that the great impact of the landless laborers' conditions on crime rates was clearly illustrated by the higher incidence of crime in the slack seasons after the planting and harvest when large numbers of laborers were unemployed and hard-pressed to feed themselves and their families (Couper, 1924: 10, 51).

Until the late 1920s, the other major form of agrarian protest in colonial Burma, communal violence, was often difficult to separate from actions which were classified as criminal. With the exception of Hindu-Muslim communal riots in the 1890s and the early 1900s, which arose from conflicts rooted in India proper rather than from conditions in Burma, there were few clashes between Burmans and immigrant groups until after the credit crisis of 1907–1908 (*RPAB*, 1907: 10; 1908: 16–17). The first anti-Indian assaults, as yet small and localized affairs, occurred in these years. In the next decade, Indian landlords, moneylenders (especially the ubiquitous Chettiers) and even poor and defenseless laborers became frequent targets of attacks by Burman dacoits (*RPAB*, 1913: 18; 1914: 21; 1915: 15; 1918: 17, 19). On several occasions, full-scale skirmishes between gangs of Burman and

Indian laborers occurred. By the early 1920s, the pressure of an ever-growing population, fed by virtually unrestricted immigration from East and South India, resulted in widespread communal tension and hostility (*RPAB*, 1919: 16–21; 1920: 15–6, 19; 1921: 16, 25). The Burman fears that, under the aegis of colonial rule, Indian and Chinese immigrants were steadily taking over their homeland—fears that appeared to be substantiated by the growth of an Indian landlord class and the vital roles played by Indian merchants, millers, moneylenders, and laborers in the export economy—would result in the early 1930s in an orgy of anti-Indian riots and assaults.

In addition to attacks on Indians, and occasionally on Chinese merchants and moneylenders in this period, there were also signs of growing tension between Burmans and other ethnic groups, especially the Karens. Karen villages were attacked, wealthy Karen homes looted, and Karen and Chin officials were murdered. Though clashes between indigenous ethnic groups would never attain the magnitude nor the intensity of Burman-Indian conflict in the 1930s, Burman assaults on members of indigenous minority groups were further signs of intensifying social tensions, as group rivalries mounted in an economy whose growth could no longer keep pace with rapid population increase.

The basic forms of Burmese protest and resistance to British rule that had emerged in the days of conquest—local risings led by *pongyis*, prophets, or pretenders, and banditry—persisted into the 1930s, and in some areas into the period of independence. Changing social and economic conditions led to the rise of·a new form of protest beginning in the early 1900s—communal rioting and Burman assaults on members of immigrant and ethnic minority groups. In the mid- and late 1920s, additional forms of protest were adopted by disgruntled cultivators and urban laborers as economic dislocations gave way to a full-scale collapse of the smallholder-based economy and Western-educated nationalist leaders sought to build a mass base for their challenges to British rule. In this period, growing numbers of *pongyis* also became involved in political agitation. Those who supported these movements of protest continued to rally to calls for the restoration of the Burman monarchy, the removal of the illegitimate and alien colonial overlords, and the defense of Buddhism and Burman culture. The breakdown of the smallholder-based export economy, however, and the class and communal tensions that it produced, gave added impetus to social and economic grievances that were felt by some groups in the late nineteenth century, but had not begun to play a major role as sources of protest until after 1900.

For well after a decade after they began to form political associations to lobby for the advancement of their interests in British official circles, Western-educated Burmese leaders had few contacts with, and in fact showed little concern for the condition of, the agrarian classes. Though many future nationalist leaders grew up in households whose prosperity and social prominence owed a good deal to sizable landholdings and successful participation in various sectors of the rice-export economy, the Western-educated Burmese were overwhelmingly urban-oriented and to a large degree isolated from the great majority of the colonized population. Caught up in endless factional struggles, quarrels with the British overlords, and hard-fought campaigns to increase opportunities for more and better education and jobs for themselves, until well into the 1920s most Western-educated Burmese gave little serious thought to organizing rural cultivators or the urban poor.

By the early 1920s, worsening economic conditions and the spread of agrarian and urban unrest, combined with a growing desire to recruit mass support for their struggles with the British overlords, led many Western-educated politicians and political factions to seek ways to involve the cultivating classes in the nationalist struggle. Though the definitive account of these efforts has yet to be completed,[11] the available evidence suggests that despite some organizational and ideological innovations, the nationalist-inspired peasant movements of the 1920s and 1930s strongly resembled earlier protest and resistance efforts in leadership, goals, and often the forms of protest adopted.

One of the strongest links to earlier protest movements was provided by Buddhist *pongyis* who played vital roles in nationalist-inspired village associations or *athins* and in arousing dissidence in rural areas. In 1921, those *pongyis* who were committed to political agitation established the General Council of the *Sangha Samettgyi* (GCSS) within the umbrella nationalist organization, the General Council of Burmese Associations (GCBA). The GCSS was to become the major vehicle of *pongyi* involvement in political action and one of the key links between the tiny minority of urban-based, Western-educated nationalist leaders and the cultivating classes (Maung, 1980: 23–6). Many of the so-called political *pongyis*, who, as Mendelson has argued, were often not *pongyis* at all (1975: 173ff.), were from rural origins and thus attuned to the grievances and outlook of the cultivating classes. The overriding concern of the *pongyi* organizers, however, was the decline of discipline within the Buddhist *Sangha* (which ironically had in part made their political activities possible under a religious cover), and especially the threat to Buddhist monastic education which the spread of Western education and the growth of a market-oriented, consumer-minded society clearly posed (Mendelson, 1975: chs. 3, 4; Brohm, 1957: 303–20; Smith, 1965: chs. 2, 3).

Pongyi orators, like U Ottama and U Wisara, who toured the rural areas of Lower Burma in 1924 and 1926 respectively, told the large crowds that turned out to cheer them, that foreign domination was the root cause of the decline of Buddhism in Burma and a vital threat to the survival of Burman culture. Reflecting their ties to Western-educated politicians in both Burma and India, *pongyi* agitators called for tax boycotts and civil disobedience campaigns to undermine the authority of the colonial regime. In some cases, their rousing speeches, whose seditious content guaranteed eventual arrest and imprisonment, touched off local riots, antitax campaigns, or the widespread posting of "no admittance" signs on village gates. More frequently, however, they inspired widespread tatooing with cabalistic designs, the manufacture of charms intended to confer invulnerability, and most ominously the collection of *dahs*, long knives, and arms for anticipated risings against the British overlords (Maung, 1980: 14–16, 51–4; Morris, 1930: 2–7; *Rangoon*, 18 Feb., 1929: 13).

Whether initiated by *pongyis* and the GCSS or by Western-educated nationalists from radical factions of the GCBA, like the So Thein group, the basic units of rural nationalist organization were village associations called *wunthanu athins*. Through these locally recruited and loosely coordinated associations, nationalist leaders of rival factions sought to arouse support for their stands in various political controversies that arose in the 1920s. With some exceptions, peasant interests were only peripherally involved in most of these constitutional and factional struggles. The most important of these exceptions was the antitax campaigns that spread to many areas in rural Burma in the mid- and late 1920s.

Because it was levied equally on all households regardless of income and collected at the worst possible time of the year for the cultivating classes, the capitation tax proved an ideal issue around which to rally widespread rural protest against colonial rule. Not only had landless laborers and deeply indebted tenants to pay the same amount as rich landlords and merchants, but also the tax was collected beginning in August before the harvest, which was precisely the time when the cultivator was the most pressed for food money and other essentials. In order to pay the tax, cultivators were often forced to borrow money at high rates of interest from Burmese and Indian moneylenders and were thus driven ever deeper into debt (Couper, 1924: 53; Saw, 1931: 7). The appeal of the capitation tax as a focus of protest was also enhanced by the fact that its payment had long been viewed by the Burmans as tantamount to an admission of the legitimacy of the overlord who demanded it. After the British conquest of Lower Burma, for example, Burman officials in many areas refused to collect the tax on the grounds that to do so would amount to a repudiation of the Konbaung monarch who still ruled in Upper Burma and to an acceptance of British rule which they vainly hoped would be temporary (*PFP*, 1853: no. 60).

The fact that the tax in the late nineteenth century was collected by village headmen gave it an additional potency as a cause for arousing rural protest. From the late 1880s, when the *thugyis* had been fully integrated into the colonial administrative machinery, they had become in most instances ever more alienated from the village populations whose interests they had once served. Saddled with onerous and unpopular tasks, such as tax collection, and granted little real power, *thugyis* became by the first decade of the twentieth century one of the major targets of rural unrest. In the 1880s and 1890s, headmen who cooperated with the government, often in marked contrast to the sullen refusal of assistance by the villagers in their charge, were condemned to death by dacoit leaders, and on some occasions executed for their collaboration with the colonizers. As economic conditions worsened after 1900, *thugyis* increasingly became the objects of dacoit attacks and growing numbers of headmen were murdered while attempting to collect taxes or quell local disturbances. As much as the capitation tax itself, the collaboration of Burman headmen was at issue in the anticapitation tax campaigns that periodically disturbed the uneasy colonial peace during the 1920s.[12]

In 1923–24, *pongyi* orators like U Ottama and Western-educated politicians like U Chit Hlaing toured the rural delta districts exhorting Burmese cultivators to refuse British capitation tax demands. In many areas of Lower Burma from Prome to Tavoy, villagers, usually led by *wunthanu athin* agitators, refused to pay the tax when the *thugyis* came to collect. In some regions, villagers responded to government measures to compel payment, with passive resistance campaigns patterned after those which had been so successfully employed by Gandhi and Indian nationalist agitators in the preceding years. In other areas, *athin* leaders used threats and violent measures, such as arson and livestock maiming, to insure widespread support for the antitax campaign. The government responded to this direct challenge to its authority by arrests of key leaders and confiscation of village and household grain supplies. In some cases villages supporting the campaign were occupied by punitive policemen. In all cases, the antitax campaign was defeated, but local outbreaks of this form of resistance flared up in 1927 and 1928, and again in 1929, on the eve of the Great Depression rebellions (*Rangoon*, 2 Feb. 1929: 11; Morris, 1930: 7; Saw, 1931: 7–8).

Saya San, who was the central figure in the series of peasant rebellions that raged in the Burmese countryside from 1930 to 1932, as a rebel leader combined both the long standing tradition of protest that had dominated Burman resistance through most of the colonial period and the new causes for unrest and nationalist innovations in protest organization that had emerged in the 1920s.[13] As a *se saya* or Burmese medical practitioner, sometime *pongyi*, and peddler of lottery tickets, Saya San had gained familiarity with conditions in many parts of Burma and a knowledge of the esoteric magical skills and modes of cult organization that were to provide much of his appeal to large numbers of cultivators. In raising the standard of rebellion, he promised to restore the Burman monarchy (in the person of himself), to defend Buddhism, to purify the *Sangha*, and to drive the "infidel" British from the land. His stress on the need to restore the monarchy was given added power by the belief held by many of his followers that Saya San was a *Mettaya* or embryo Buddha, a belief that Saya San himself appears to have shared. He prophesied that the victory of his *galon* (serpent) armies over the British would usher in a utopian age of social harmony and religious bliss. All of these key themes had persisted through the decades of colonial rule and their powerful hold over the peasantry was amply demonstrated by the number and size of the rebellions that were initiated by Saya San or led by his disciples.

Saya San was, however, more than a prophet-pretender in the traditional Burman mode. He was a leader with extensive links to the radical So Thein wing of the GCBA and widespread contacts with *wunthanu athin* leaders throughout the Irrawaddy delta region. In the years before the outbreak of the depression risings, he frequently spoke to *athin* gatherings, carried out a special enquiry for the So Thein GCBA into alleged police brutality involved in the suppression of the antitax campaigns, and made fiery speeches demanding full independence for

Burma. In recruiting support for the rebellion that he plotted for nearly two years, Saya San made frequent references to peasant distress arising out of the indebtedness, land alienation, and rack renting that had led in the 1920s to the final disintegration of the smallholder economy of colonial Burma and had culminated in the Great Depression. Displaced landholders, disgruntled tenants, and unemployed laborers—many of whom had previously joined *wunthanu athin* associations—responded to his call to drive the British and their Indian allies from Burma and to restore indigenous rule.

Although the causes which gave rise to the 1930–32 disturbances were a mix of appeals for monarchical and religious restoration, and grievances arising from the breakdown of the export economy, the forms which agrarian protest took in the turbulent decade of the 1930s were the same as those which had been dominant since the first decades of resistance to British conquest. Localized rebellions led by *pongyis* or princely pretenders like Saya San received the most attention in government enquiries and the contemporary press. More widespread, however, and more difficult for the British to suppress was the resistance offered by dacoit bands that were often formed after attempts at open rebellion had failed. During the 1930–32 disturbances, assaults on Indian moneylenders, landowners, and laborers were also widespread and indiscriminant with regard to victims within the Indian community, as had been the communal riots in Rangoon in May of 1930. Though bloody communal riots would again erupt in the towns, especially in Lower Burma in 1938, Indian-Burman conflict in the rural areas peaked during the 1930–32 rebellions. These clashes were paralleled by Burman assaults on minority ethnic groups like the Karens and Chins.

Perhaps no incident in this period of unrest better epitomized the persistence of traditional protest forms than the petition that was presented to the acting Governor of Burma, Joseph Maung Gyi, on the eve of the first Saya San rising. The complaints set forth in the petition focused on the problems of debts to foreign moneylenders, especially the Chettiars, and the spread of land alienation. The petitioners demanded government relief through the establishment of a land mortgage bank and official measures to check land alienation (Saw, 1931: 1–2). Though Maung Gyi curtly rejected the petition, those who offered it were acting in accordance with well-established Burman traditions. The peasants' right to petition the throne or high officials for tax reductions or to draw attention to the excesses of state officials was well established in precolonial Burma and there is evidence that in some instances such petitions brought relief to the groups involved (Scott and Hardiman, 1900: 432; Mya Sein, 1938: 67). The petition presented to Maung Gyi in December of 1930 may have been in part a device to rally wavering peasants to the rebels' cause, but its use demonstrates the strong hold ancient forms of peasant action and the peasants' sense of political legitimacy still had over the cultivating classes. It also illustrates the way in which peasants attempted to deal with grievances arising from new forms of social and economic organization with longstanding modes of protest expression.

Not only the forms taken by peasant protest in the depression era, but the causes espoused by those who supported it, indicate that the major approaches developed thus far for the study of anticolonial protest on the part of peasant groups may not be appropriate for Burma. At the very least, the great emphasis in the literature on colonial societies on the role of Western-educated nationalist leaders in arousing the colonized to rise against their alien overlords is misplaced, with the possible exception of the late 1930s when the *Thakin* movement gained widespread support in rural Burma. After over a hundred years of British rule in some areas and from fifty to eighty years in others, peasant rebels fought to restore Buddhism and the Burman monarchy, rather than to win independence and gain government by parliaments and Western-educated lawyers and journalists. They rallied to monks and princely pretenders, rather than to nationalist agitators. They also strove to put an end to the stifling control that railways, telegraphs, and European bureaucratic organization had given the colonizers over their once quasi-autonomous village communities.[14] Though rebel organizers made use of nationalist-inspired village associations, many of these had come under the influence of *pongyis*, and during the 1930–32 rebellions the *athins* functioned more like sectarian or *gaing* organizations than branches of nationalist parties. The peasants' adherence to millenarian prophecies and their pervasive reliance on magical talismans (with disasterous results) further distanced them from the urban-based nationalists who would have had little place in the new society which rebel leaders like Saya San envisioned.

The deep attachment felt by those who rose in rebellion for religious leaders, whether *pongyis* or royal pretenders, the heterogeneous composition of rebel bands in terms of the social strata from which they were recruited, and the targets of rebel assaults—all these indicate that a class-based, much less a Marxist, analysis of rural protest in colonial Burma would distort rather than advance our understanding of the meaning of rural unrest. Though tensions between landlord groups, and tenants and laborers had been on the rise since the first years of the twentieth century, government officials, policemen, and migrant Indians (*both* moneylender-landlords and poverty-stricken laborers), were the major targets of rural protest in the 1920s and 1930s. Insofar as group clashes were involved, communal not class divisions were decisive. Except for the urban laborers, who also vented their hostility primarily through communal rioting, there was little sense of class identity among the landless laborers or tenants whose ranks swelled as the smallholder economy declined in the early twentieth century. Members of these social groups worked in small bands, identified primarily with kin and household, and dealt with landlords and estate managers or moneylenders as individuals rather than as representatives of hostile classes. As in precolonial Burma, cultivators tended to be vertically, not horizontally, oriented, and in search of meaningful hierarchies of dependence rather than peasant-dominated utopias based on equality and communal sharing. Thus, though many of Eric Wolf's arguments concerning the impact of capitalism and colonialism on non-

Western peasant societies work well for Burma, neither "middle peasants" nor any other single agrarian social group dominated the ranks of those who rose in protest (1969a: 278–302).

Despite the fact that Burma provides a prime example of the sort of export economy identified by Jeffrey Paige, those who supported movements of protest were a mix of tenants, landless laborers, and smallholders, rather than a homogenous force representing one social strata as is suggested by Paige's theoretical formulations (Paige, 1975: ch. 1). These groups rose in protest neither against the rigid oppression of a landlord class locked into the agrarian sector nor against more diversified entrepreneurial groups with investments in the rural sector, but primarily against alien and illegitimate colonial overlords and their immigrant and indigenous allies. The protest options of the cultivating classes were not limited to strikes or full-scale rebellion, but displayed a wide range of longstanding modes of response from arson and flight to banditry and sect formation.

When they rose in rebellion, laborers joined tenants and indebted smallholders, and they all turned to *pongyis* or dacoit chiefs for leadership. Though the expulsion of the British, the end of taxation, or the cancellation of all debts re-occur as the goals of peasant risings, I have found no rebel references to the destruction of the landlord class, the redistribution of land, or even to the elimination of the market economy that one might expect if class considerations were in fact central to peasant protest in rural Burma.

Insofar as it was generated by economic grievances, protest in rural Burma in the colonial period arose primarily from frustrations resulting from market dysfunctions and slumps, rather than from peasant concerns for subsistence or survival that have been stressed in James Scott's recent study on *The Moral Economy of the Peasant* (1976). Because the vast majority of cultivators of all kinds in Burma grew rice, the staple food, the threat of starvation was rarely an issue, except for the small percentage of landless laborers who could not find employment. For landowner peasants, market slumps and not colonial taxes (which were on the whole quite low in relation to the productivity of the cultivated lands) were the major source of discontent. Smallholders and tenants were not faced with starvation. On the contrary, they had too much rice to eat because they could not sell it at a decent price or at all. The vast majority of peasants in Lower Burma, where most rural protest and the Saya San rebellions were centered, were market, not subsistence, oriented. Market slumps and a shortage of open land, and not government taxation, were the key causes of the indebtedness, land alienation, and the declining wages and profits that undermined the cultivators' ability to purchase the consumer amenities and maintain the high standard of living (relative to other peasant societies) to which they had become accustomed in the late nineteenth century. For landless laborers, declining wages and unemployment and not land revenue payments were the major threat to survival.

The anger of the cultivating classes came to be focused on the colonial state not because the British overlords had violated the moral or ethical precepts which

Scott argues regulated state-peasant relations in the precolonial era, but because without the compensation of consumer rewards and economic well being, the peasants came to view the British as illegitimate and infidel rulers whose presence was a vital threat to Burman culture and traditions. The fact that protesting groups focused their economic complaints on capitation taxes, rather than on land taxes which were much higher, indicates that legitimacy rather than economic survival was the major issue employed by those who sought to recruit peasant supporters for rebellion. The importance of political and closely-related religious concerns for rural dissidents was also reflected in the repeated references by those who took part in rural protest to the restoration of the Burman monarchy and to the restoration of Buddhism as the state religion. To the extent that the dissidents' grievances were economically based, debts to Indian moneylenders and competition from Indian laborers were far more important sources of rural unrest than the allegedly rigid land revenue policies of the colonial government—which in fact were quite flexible and remarkably sensitive to local variations—or the colonial regime's hardhearted refusal to grant remissions in times of crisis—which in fact it did, in addition to providing rural relief works.[15]

The persistence of precolonial modes of protest in colonial Burma, the limited impact of nationalist leaders and ideas on agrarian movements, and the problems involved in applying recent general theories on the origins of agrarian rebellion to the Burmese experience—all indicate a need for a reappraisal of some of our basic assumptions about the character of anticolonial resistance on the part of peasant groups. Admittedly, it can be argued that this caution may need only be applied to Burma which in the degree of its precolonial isolation, the intensity of its xenophobia, the far reaching impact of its colonial change, and the extent of its postcolonial retreat back into isolation, is atypical. Recent work on local conditions and rural movements in India, Africa, and other areas in Southeast Asia, [16] however, indicate that many of the patterns discussed in this essay can be found beyond Burma. These studies also represent a much-needed shift in our approaches to and vision of the impact of colonial rule on the cultivating classes of Africa and Asia and the roles of different strata of the peasantry in the process of decolonization.

6. Peasants, Proletarians, and Politics in Venezuela, 1875–1975

William Roseberry

This essay is an attempt to interpret the political activity of peasants in the Venezuelan Andes during the nineteenth and twentieth centuries. These peasants represent something of an anomaly in comparison with some of the others described in this book in that they have not been particularly rebellious or revolutionary. Nonetheless, I do not approach them as representative of a negative case; nor do I consider the lack of rebellion the central problem of this analysis. Rather, I take as my problem the formation of the peasantry as a class, the nature of their relationships with each other and with members of other classes, and the development of forms through which their political activity was channeled. This is, then, an exercise in political and economic history.

In terms of the issues which inform this book, I approach this peasantry through an analysis of the processes of capitalist development and state formation. No attempt is made to disentangle these as separate factors or to talk about capitalist development and state formation in terms of economic and political levels. Such a separation might make for a neater explanatory analysis, but it would distort Venezuelan social reality. In Venezuela, as will become clear, the state cannot be understood without an analysis of capitalist development, and capitalist development cannot be understood without an analysis of the state. This is not to say that economic and political factors have a reciprocal influence on each other; they simply cannot be treated as factors. They are aspects of a *totality*. To treat them as factors or levels breaks up that totality and precludes historical understanding.

In stressing the importance of the totality, I am following Lukacs' (1971) contention that such an emphasis is the central feature of the dialectical method coming to us from Hegel through Marx. Nonetheless, it should be noted that the attempt to grasp society as a totality does not imply that we see society as an undifferentiated whole. Indeed, the conception of totality that comes from Marx and Lukacs is quite different from the holism of American anthropology. Nor does the problem of grasping a *differentiated* whole reduce itself to the whole/part problem as it is normally conceived. For example, it would be inadequate to take a particular society as a totality and conceive economics, politics, culture, etc. as its constituent parts. Likewise, it would be inadequate to take the "world-system" as the totality and then look at core, semi-peripheral, and peripheral nation-states (or articulating capitalist and noncapitalist modes of production) as the significant parts. Everything hinges, then, upon how we conceptualize the whole and its parts.

To explicate this problem further, I will examine Marx's discussion of it in his famous "Introduction" (1973a).[1] In the section entitled "The Method of Political Economy," he notes that when we examine the political economy of a particular country, it would seem that the proper place to begin would be with the population as a whole. But then he observes that population is meaningless unless one talks of the classes that exist within it, and the notion of classes is meaningless unless one can examine, through apparently more simple categories, the basis for the social existence of particular classes. he observes: "Thus, if I were to begin with the population, this would be *a chaotic conception of the whole*, and I would then, by means of further determinations, move analytically towards ever more simple concepts, from the imagined concrete towards ever thinner abstractions until I had arrived at the simplest determinations" (Marx, 1973a: 100; emphasis added). He then claims: "The concrete is concrete because it is the concentration of many determinations, hence unity of the diverse" (1973a: 101).

According to Marx the "population" would be a "chaotic conception of the whole" and therefore an inadequate notion of the concrete because, as a starting point, it would not be "the concentration of many determinations." He then begins looking for a starting point for the analysis of capitalism that would be simple, tangible, concrete and yet would simultaneously be abstract. It would be a "part" that would simultaneously allow one to grasp the whole because it would be "the concentration of many determinations."[2] After discussing exchange and labor as potential starting points, he appears to settle on capital in the "Introduction." But with the publication two years later of his *Contribution to a Critique of Political Economy* (and in volume 1 of *Capital*, published ten years after the drafting of the "Introduction"), he begins with a seemingly insignificant part: the commodity. This was a strategic starting point for several reasons. It referred to a visible, tangible object, an apparently simple part; yet the analysis of the commodity in terms of value and the analysis of the social relations embedded within commodity relations allowed Marx to analyze the deepest contradictions of capitalist society. For this reason, he considered the commodity to be "the economic cell-form" of bourgeois society. It could serve this function because although the commodity form was not specific to capitalism, capitalism represented a particular type of commodity economy in which the commodity form was so pervasive that even labor power had become a commodity. Social relations took the form of commodity relations. And this particular development implied historical process; to discuss commodity production and exchange was simultaneously to write the history of a particular type of society.

Rather than beginning his analysis with an abstractly conceived totality, or with economic or political parts, he began with a deceptively simple concrete part which (1) implied an historical process, (2) illuminated (*and obscured*) basic social relations of appropriation, and therefore (3) allowed him to mediate the apparent antinomy between part and whole and grasp capitalist society as a totality (cf. Nicholas, 1973: 36–38).

In this essay, I do not pretend to have such a strategic starting point, but I do attempt to analyze a part of Venezuelan society in such a way that our understanding of the totality is enhanced. I concentrate on the formation of the peasantry in the Venezuelan Andes. The attempt to understand the peasantry requires an analysis of the class structure of Venezuela, the position of the peasantry within that structure, and their interrelationships. Although I concentrate on a particular class, then, I have to talk about peasants in terms of their relationship to other classes. To write a history of the Venezuelan peasantry is to write a history of Venezuela. It is in the process of class formation that capitalist development and state formation, the economic and the political, are joined.

But if we encounter serious problems in the analysis of totalities, we encounter even more vexing difficulties in attempting class analysis. One would have to look a long time to find a Marxist who did not take class analysis as a point of departure. Our histories, after all, are written in terms of class relations and class struggles. But within the Marxist tradition, there are serious disagreements regarding how social classes are to be conceived. The disagreements go to the heart of a Marxist approach. In Althusserian Marxism, humans are little more than supports of structured social relations, and social classes can be deduced from abstractly conceived modes of production. The analysis of modes of production (however they are defined) then becomes a crucial step in the *investigator's definition* of social classes. Another tradition, which has recently been quite vocal in its criticism of Althusser, stresses that *classes define themselves* in concrete historical processes and struggles. Central to this tradition is a refusal to define classes in terms of their structural position without considering their action as social groups, in other words, a refusal to separate class situation and class consciousness. E. P. Thompson expresses the fundamental assumption of this tradition:

> Class formations . . . arise at the intersection of determination and self-activity: the working class "made itself as much as it was made." We cannot put "class" here and "class consciousness" there, as two separate entities, the one sequential upon the other, since both must be taken together—the experience of determination, and the "handling" of this in conscious ways. Nor can we deduce class from a static "section" (since it is a *becoming* over time), nor as a function of a mode of production, since class formations and class consciousness (while subject to determinate pressures) eventuate in an open-ended process of *relationship*—of struggle with other classes—over time (Thompson, 1978: 106).

The issue should not be seen as a choice between the extremes of deducing classes from modes of production or of defining them in terms of specific and concrete struggles. The central lesson of Thompson's critique (and this is sometimes blurred by his style) is that classes emerge "at the intersection of determination and self-activity."

In writing a class analysis which would place itself between extreme deductive and inductive styles, I first turned to Georg Lukacs, who clearly understood that class implied more than a structural position but that class consciousness could not be reduced to the naive description of what men *in fact* thought, felt, and wanted at any moment in history and from any given point in the class structure" (Lukacs, 1971: 51). Lukacs attempted to resolve this dilemma by "imputing" "the appropriate and rational reactions . . . to a particular typical position in the process of production" (Lukacs, 1971: 51). He began by noting that any concrete analysis must grasp society as an historically constituted whole (1971: 50). Within that totality, and defined in terms of it, we may identify particular types or classes. We may then consider the extent to which specific classes, given their particular position within the totality, are able to envision the social whole. Thus, we may impute a certain class consciousness, not in terms of what is actually thought or felt, but in terms of the objective possibilities and limits given to a particular class within an historically constituted totality.

The first question we must ask is how far is it *in fact* possible to discern the whole economy of a society from inside it? It is essential to transcend the limitations of particular individuals caught up in their own narrow prejudices. But it is no less vital not to overstep the frontier fixed for them by the economic structure of society and establishing their position in it. Regarded abstractly and formally, then, class consciousness implies a class-conditioned *unconsciousness* of one's own socio-historical and economic condition (Lukacs, 1971: 52).

The analysis of imputed consciousness should not be a mechanical attempt to see that consciousness as arising automatically (1971: 208–09, passim). Rather, one should be outlining the possibilities for and limitations upon conscious activity by particular groups within a concrete whole. The analysis here envisioned, then, would first require an understanding of a totality within history, an examination of its characteristic class structure. Second, it would require the imputation of a consciousness (a vision of the whole and one's position within it) to particular classes. Third, it would require an evaluation of the nature of that particular consciousness in terms of the whole.

There are, however, some problems with Lukacs' position. The first concerns his understanding of class as a structural position. As he moves into a discussion of particular classes, he is thinking of the evolution of capitalism in general rather than of the historical development of particular capitalisms. Despite his call for analysis of historically constituted concrete wholes, then, his own analysis, in practice, is far from concrete. Moving from a discussion of precapitalist estates to capitalist classes, he sees the bourgeoisie and the proletariat as "the only pure classes in bourgeois society." More importantly for our purposes, he claims: "The outlook of the other classes (petty bourgeois or peasants) is ambiguous or sterile because their existence is not based exclusively on their role in the capitalist system of production but is indissolubly linked with the vestiges of feudal society. Their aim, therefore, is not to advance capitalism or to transcend it, but to reverse its action or at least to prevent it from developing fully" (Lukacs, 1971: 59).

Without doubt, this interpretation is relevant for *some* peasantries, and other writers have looked at peasant politics in similar terms to good effect. In an analysis which does not cite Lukacs but starts from similar assumptions and carries them to different conclusions, Wolf shows how the past, as tradition, could be an important organizing force for segments of a peasantry. An attempt to "reverse the action" of capitalism could also constitute an attempt to "transcend it"; or, ". . . it is the very attempt of the middle and free peasant to remain traditional that makes him revolutionary" (Wolf, 1969a: 292). Of course, through both general and historical discussions, Wolf also shows the limited and contradictory nature of such action.

But what of situations in which peasants are not tied to a precapitalist past but are precipitates of capitalist development? In imputing a consciousness to peasants, we need to consider the concrete historical processes which have created them, which have placed them in particular relationships with other classes, and which have provided particular arenas and moments for political action. An analysis of class structure in Venezuela, for example, will always be insufficient so long as it begins and ends with a list of West European classes. Labels like peasant and proletarian provide convenient markers or points of departure, but we can only impute a consciousness to the people, to which those labels refer, in terms of specific circumstances and relationships.

In broad terms, the process that has created peasants and proletarians in Venezuela has been world historical: the incorporation of Venezuela within the capitalist world system. But capitalist penetration of Venezuela did not encounter a peasantry on the ground to be destroyed or maintained. There were no people standing neck high in the water for whom capitalism was like a ripple which drowned them (Scott, 1976). Nor were peasants in Venezuela able to organize around a precapitalist tradition that could serve as a vision of the future (Wolf, 1969a). Rather, Andean peasants, like other Venezuelan toilers, were themselves precipitates of the process of capitalist development. Their class position and their politics were therefore quite distinct.

In discussing the class position and politics of particular peasantries and proletariats, we are confronted with the second major problem with Lukacs' analysis, that associated with the exercise of imputation. In practice, Lukacs' analysis of the position of particular classes defines that position in economic terms. In large part, this is a consequence of the lack of historical specificity, or concreteness, in his definition of totalities, thus purging the analysis of social, political, and cultural detail.[3] We are left, then, with a form of analysis which is similar to the automatic ascription of consciousnes on the basis of economically defined structural positions.

In my own analysis, I have not resolved this problem by moving from imputation to an empiricist description of what people in fact thought and felt at any particular moment. Rather, I try to deepen our understanding of the totality so that we can assess the contradictory structural positions occupied by particular classes and their contradictory visions of the totality and their positions within it. I then talk about how those contradictory relations were resolved in the context of specific political events or movements. In my analysis of the processes of capitalist development in the Venezuelan Andes, I concentrate on the formation of what could broadly be defined as the working classes. In each historical period, the process of their formation has implied increasing social and economic fragmentation, or heterogeneity. Among the peasantry of the nineteenth century, we find economic and social differentiation. In the twentieth century, proletarianization and migration have resulted in a working class that is split along many lines.

My analysis, then, points to a heterogeneous working class, split along lines that can be precisely defined in each historical period. Consideration of class consciousness, or the move from the examination of class as a structural category to the analysis of class in terms of group activity, involves an examination of economic, social, cultural, and political relations that promote a feeling of homogeneity or community. That is, around what banners and in terms of what goals would a heterogeneous class coalesce? In what circumstances would they form a community? In imputing a consciousness to a particular class we need to look at the forces which promote a feeling of homogeneity. We need to examine relationships that unite members of one class to each other or to members of another class in the context of particular movements, paying attention to the ties that bind as well as those that are severed. With such considerations in mind, we may now turn to an account of the formation of a Venezuelan peasantry.

In outlining the Venezuelan problem I must place some limitations of time and space on my considerations. I will be examining three moments in Venezuelan history that are central to an understanding of the development of capitalism in that country: the late nineteenth century, characterized by the dominance of a coffee economy; the transition from a coffee-export economy to a petroleum-export economy in the third and fourth decades of the twentieth century; and the consolidation of the petroleum economy in the mid-twentieth century. At each moment, peasants have been politically active, but at no moment have they taken the political initiative. Moreover, only one of the political movements could be classified as a rebellion: the Gabaldón episode of 1929. But even that movement was not a *peasant* rebellion, as we shall see. Their participation in caudillo wars of the nineteenth century may have been their most conscious and least rebellious activity. With the consolidation of the petroleum economy, peasants have been "mobilized from above" (see Powell, 1969; 1971) by state-building political parties and have sidestepped the *guerrillero* movement of the 1960s.

Such statements can only be understood in terms of the spatial restrictions that have been placed on the analysis. I will be concentrating on Andean peasants rather than considering a "Venezuelan peasantry" as a whole. This limitation reflects, in part, the particularity of my own understanding. My field research was conducted in the Andes, in the Boconó District of Trujillo State, and that is the region I can most comfortably examine. In fact, while the Andes, defined as the states of Táchira, Mérida, and Trujillo, constitutes a certain unity, I am acutely aware of the regional differentiation that exists within the mountain states.

More importantly, however, the spatial limitations have been imposed on us by history. Domingo Alberto Rangel points to three foci of development in nineteenth-century Venezuela. The coffee-producing Andean states in western Venezuela were part of the economic orbit of the port city of Maracaibo. The second regional orbit was eastern Venezuela, around Carúpano, and was based on cacao production. The third focus was centered in the jungles of Guayana and depended upon gold extraction. A fourth region, the cattle-producing llanos, suffered a long decline in the nineteenth century, in part due to the destruction of both the War of Independence (1810–1823) and the Federalist War (1859–1863), and it provided migrants for the developing centers. Each of these regions was integrated separately with the centers of world capitalism and was weakly articulated with other areas of Venezuela (Rangel, 1969: 73–81). This internal disarticulation was reflected in a weak central government which was unable to form the diverse sectors into an integrated whole or to contain a series of regional and local caudillo wars. Despite long periods of stable government at the center (e.g., the governments of Paez or Guzmán Blanco), the fundamental Venezuelan reality in the nineteenth century was regional and local instability and violence. Venezuela did not constitute an integrated social formation; rather, particular regions were integrated into European social formations as export economies. That disarticulation characterized particular regions as well: each of the Andean states was more closely linked to the port city of Maracaibo than to any other Andean state. The Andes never constituted a regional economy but rather a group of regional economies, each producing similar products but maintaining separate ties with trading centers within and beyond the Andes.

Such regional differentiation at the national level affected the formation of a peasantry as well. Unlike, e.g., the cacao sector and the remnants of the llanos ranching economy, which were characterized by large landholdings and dependent peons, the coffee economy in the Andes was forged with a relatively independent peasantry. Rangel (1969; 1974), who concentrated on Táchira, indicated that its coffee economy was created by migrants from the llanos who established small- and middle-sized farms and, until the beginning of the twentieth century, depended primarily on family labor. I, in turn, have shown that the coffee economy in Boconó, Trujillo, was built in part on colonial foundations and in part on the migration of pioneers into previously unsettled territory. The result in both areas was similar, in that an independent peasantry was created. In Boconó, however, it was formed from disparate elements: Indians on disintegrating *resguardos*, white descendents of original settlers on colonial properties, which were in the process of dissolution, and migrants from the llanos (Roseberry, 1977; 1979; 1980; 1982). If the coffee economy in both Táchira and Trujillo circumvented the latifundia structure of the rest of Venezuela and established a relatively independent peasantry, it also facilitated the rise of a merchant class that tied local producers to German commercial houses in Maracaibo. Like the new peasantry, this merchant class was formed partly by the descendents of colonial settlers and partly by the immigration of new settlers, in this case from the llanos and from Spain and Italy (Roseberry, 1977; 1979; 1980; 1982).

The fact that the coffee economy was built on colonial foundations in Mérida and Trujillo and on a relatively blank slate in Táchira had important political implications. The class configurations in Mérida and Trujillo, on the one hand, and Táchira on the other, were distinct. Small-scale producers and merchants who were active in the coffee economy became the basis for the liberal movement in the Andes. They were opposed by a conservative movement rooted in the areas and classes that had been dominant in the colonial era. Large landlords, who had bases of operation in the higher elevations of the Andean cordillera and had been producing wheat and other crops for regional markets, were threatened by the influx of population into temperate zones and the disruption of their regionally closed monopolies. The struggles that erupted opposed conservatives (*godos*) to liberals, cold zone to temperate zone, wheat to coffee, regional markets to world market, Trujillo to Táchira. For a good bit of the last quarter of the nineteenth century, they coalesced around a struggle for control of the Great State of the Andes, an administrative creation of national President Guzmán Blanco, who was attempting to assert central control over regional rivalries. Early on, the upper hand was held by Trujillo conservatives of the cold zone. Even within Trujillo, however, they were opposed by liberals based in such coffee producing areas as Boconó. By the end of the nineteenth century, the balance of power had shifted from wheat to coffee, from conservatives to liberals, from Trujillo to Táchira.[4]

The political struggles took the form of caudillo wars. Rangel's exaggerated claim that "there were as many generals as there were villages" (Rangel, 1974: 55) is given some support by the 1891 census. In Trujillo, for example, there were 35 generals, 63 colonels, 55 commandants, and 188 minor officers among a total population of a little over 145,000. The soldiers in these struggles were peasants. I shall pose two questions regarding peasant participation in these wars: was peasant political activity "conscious"? why did it take this particular form? With regard to the first question, Rangel claims: "The caudillo, of the type we suffered in Venezuela, was a survival of primitive times. In rudimentary societies, political ties are established through a person. Social classes do not have a clear consciousness of their interests and act with a certain slowness to events. In an advanced society, classes have a lucid consciousness which carries them to prompt action. Each one of its members intuits the meaning of social facts and reacts actively. . . . Backward societies lack similar mechanisms" (Rangel, 1974: 53).

Leaving aside the rather mechanical treatment of class consciousness in "advanced" societies, one must question Rangel's treatment of the level of consciousness of peasant participants in the caudillo wars of the Andes. Certainly some of them were so economically dependent upon the notables who became generals that they had little choice but to follow them into battle. This would be particularly true for those who supported the conservative landlords who controlled large tracts of land and could call upon dependent tenants. It would be true as well of the liberal armies. Merchants and smaller landlords could call upon people who were tied to them through a variety of economic, social, and cultural relations (e.g., debt and ritual co-parenthood). Moreover, there were probably multiple personal and regional loyalties which motivated peasant participation.[5] It is also true that the movement did not demonstrate a lucid consciousness of the divergent interests of merchants and peasants. Nevertheless, those differences could hardly have been central as the coffee economy was being formed. Rather, their interests converged in opposition to the regional economy of the colonial period. They were attempting to forge something new, from which they all expected to benefit, and they formed a common cause to do so. At this moment, there was little for peasants to rebel against and much for them to fight for. If we penetrate the caudillo myth of personal charisma and clientelist politics, we are struck with how much this struggle had to do with conflicting economic interests. This is not to simplify a confusing situation or to deny that conservatives fought conservatives and liberals fought liberals, as individual notables attempted to strengthen their own positions. Despite such factionalism, there is little evidence to support Rangel's claim that this represented an atavistic reliance on purely personal relations.

I would therefore maintain that peasant activity was conscious in that it was promoting particular economic interests. It must be emphasized, however, that this consciousness was of particular rather than class interests. Why did their activity and their consciousness take this form? If we take a broad view, the differentiation of what was to become the Venezuelan social formation into various poles of development contributed to the formation of heterogeneous working classes. Here a small holding peasantry; there dependent peons or tenants. Even within a particular region, class heterogeneity was a central characteristic. In the Andes, the peasantry was never an undifferentiated class; formed of disparate elements, it included migrants settling on national lands as well as people from colonial forms in the process of dissolution. In Boconó, Indian reserve lands and European properties were parceled and alienated (Roseberry, 1977: 91–96; 1979; 1980; 1982). In both cases, a community of producers was dissolved.

In the indigenous reserves, the community was defined by ownerhsip of land, and the Indian was defined by membership in a community which owned land. Dissolution of reserves was simultaneously the dissolution of the community and the destruction of the basis for indigenous identity. Residents of colonial properties held rights to particular properties because they were descendents of the original owner. The community was based on descent. Although neither situation was characterized by communal production, each had a social and ideological network which bound individual families to each other. The establishment of small scale private property dissolved the network, promoting greater heterogeneity. Community dispersal was reflected in a residence pattern in which farmers lived on their farms. With the move to private property, some individuals within the old communities were able to dispossess other individuals.[6] Differentiation among small producers was enhanced, and a communal ideology was replaced by one of conflict and competition. This differentiation within communities was rendered more complex by regional differentiation between communities. For example, the sources of these communities were various (indigenous reserves or European properties, migrants from other regions, etc.). Regional and ethnic identities divided the peasantry, and some peasants produced wheat for regional markets while others produced coffee for the world market.

When these sources of division are placed in the context of expanding commodity production, in which some are favored and some are not, in which some occasionally need workers and others need work, the picture of a heterogeneous peasantry is complete. The ties that promoted a feeling of homogeneity or community were vertical rather than horizontal. These could be economic and social relations with merchants to whom peasants were indebted, with locally prominent small landlords, or with rich peasants who bought their neighbors' coffee and carried it to a nearby town. Or they could be regional or ethnic affiliations, both of which tied into a vertical orientation. There were some horizontal ties, such as reciprocal labor arrangements, but these tended to be dyadic (e.g., *mano vuelta*). The more inclusive forms of reciprocal labor (e.g., *convite*) were asymmetrically vertical. Thus the dominant forces of cohesion were vertical, and the forces promoting a feeling of homogeneity in the coffee economy favored the formation of local factions.

In the nineteenth century, then, Andean peasants came close to resembling the French peasants described by Marx in the *Eighteenth Brumaire*. The oft-quoted passage from Marx is as follows:

The small peasant proprietors form an immense mass, the members of which live in the same situation but do not enter into manifold relationships with each other. Their mode of operation isolates them instead of bringing them into mutual intercourse. This isolation is strengthened by the wretched state of France's means of communication and by the poverty of the peasants. Their place of operation, the smallholding, permits no division of labour in its cultivation, no application of science and therefore no diversity of development, variety of talent, or wealth of social relationships. Each individual peasant family is almost self-sufficient; it directly produces the greater part of its means of life more through exchange with nature than through intercourse with society. The smallholding, the peasant, and the family; next door, another smallholding, another peasant, another family. A bunch of villages makes up a department. Thus the great mass of the French nation is formed by the simple addition of isomorphous magnitudes, such as potatoes in a sack form a sack of potatoes. In so far as millions of families live under economic conditions of existence that separate their mode of life, their interests and their cultural formation from those of the other classes, they form a class. In so far as these small peasant proprietors are merely connected on a local basis, and the identity of their interests fails to produce a feeling of community, national links, or a political organization, they do not form a class. They are therefore incapable of asserting their class interest in their own name, whether through a parliament or through a convention. They cannot represent themselves; they must be represented. Their representative must appear simultaneously as their master, as an authority over them, an unrestricted governmental power that protects them from the other classes and sends them rain and sunshine from above. The political influence of the small peasant proprietors is therefore ultimately expressed in the executive subordinating society to itself (Marx, 1973b: 238–39).

This passage is quoted by Marxists and non-Marxists (and anti-Marxists) alike. For the orthodox Marxist, it can be used to disparage the revolutionary potential of a peasantry and can contribute to an attitude which makes possible the forced disappearance of a peasantry after the revolution. For the anti-Marxist, the passage can be used as one of many to show that Marx was "against" the peasant. Both usages lift the passage from its context and distort its meaning.

Regarding that context, it is important to note first of all that the passage refers to mid-nineteenth century French peasants. While there are aspects of the discussion that are relevant to other peasantries (indeed, I maintain that nineteenth century Venezuelan peasants were similar in some respects), that relevance must be established historically. Moreover, he looks at the mid-nineteenth century French peasant as the product of a specific historical development—the French Revolution. In this section of the *Eighteenth Brumaire* and in corresponding sections of *Class Struggles in France*, he examines the strains placed upon the new small holders, the debt burdens they encountered, and the manner in which they might see their support of Bonaparte as a protest against their creditors and other apparent representatives of the forces that oppressed them. This points to the second aspect of the passage's context that is important. It is part of a discussion of the support of Bonaparte among the peasantry. It is an attempt to understand political consciousness in terms of class situation, and it is full of insight. I might point to a passage which follows by a few pages the paragraph cited above. In it, Marx claims: "[T]he Bonaparte dynasty represents the conservative, not the revolutionary peasant. . . . It represents the peasant's superstition, not his enlightenment; his prejudice, not his judgement; his past, not his future; his modern Vendee, not his modern Cevennes" (1973b: 240). In a commentary, Hal Draper has drawn this lesson: "This, qualified Marx, was true only of the conservative bulk of the peasantry, not of its radicalized elements who were able to look beyond their small land-parcels" (Draper, 1977: 402). I suggest that it is time we stopped thinking of peasants in such vanguardist terms. When Marx talks of the conservative and the revolutionary peasant, he is not referring to a conservative bulk and radicalized elements. Rather, the peasantry as a whole, because of its class situation, was Janus-faced. It could be *both* conservative and revolutionary. All depended upon the presence or absence of connections which could promote a "feeling of community, national links, or a political organization." In mid-nineteenth century France, those connections were vertical rather than horizontal, and Bonaparte was able to make himself the symbol and apparent force of their liberation. Likewise, in mid-nineteenth century Venezuela, or at least in parts of the Andes, the connections that created "a feeling of community" were vertical, and they ran through caudillos. This should not suggest, and I contend Marx did not mean to suggest, that such a feeling of community and such a political organization could not be created in, say, twentieth-century China. Not all peasants live in a "baseless triangle."

There were, of course, some differences between French and Andean peasants in the nineteenth century. Andean peasants hardly constituted a "vast mass whose members live in similar conditions but without entering manifold relations with each other." Nor did peasant families "[acquire their] means of life more through exchange with nature than in intercourse with society." Were this the case, we would have little more than a cataloging of complexity or heterogeneity. Rather, the manner in which they entered into "intercourse with society" pushed them into vertical alliances. Because of this particular direction of the forces promoting a feeling of community, however, there was no "identity of their interests . . . no national union and no political organisation." In this sense, they do not form a class. The forces promoting a feeling of homogeneity tended to forge relations (based at least in part on conscious recognition of similar interests) between segments of the peasantry and segments of dominant classes. Regionally based conservative and liberal factions represented the limits to the formation of political communities.

In the twentieth century, however, new forces were set in motion which created new limits and possibilities. Táchira liberals, dominant in the Andes by the end of the nineteenth century, gained control of the central government in 1899. While in power, they presided over the transformation of Venezuela from an agricultural-export economy to a petroleum republic. More specifically, much of this transition was made under the rule of Juan Vicente Gomez (1908 to 1935), who granted the first petroleum concessions and saw petroleum far outstrip all other exports. He also appointed economic ministers who, in the middle of the depression of the 1930s, revalued the Venezuelan currency in a manner that was disastrous to agricultural exporters and favorable to the importers of capital goods (i.e., the petroleum interests; I refer to the Convenio Tinoco of 1934). Contradictions abound in this period. Gomez initially became prominent as a coffee hacendado and then presided over the demise of the coffee economy. He rode the crest of regional power and caudillo influence and set in motion the processes by which a centralizing state machinery integrated the Venezuelan social formation for the first time and suppressed regional bases of political and economic strength. He peopled his adminstration and army with Andeans and allowed political and economic power to pass to others.

In order to understand this transformation and the response of Andeans to it, we must first understand something about the manner in which Cipriano Castro and Juan Vicente Gomez came to power. Theirs was not an undifferentiated movement by Andeans. Although Castro and Gomez gained local influence among Táchiran (and Colombian) liberals and through the coffee economy, their movement did not represent the conquest of political power by coffee merchants and peasants. While Gomez had been a coffee hacendado, Cipriano Castro (who led the 1899 invasion from Colombia which captured state power with sixty men) had grown up in the town of Capacho in Táchira and had been educated in the

Colombian town of Pamplona. Rangel notes that this urban, urbane, middle-class man did not develop the clientele needed to conquer state power in the countryside. He claims that Castro could not do so because the Andean peasantry was not dissatisfied, as were peasants in other regions (Rangel, 1974: 66). Certainly, for them, the coffee economy was still vigorous and offered a level of autonomy and standard of living which, despite growing debts, was better than that achieved by rural producers elsewhere in the country. There is strong evidence, however, that the coffee economy was beginning to stagnate by the end of the nineteenth century, that the top-quality open land that had served as the fuel for expansion was filling up (Roseberry, 1977: 132–42). An urban population composed of merchants and professionals would probably be the first to sense the potential crisis.

> Cipriano Castro found his clientele in the cities of Táchira where middle class youth confronted acute problems. Toward the last years of the century Táchira was overflowing with high school graduates who could not afford a university career. They were members of an ambitious middle class which could no longer prosper. The region had no industries to offer a promising future to these people. The graduate had to settle for being an artisan, teacher, or modest employee. . . . Castro does not have peons or discontented rural masses. But in each town there is a half-educated young man who reads his articles and enlists in his cause. . . .
>
> The movement with which Táchira—led by Castro—invades Venezuela . . . is the rebellion of a middle class matured by the prosperity of coffee but for which the horizons in view were not sufficiently tempting (Rangel, 1974: 67, 68).

Just as Castro had grander visions and was not tied to the Andean economy, he was opposed by some Andeans in his drive to Caracas. While in power, he was opposed by several Andean caudillos who did not see in Castro a worthy spokesman. But Castro had named as his vice president a more typical Táchirense, Juan Vicente Gomez, who deposed Castro in a coup in 1908. On the surface, it would appear that his was the most Andean of administrations. He named Andeans to positions in the central government, to state presidencies, and to the army. Furthermore, as a coffee hacendado of moderate scale, he was the economic and cultural heir of the Andean countryside. Nevertheless, by the time Gomez took power in 1908, his Táchira coffee hacienda was no longer his major source of wealth. As Vice President under Castro, he had accumulated commercial monopolies in meat and/or liquors in Caracas, Valencia, and Puerto Cabello. To supply the meat for his monopolies, he began accumulating large cattle ranches. This allowed Gomez to break out of agricultural export production, and it brought him into new alliances with those Caracas merchants with whom he shared power. Shortly after deposing Cipriano Castro, Gomez re-established diplomatic relations with the various foreign governments Castro had offended (including the United States). Soon, foreign asphalt concessions which had been annulled by Castro were re-established, and new petroleum concessions were granted to Venezuelans who sold them to foreign companies. This mechanism allowed those in government and their allies to enrich themselves, and it meant that they had a personal stake in the petroleum future. The basis for political and economic power in Venezuela was being altered. Thus, although Andeans were visibly present in the government, the interests of coffee producers or merchants were poorly represented. However tyrannical the dictators may have been politically, their rule represented a period of shared economic power in which some Andeans were favored along with Caracas merchants and foreign companies. The entire period of Andean rule (1899–1945) represents a progressive loss of national power by the producers and merchants who had been dominant in the expanding coffee economy.

The signs of discontent were many and, as they spread, a specifically Andean politics began to dissipate. Gomez recognized many rivals among the old caudillos within and without of the Andes. Some rose up against him; others were imprisoned or exiled or neutralized because they might rise up against him. While prisons overflowed, however, it seems that much of the peasant discontent was localized. Specific individuals in particular regions benefited from the Gomez peiod, even if the agricultural economy as a whole was disintegrating. For example, in 1920 and 1923, Gomez granted large sections of the national lands in the Boconó District, which had been so important in the formation of the coffee economy, to merchants and locally prominent farmers. As coffee farmers entered into a period of crisis with the depression, merchants in Boconó and Maracaibo foreclosed on farmers and smaller merchants who could not pay their debts. If they had the power of the state behind them in their foreclosures, they were also the most visible villains. When people reminisce about that period, they speak of the tyranny of dictatorship in comparison with the liberty of democracy, but their most bitter comments are reserved for those families who benefitted from the period.

What is most remarkable about the period, however, is the relative lack of political opposition to Gomez. Peasants suffered, some were imprisoned (along with notables who opposed or threatened Gomez), but for the most part they did not rise up against the Gomez state. There were important exceptions, and I will examine one of these shortly. In considering the relative lack of activity on the part of peasants who had once been so active, Rangel points to a kind of exhaustion (1974: 198). He feels that after years of struggle with no positive result in the nineteenth century, they could fight no more. Such an explanation hardly seems sufficient. Perhaps it was also due to the fact that no one, except for an occasional Alberto nature of Gomez's rule. He was an Andean, a caudillo, and had acted as a caudillo was expected to act in government: he had enriched himself and his friends. Perhaps it was also due to the fact that no one, except for an occasional Alberto Adriani (see his 1937), could recognize the crisis of the agricultural economy as its final crisis. The period of growth in the coffee sector was characterized by boom-and-bust cycles as international prices rose and fell. There was, perhaps, little reason to expect this to be any different. The petroleum transformation was occurring behind the backs of everyone. A future was being created that few could envision. Of course, that future also held out the possibility of new wealth, and the petroleum camps in the Maracaibo basin attracted Andean migrants. This may have taken the cutting edge off some of the despair.

I think, however, that the more fundamental reason for a relative lack of political activity has to do with the transformation of the forms through which that activity had traditionally been channeled. The state structures were hardly in crisis during this period; rather, they were in full expansion and consolidation. With the greatly increased revenues from petroleum earnings, the central bureaucracy was growing at a remarkable rate. New agencies were created, old ones modernized. Roads were built and communications systems improved. Gomez was attempting to maintain his control by being able to check developments in particular regions. In the process, he laid the foundation for the integrated society and state that Venezuela became as a petroleum republic. By this I do not mean that it became a smoothly functioning system. I simply mean that the regionalism of the nineteenth century was superseded, and the caudillos who thrived in regional environments were displaced.

The displacement of the caudillo began early in the Gomez period, before the petroleum transformation. In 1913, at the end of the first constitutional period, at which time Gomez was expected to step down, he consolidated his rule. In response, caudillos rose up in various parts of the country in a series of localized rebellions. At the same time, Gomecistas fabricated an invasion by Cipriano Castro to which the state had to respond. The popular phrase repeated by Heredia captures the spirit of state action: *se alzó el gobierno* (the government rebelled) (Heredia, 1974: 14). From 1913 to 1915, caudillos were exiled or imprisoned, or they submitted. Those who submitted were disarmed, as Gomez pursued and established peace in the countryside.

Thus, quite early in Gomez's rule, he crushed the traditional forms through which protest and rebellion could be channeled. When peasants turned again to political action in 1929, they did so through the forms that were embedded in a Venezuela that was disappearing. One can point to one of the most famous revolts: the Gabaldón episode of 1929. It is interesting because it occurred during a period of a year and a half characterized by insurrections, a period that at once marked the end of caudillo politics and the beginning of national political parties. Of more immediate interest, however, is the fact that it emerged in an area near Boconó. Although General José Rafael Gabaldón began the revolt from his hacienda in Portuguesa State, it was in a region just across a political boundary from the Boconó District of Trujillo State. More importantly, Gabaldón was himself a Boconó notable, a member of one of Trujillo's most interesting families, which had provided both conservative and liberal caudillos in the nineteenth century. Gabaldón was an early follower of Gomez and was appointed president of Portuguesa State. When, however, Trujillo politico Leopoldo Baptista fell out of favor with Gomez in the events of 1913, Gabaldón, as a protege of Baptista, was implicated in Gomez's purge and had to hide in the mountains of Boconó. In the *Sagrada* of 1914–15,

Boconó was visited by Gomez's assassins, who were looking for Baptistas, primarily José Rafael Gabaldón. He was never captured, and it is said that while being pursued he went to a *carnaval* party at the house of the Jefe Civil of Boconó, in an elaborate disguise (Baptista, 1962: 135–38).

So began, in characteristic fashion (i.e., the state creating the dissident), a long period of opposition to Gomez. There was an early reconciliation between Gabaldón and Gomez, with Gabaldón returning to the hacienda Santo Cristo in Portuguesa State in 1915. It is fascinating to read Heredia's account of the Gabaldón uprising in 1929 and the period of quiet from 1915 to 1929. It illuminates the nature and limitations of caudillo politics during the Gomez years. One sees how relationships are formed among notables (merchants, hacendados, doctors, lawyers, school teachers, etc.), and within and between a variety of regional centers, all linked by ties of friendship and kinship. One senses a certain ambiguity and *inquietud* in their relationships with those in power. Gabaldón himself enjoyed an uneasy friendship with Gomez during this period. The notables, the group from which caudillos had arisen and to which they had fallen, were at once tied to localities and in a position to transcend them. Their sources of authority and influence were local; yet they maintained networks of relations with notables from other localities. Their room for maneuver was therefore greater than that of the peasants on whom they might depend in political action.

The events which eventually broke the long quiet of the 1920s are indicative of the forces which were creating a new Venezuela. They emanated not from a peasant rebellion or a caudillo uprising but from a student movement at the central university in February to April of 1928. The leaders of that movement, known as the Generation of '28, became the founders and grand old men of the modern political parties of this century. The student movement itself was suppressed, and the leaders fled into exile or were imprisoned. This was not the first such student movement. Earlier action by Gustavo Machado, Salvador de la Plaza and others had brought early imprisonment and exile and had closed the central university from 1912 to 1923. What was new in 1928 was the popular response to the student movement. The action of the university students, and the speed and violence of the government response, provoked demonstrations of support and resistance in the growing cities and in the petroleum camps. And it provoked the re-awakening of caudillo politics.

One of the students who participated in the events of 1928 (who later became one of the recognized notables of the Generation of '28) was Gabaldón's son, Joaquin Gabaldón Márquez. Through letters, Gabaldón had been apprised of events in Caracas. Shortly after the strike, Gabaldón visited Gomez to ask for the release of imprisoned students and to push for a more open administration.[7] After the interview, he sent Gomez a public letter dated 7 September 1928. This action finally broke the uneasy truce between Gabaldón and Gomez. From that point it was known that Gabaldón would rebel or be imprisoned.

Heredia's discussion of these and subsequent events demonstrates clearly the contradictory nature of political action during this period. In the first place, it is interesting to note the time span between the 7 September letter (when Gabaldón was once again classified as an enemy) and the actual uprising of 28 April 1929. Of this period, Gabaldón has written: "Because of my public letter to General Gomez, I could no longer leave "Santo Cristo," since the dictator had given orders to capture me should I leave. Yet my detention was not simple then, in those mountains, where I had for ten leagues around everything prepared so that I could not be surprised, and in the hacienda I was accompanied by a growing number of loyal and brave men capable of repelling any attack" (quoted in Heredia, 1974: 82–83).

One sees here the limits of state power in 1929, even as state structures were being consolidated. Gabaldón was able to create a space into which agents of the state dared not enter. One also gets an insight into the nature of caudillo power. Gabaldón was simultaneously able to depend on others for protection and offer protection to those who were defending him. The lack of peasant rebellion from 1913 to 1929 becomes less mysterious, for the disarmament and incapacitation of the caudillos had destroyed the mechanisms through which peasants could coalesce and create a structural space for organization and rebellion. The nineteenth century had established a heterogeneous peasantry, and the ties that bound them ran through caudillos. The forces promoting a feeling of homogeneity in the nineteenth century had been superseded and had not yet been replaced by new ones.

The attempt to re-establish those old political forms was less a response to the new Venezuelan reality and more an attempt to recreate what had been. That this attempt was fraught with contradiction is apparent from Heredia's account. As it became apparent that a movement against Gomez was imminent, there was, on the one hand, an attempt to turn to regional cadiullos, and, on the other hand, an attempt to coordinate their activities on a national level. In a series of letters and meetings between student leaders and caudillos in Venezuela and in exile, as well as with members of the government,[8] plans were laid for a series of simultaneous uprisings and invasions. In a flurry of conspiracies and betrayals, alliances were formed and broken. The date of 28 April 1929 was set for the coordinated uprisings, but they were later postponed until 5 May. For reasons which are obscure, Gabaldón never received notification of the postponement and began the rebellion on 28 April by taking Guanare with thirty men.

The 28 April uprising was limited to the states of Portuguesa, Lara, and Trujillo. Upon learning that the other uprisings and invasions had not occurred, Gabaldón took his little army into the mountains, where he attracted peasant recruits. Government forces in pursuit estimated his strength at 2,000; Gabaldón himself estimated it at 300 (Heredia, 1974: 105). By 7 May, he had returned to Guanare, where the only major battle with government forces was realized. Despite the fact that the rebels had few arms, they defeated the government forces. In the moment of victory, however, Gabaldón decided to retreat. With the knowledge that his force was alone and that his own victory had been costly,[9] he decided he could not capture state power and tried to escape to Colombia. It was a move that can be questioned and in fact was questioned by some of his followers (Heredia, 1974: 112–14); in any case, it meant the end of the rebellion. Their escape route blocked; the army dissolved into small groups seeking refuge. Gabaldón, along with his son Joaquin, was taken prisoner two months after the uprising. The other caudillo uprisings, or invasions from exiled caudillos, arose individually during 1929 and were suppressed.

This failed movement was the closest the Andean peasants came to rebelling against the state during the crucial years in which Venezuela was transformed from an agricultural-export economy to a petroleum-export economy. They did not initiate the movement but coalesced around a disaffected hacendado. It can be seen as one of the last of the caudillo movements, and like the movements of the nineteenth century, it was contradictory. It centered around the leadership of a person; it was a factional rather than a class movement. It was not a peasant rebellion. Like the factional struggles of the nineteenth century, however, this one was not without political and economic content. Just as liberal factions in the nineteenth century crossed class lines to create a new economy in which they all had a stake, the Gabaldón rebellion crossed class lines to protest the Venezuela that was being created and to recreate the past. While the revolt occurred in 1929, the price crisis of the coffee economy had not yet set in. But the coffee economy was no longer dominant by the mid-1920s. Gabaldón and the peasants that followed him had been politically and economically displaced.

After the Gomez years, Gabaldón collected a good bit of moral capital for his role in the rebellion. He held occasional political and ambassadorial posts and died an honored man. He, like coffee, like the peasant, and like the countryside, had become symbolic of a prepetroleum, preurban, premodern Venezuela. All of that symbolic weight was contained within the revolt itself. In Wolf's terms, we might say they were attempting to "remain traditional" (Wolf, 1969a: 292). Yet what is perhaps most interesting about that attempt, and the symbolism that attaches to coffee and agriculture, is how nontraditional that tradition was. It too was a product of capitalist development, setting in motion forces which were in conflict with a new moment of capitalist history in the twentieth century.

That the movement (like other regional movements that arose during the period) was doomed in the face of what was happening in Venezuela at that time should be, I hope, apparent. They were regional rebels in a national society. The attempt to turn their regional movements into a unified national one by aggregation seems to have failed, in part, because of their mutual distrust. Even had they coordinated their uprisings, however, it is unlikely that simple aggregation could have responded to the new Venezuelan reality. National forms of political action only emerged with the formation and growth of political parties in the 1930s and 1940s.[10] We are now on ground that has been thoroughly trod by North American political scientists in celebration of Venezuela's "democratic experiment," and I do not intend to further turn well-worn paths into ruts. The important point is that as the parties were formed, they were in a position to respond to and eventually to capture the new Venezuelan state: as students, they were imprisoned and exiled; as political leaders, they consolidated the infrastructure created by Gomez and gave it a democratic form.

A proper understanding of the transformation of politics in Venezuela requires an understanding of the economic and social transformations that constituted the petroleum era. Because this has been discussed in some detail elsewhere (see Rangel, 1970; Brito Figueroa, 1966; Malavé Mata, 1974; Córdova, 1973; Roseberry, 1977: 143–70; 1982), I will only summarize the results here. Structurally, Venezuela is no longer dependent upon agriculture and is now dependent upon petroleum. Nevertheless, the petroleum industry itself is spatially confined to two zones and absorbs a minuscule percentage of the population. Although a wide variety of support services emerged in conjunction with the petroleum sector, its principal ramifications have been indirect. Earnings from petroleum have been funneled through the state, which has attempted to "sow the petroleum" in other sectors with government-initiated and government-controlled industrial and agricultural enterprises. With direct investment and with the establishment of marketing control boards and mixed public-private cooperatives, the government has established greater control over the economy. For example, in the coffee sector private merchants have been largely displaced by government credit and marketing programs. With the nationalization of the petroleum companies in 1976, the central government has become the major economic actor in Venezuela. With the expansion of the bureaucracy in Caracas to administer these programs, there has been a concomitant expansion of the urban middle class and of the commercial sector.

If one were to trace the country's economic evolution in terms of primary (agriculture and mining), secondary (manufacture, construction, and utilities), and tertiary (commerce, transportation, and services) sectors, the results would be remarkable. Distribution of GNP among sectors has been relatively stable because of petroleum earnings (in the primary sector). Nevertheless, from 1950 to 1969, there was significant slippage in the primary sector (from 38 to 28 percent of total GNP), a minor proportional increase in the secondary sector (from 17 to 20 percent), and a larger proportional increase in the tertiary sector (from 45 to 52 percent) (Venezuela, Banco Central, 1971: 54). As was noted earlier, however, the petroleum sector does not absorb much of the population.

If we divide the economically active population among those same sectors, a different picture emerges. In 1950, 46 percent were working in the primary sector; by 1971, only 22 percent were. The secondary sector remained relatively stable (from 17 to 20 percent), and the percentage of the population working in the tertiary sector increased from 34 to 42. The major increase was in a group the census takers did not know what to do with. The residual others increased from 3 to 16 percent (Venezuela, Ministerio de Fomento, 1971). The remarkable decline in the percentage of people engaged in the primary sector, which is accounted for by decline in the agricultural sector,[11] is reflected in figures on migration. From 1936—a year after Gomez's death—until 1971, Venezuela was tranformed from a country in which 35 percent of the population lived in urban areas to one in which

77 percent of the population did so. Over the years we have been considering, Venezuela was 54 percent urban in 1950 and 77 percent urban in 1971 (Venezuela, Ministerio de Fomento, 1971; Paez Celis, 1975).

Enough numbers. What does this mean in class terms? For one thing, it means that to look for a peasantry in Venezuela in this half of the twentieth century is to look at Venezuela from a romantic point of view.

Although one will still find farming families in the countryside, one will find very few who have not been affected by the transformation. An older farmer may have seen all his sons and daughters move to Caracas or other urban areas. Or a farmer (and/or members of his family) may work off the farm in Boconó (or Caracas) for all or part of the year. When one combines this trend with the long decline in productivity and income from the farms themselves, it becomes clear that the farm is increasingly relegated to garden status. Wage labor, if it can be had, is an increasingly attractive alternative. As one informant expressed it (with some exaggeration): "Today a fixed worker, in public works, is better than a farmer. Much better. Because he has savings. He is working but he has savings. He has fifteen, twenty years of service and already has thirty thousand or twenty thousand bolívares saved up [here he exaggerates—WR]. . . . The ones who get ahead nowadays, in working, are the laborers." Andean farmers have been trapped within historical processes they have not created. Many of their farms no longer provide for their livelihood, but most of them are only able to find work off the farm on an irregular basis. They stay on the land, and they work for others when they can. They are caught between peasant and proletarian categories as they are traditionally defined.

Looking beyond the local farmers and examining what has been happening to their sons and daughters, we see that they have been the recruits for expanding urban occupations (e.g., in services and the remarkable residual category). The integration of the Venezuelan nation-state has also made for a certain integration of its working classes. What has been happening to Boconó families is a microcosm of what has been happening nationally. A peasant rebellion, like a regional caudillo uprising, would be anachronistic in Venezuela today, for peasants are increasingly disappearing into a broad working class.

Given these developments, one can easily see structural reasons for the failure of the *guerrillero* episode of the 1960s. Using a Cuban model, left-wing parties were attempting to organize rural peoples into a revolutionary force during a decade in which an economically active population engaged in agriculture (only a portion of whom could be considered peasants) was declining from 31 to 20 percent of the national total. Peasants were romanticized and organized at a time when they were disappearing.[12] Of course, the strategy and the movement itself were imposed upon the left by a government which was attempting to purge them. I am simply indicating that the movement was doomed because it did not address the increasing integration of the peasantry within the proletariat, and because it did not articulate the essential unity of town and country, proletarian and peasant.

Discussion of politics at present would have to consider the forces that promote fractionalization and those that promote integration (or, in terms expressed earlier, the forces that promote heterogeneity and the forces that promote a feeling of homogeneity). The broad working class to which I referred is incredibly fragmented. Workers can be divided along many lines: those in the country and those in the city; those with land, those without land; those with work and those without work. Yet because the urban proletariat and subproletariat is of such recent vintage, there are ties which crosscut fractional divisions, e.g., those of kinship and regional affiliations.

The most important integrative ties, however, are those of the state. Part of this integration is evident from what has already been said about the political and economic role of the government. It is at this level that the importance of the political parties established by the Generation of '28 can be seen. From 1945, when Acción Democrática first came to power,[13] the political parties have been the principal channels for political activity. Venezuelan peasants, like proletarians, industrialists, merchants, etc., have expressed themselves politically through the parties and the unions and organizations created by those parties. In this way, political activity broke its regional fetters and became a national force. Yet as Powell has demonstrated, the peasantry (as well as other groups) was mobilized from above (Powell, 1969; 1971). That mobilization has at once promoted integration (as it has emanated from central sources) and perpetuated fractionalization (as it has divided its organizations and unions into peasant, labor, and other categories).

The role of political parties in local and national processes has numerous implications. Government penetration of the economic sphere has provided enormous opportunities for new forms of clientelist politics. The government is the most important employer of wage labor in rural regions. In order to obtain work (or in order to obtain agricultural credit) there is often a tacit requirement that one must be a member of the political party in power. That party—through the government—becomes the most important source of patronage. The peasant, then, in attempting to improve his position, has a stake in the maintenance of the system and the positions of the people who dominate it. This is not to argue that peasants will always be nonrevolutionary (though in Venezuela the question is somewhat moot as the peasantry has declined in economic importance). Indeed, if the government (which increasingly is coterminous with capitalist power as it extends its control over the economy) fails to meet the expectations of peasants and proletarians for improved living standards, its system of patronage will have a weaker hold on the loyalties of its clients. This, of course, is the hope of various socialist movements in Venezuela (cf. Roseberry, 1978: 15).

Mobilization from above has also meant that political activity can be channeled by party cadres into relatively safe areas like election campaigns, rallies, etc. And one gets the distinct impression that protest itself is managed. I could point to numerous points of indirect evidence to support this, but one in particular seemed obvious. While I was in Boconó, the president's wife came to Trujillo and Boconó for an inspection visit. While there, she conferred with an invited group of peasants and listened to their version of the problems they confronted. I quote from *El Nacional*, 16 July 1975:

> The peasants of the municipalities which form the Boconó District, in an organized manner, were explaining their problems and hopes. With complete courtesy, but with force, the peasants told the First Lady they felt cheated.
>
> "Come see our miserable houses, Doña Blanca. Come see them so you can tell the President of the miserable conditions in which we Trujillan peasants live."
>
> The community representatives, one by one, demanded rural roads but above all a housing plan.

That the two problems mentioned by the selected protesters had to do with government projects was not, I suggest, entirely accidental. Both supported programs of government construction. For example, the government was, in several localities, building *nucleos* of rural houses in a uniform fashion: cement blocks on concrete slabs. Of course, each family who purchased a house and moved from an old *bahareque* house on its farm to the new *nucleo* was tied more closely to the government. And at each project, be it a road, a housing project, or a chapel,[14] the government would erect a sign saying, "*El Gobierno Democrático Construye. . . .*"

The new forms through which political activity is channeled once again make for political communities which are vertically rather than horizontally based. That is, organization along "class" lines is difficult today, just as it was in the nineteenth century, although the basis for present-day political communities is entirely different and contains within it more dynamic possibilities. The peasant or proletarian who participates in the state-building parties may find his political activity constantly frustrated. This was reflected in a series of conversations I had with one worker/peasant in Boconó.

A long-time member of Acción Democrática, the dominant party, but one who has never enjoyed any of the major spoils of electoral victory, he reflected on the control of his party by people he does not identify with. The interview took place early on in our friendship, when he seemed to think that because I was an outsider doing a study in the region I had an inside track to governmental authorities. The early interviews took the form of reports from the countryside to the president, whom he admired. He wanted to warn the president that he and his party were being betrayed because Copeyanos (members of the other dominant party) were entering his government. His rationale: the Copeyanos were the merchants and industrial capitalists; Acción Democrática was born in the countryside and was identified with "the people" but was constantly being infiltrated and frustrated by Copeyanos (i.e., *burgueses*). Yet, *Adecos no son burgueses* (Adecos are not bourgeois).[15] On the other hand, he also recognized that there is a wealthy group of individuals, some of whom are Adecos, who are influential in every government, regardless of party:

. . . when this government changes, they go to the next government and are received, because they work in bands. They're like music; they work in various bands. . . .

In my opinion, this has existed for a long time because during the dictatorships—I'm going to talk about the dictatorships; I'm very old and I have read. All those that are doctors today, the older ones and the sons of doctors that were—they had money to pay to be taught. There were no free schools like there are today. The schools had to be paid. . . . And those are the same people with the same wealth, those rich. And you know that rich man leaves his inheritance when he dies . . . it's like a chain, leaving his inheritance to his wife and the children, and he carries the same ideas as the father that was. So that these people never change since they know nothing of progress, they don't know about liberty, what they're interested in is money. . . . So that there's not, there's not a feeling of, "We're going to help out this one or this one." No. "My father is rich and my father let me learn everything, I have an inheritance from my father, and I'm going to get myself a ministerial job or join an institute of those rich . . ." So that nothing ever happens here, so that this is the backwardness of this country. Until they change those people, send them to another country, those rich, this won't change. What's happening now has to keep on happening. And this happens in all the governments and governments are never bad. The bad governments—the bad is in us, the Venezuelans, the capitalists are the ones that knock us over the head.

But the situation is not as non-contradictory as my friend might think. There is an inherent weakness in the politics of patronage practiced by the parties in power: they must deliver on their promises. For reasons that have as much to do with Venezuela's position in the world system as with the politics of the parties that achieve state power, governmental parties have been unable to keep such promises. At the moment, this is leading to a trend in which two centrist parties (the social democratic Acción Democrática and the christian democratic COPEI) exchange positions every five years. The party out of power capitalizes on a large protest sentiment and throws the party in power into the opposition in each presidential election. Both parties (COPEI with less success than AD) promote integration by organizing diverse class fractions into a central organization and promote fractionalization by maintaining distinct organizational sectors. That is, the parties promote a feeling of homogeneity by integrating a fractionalized working class into a multi-class organization oriented toward the development of the Venezuelan state.[16] But they attempt to maintain heterogeneity within the working classes.

If political communities are still vertically based, however, they are fundamentally different from those of the nineteenth century and offer more room for maneuver. For one thing, now they are national rather than regional or factional. In addition, there is a material basis for the creation of horizontal ties between segments of an unevenly developed but increasingly national working class. Socialist parties (themselves fractionalized) have been actively involved in the attempt to create such ties. Much will depend upon their ability to take a heterogeneous proletariat (including a proletarianizing peasantry) and make it act as a homogeneous force. In doing so, they can utilize the centralizing forces of the state itself. For example, left-wing parties have been active in rural regions but have been most successful in organizing students in high schools. But the expansion of public education has meant that some of the students are sons and daughters of a proletarianizing peasantry. A more immediate example is the demonstrated ability of some left-wing parties to win union elections.

In short, there is some room for maneuver in present-day Venezuela, which is simply another way of saying that the situation is contradictory. The forces promoting a feeling of homogeneity have been those associated with a centralizing state. But the centralizing state has created possibilities for the development of new and potentially explosive homogeneous forms.

The reader no doubt will have noted that, despite my criticism of reference to economic and political factors, I have indeed talked about, and differentiated between, economics and politics. But they have not been conceived as levels, and the state has not been conceived primarily as a political institution (or set of institutions), the relationship of which to capitalist economics can be treated as problematic. Rather, the analysis of capitalist development as a process has forced us to consider the state in economic terms. This is particularly true in the twentieth century with the creation of a petroleum economy under Gomez and its consolidation in mid-century under Acción Democrática and other pretenders to power. Capitalist development in twentieth century Venezuela has been defined first of all by the relationship of Venezuela to the multinationals, a relationship which was first set in the petroleum industry and has subsequently ramified through an industrial and commercial infrastructure directed toward the internal market. Second, it has been defined by the Venezuelan state, which granted the first concessions, set the conditions for exploitation, shared unequally in the profits of that exploitation, attempted to "sow the petroleum" throughout the economy, and defined the relationship of multinationals to subsequent industrialization processes. National capital flows into the interstices of a structure created by multinationals and the Venezuelan state: industrial and banking partners to the multinationals, industries complementary to state projects (e.g., construction, building materials), or commerce. The current situation is increasingly characterized as an entrepreneurial state, acting to promote development, often in cooperation with multinational capitals. As it pursues such policies and relationships, it is increasingly separated from the nation, although it creates the illusion of identification and incorporation. Indeed, the democratic form of the Venezuelan state facilitates the creation of such an illusion through state-building political parties. Here I am in substantial agreement with (and dependent upon) the analysis of Cardoso and Faletto in their postscript to the English edition of *Dependency and Development in Latin America* (1979: 177–216).

Similarly, the analysis of politics cannot proceed without an understanding of capitalist development. In the nineteenth century, the nature of the state can not be understood without an analysis of uneven regional development. This requires an examination of the creation and occupation of space, of the classes and class fractions which emerged in particular regions, the issues which engaged their attention, and the manner in which those issues were addressed. In the twentieth century, as I have already indicated, the state took the form it did (in part) because of the nature of capitalist development. Its growth and ramification is due to its mediating position between multinationals and the Venezuelan nation.[17]

To the extent that I have been willing to differentiate between economics and politics, I have talked about uneven economic processes which have torn apart a whole series of social relationships and connections, or created heterogeneity. Simultaneously, I have talked about political relationships which have made for new connections in the formation of political communities based upon a feeling of homogeneity. Even here, the distinction between economic processes and political relationships can only be made when we recognize that it is a way of talking about relationships. In the relationships themselves, the economic and political are once again united. Just as the economic process destroys connections, it creates new ones (e.g., between merchants and peasants in the nineteenth century, between the state and peasants in the twentieth) around which political communities are formed.

With such considerations, I have approached the Venezuelan peasantry, a peasantry which has been fractionated for quite different reasons in the nineteenth and twentieth centures, and which participated in the formation of vertical political communities. I have also tried to indicate those economic and political processes and relationships which make possible (if unlikely) the formation of class-based political communities. As Cardoso and Faletto conclude:

> The course of history depends largely on the daring of those who propose to act in terms of historically viable goals. We do not try to place theoretical limits on the probable course of future events. These will depend, not on academic predictions, but on collective action guided by political wills that make work what is structurally barely possible (Cardoso and Faletto, 1979: 176).

Acknowledgement

Much of this essay is based on material gathered during field research in Venezuela conducted between October 1974 and August 1976, under the institutional sponsorship of the Instituto Venezolano de Investigaciones Científicas. Research was supported at various stages by an NSF Graduate Fellowship, a Doherty Fellowship for Latin American Studies, and an NSF Dissertation Improvement Grant (SOC 75–18655). I am especially indebted to the organizers of the conference on peasant rebellions at The Johns Hopkins University, Robert Weller and Scott Guggenheim, for their critical comments on an early draft.

7. Mao Zedong, Red *Misérables*, and the Moral Economy of Peasant Rebellion in Modern China

Ralph Thaxton

Ever since Engels penned his great study of *The Peasant War in Germany*, Eurocentric social scientists have viewed peasant rebellions as defensive movements that have rested their case for survival on the allegedly reactionary values of traditional society. Although it is generally acknowledged that peasants played an important part in the Chinese revolution of 1 October 1949 most Western scholars have assumed that the success of the revolutionary mobilization in which the rural people were substantially involved was mainly the project of the Chinese Communist Party (CCP), and that the party itself provided the impetus and ingenuity for revolutionary mobilization and victory.

Post–World War II social scientific research on China produced countless versions of the process whereby the CCP *allegedly* mobilized the peasants for revolution and established its institutional hegemony over the countryside.

One variant of political mobilization theory assumed the Chinese Revolution was made in Moscow. It portrayed the CCP as an elite corps of professional Bolsheviks subverting the legitimate political institutions of Chiang Kai-shek's Republic of China and asserting superiority over a passive rural people. Although the publication of Robert C. North's *Moscow and the Chinese Communists* made clear that Mao Zedong and the CCP rose to power in spite of rather than because of the Comintern (1953: 167), the Western scholarly preoccupation with what seemed a natural ideological alliance between Communist China and Communist Russia tended to overshadow the inconvenient fact that Stalin and the Soviet Union gave massive financial and military assistance to Mao Zedong's major enemy—Chiang Kai-shek—and that the Comintern opposed the CCP attempt to create an armed peasant movement independent of Guomindang power in South China from 1925–1927 (Feigon, 1982: 141–142).

In a bold stroke of scholarship Benjamin I. Schwartz put forth the notion that Mao Zedong's strategy and tactics were different from orthodox Marxism-Leninism, and argued that Mao rose to power in opposition to a Comintern-directed–urban-based proletarian insurrection (1951: 5, 187–200). Mao was taken as the unorthodox Leninist whose elite party rose to national power by capturing a discontented peasant base. According to Schwartz, the CCP was the bearer of revolutionary mobilization and consciousness, and the membership of the CCP consummated a Leninist style takeover by instilling its own centrally articulated ideology in peasant followings within territorially secure base areas (1951: 198–200).

Working from Schwartz's premise, a generation of Western scholars placed great emphasis on the CCP as an ideological agent of mass reeducation. But they slighted the significance of the fact that the CCP had its origins in a mass movement whose leadership explicitly rejected the notion that Western style political parties could resolve the problems of imperialist penetration and mass poverty in China. For the generation of Chinese Communist Party members with whom Mao Zedong was closely associated, the May Fourth movement—a popular anti-imperialist movement against the Versailles Peace Conference decision to reward Japan with German concessions in Shandong province—offered a critical lesson to dissenting Marxist intellectuals: the lesson was that concrete political results could be guaranteed only by getting involved in the street level politics of student protests, worker strikes, and peasant demonstrations that were not the product of young Marxist intellectuals themselves but rather spontaneous demands for survival and national sovereignty.

Though Mao Zedong reiterated the importance of this political lesson in his 1927 *Report on an Investigation of the Peasant Movement in Hunan*, the lesson was not taken to heart by the erstwhile intellectual leadership of the CCP in the early 1920s. Thus new difficulties and a nearly total disaster befell the CCP. By attempting to organize various peasant movements within the narrow institutional limits of the CCP-Guomindang alliance, rather than base itself in the self-generating popular revolts of the countryside, the Chinese Communist Party exposed itself and its mass base to the counterrevolutionary violence of Chiang Kai-shek's Soviet-nurtured Guomindang army (Meisner, 1977: 25–27). In the first two years of Guomindang counterrevolution, 1927–1929, CCP membership fell from 58,000 to 10,000 (Garavente, 1978: 57). The national level organization of the party was literally shattered and left in shambles, and the party members escaped with their lives only by fleeing to the remote countryside where they survived alongside dispossessed and desperate rural people.

A third political mobilization thesis depicted the Chinese Revolution as the product of peasant involvement in the patriotic warfare of the CCP. According to Chalmers Johnson, the leading advocate of this thesis, the mobilization of the peasantry was precipitated by the brutal impact of the Japanese invasion, and the CCP took advantage of the warlike stance taken by peasants against the presence of the "pacifying" Japanse army. The CCP, in effect, rallied the war-mobilized peasants to its own revolutionary banners on the basis of patriotic appeals to resist the Japanese invaders, and class warfare, which the CCP had advocated prior to the Japanese invasion, thus took a backseat to the anticolonial struggle, or so it was said (Johnson, 1962: 1–14).

Mass nationalism was a significant departure from the conceptions that stressed Comintern-orchestrated conspiracy and the CCP as the Marxist-Leninist teacher of an untutored peasantry. But it was flawed in two fundamental respects. On the one hand, the masterful narrative of peasant nationalism failed to deal with the fact that peasants in Hunan and Henan had taken up arms against foreign-backed Chinese warlords long before the Japanese invasion, and that the popular secret societies sponsoring these armed mobilizations in the 1910s and 1920s proved to be valuable allies of the CCP during the anti-Japanese war of resistance. It was not merely the coming of the Japanese but rather the Japanese intensification of the preexisting plunder of warlord-gentry rulers that reactivated peasant-based secret society collaboration with the CCP during the war of resistance. We shall trace the pre-war lineages of this collaboration in a moment.

On the other hand, it is moderately well established that the CCP-led peasant movement grew in the regions, districts, and villages where the Japanese presence was relatively weak or nonexistent (Selden, 1971; Thaxton, 1982). Conversely, the assumed positive correlation between Japanese presence and CCP power does not hold up for all of China. In fact the CCP suffered painfully slow growth and serious setbacks in those North China base areas under the surveillance and control of the Japanese Imperial Army. The peasants in the Japanese-held North China Plain counties of the Shanxi-Chahar-Hebei base area, for example, were subjected to continuous savagery from 1938–1943 (Van Slyke, 1968: 168–169), and the CCP armed forces were all but driven out of this forward base area when the Japanese intensified the pressure of their occupation around 1940. Most interestingly, Fuping county, the one county where the CCP was able to escape Japanese savagery, was located in a remote mountainous area that evidently was a low strategic priority for the Japanese army (Band and Band, 1948: 98). Mao Zedong's early writings leave little doubt that the CCP had learned that its survival and growth were dependent on locating in geopolitical sanctuaries such as Fuping, and that this lesson had become an important element in the CCP's theory and practice of rural revolution long before the Japanese presence underscored its logic.

Each preceding variant of political mobilization theory neglected the importance of peasant values in the Chinese revolution, and each assumed that the victory of the CCP naturally reflected what peasants were struggling for. This was entirely understandable. Few Western academics worked and lived among China's rural people, and few had any hope of exploring the connection between the enduring social values of the country folk and the popularity or unpopularity of the Chinese Communist Party. To be sure, Herbert Butterfield (1981: 17–21) has reminded us of the difficulty in recovering any history that has been lost and in reconstructing folk history and folk politics within the framework of a comprehensive theme or theory. The elusiveness of the modern revolutionary history of China's Little Tradition underscores this difficulty. The cracks in the conceptual paradigm offered to comprehend this history by political mobilization theorists are extremely wide. Perhaps then it is time to abandon political mobilization theory, and to move to an alternative set of premises that pays more careful attention to the popular wellsprings of revolutionary action and legitimacy in the countryside.

This essay questions the received intellectual wisdom which holds that China's rural people could proceed from rebellion to revolution only because they fell under the moral hegemony of CCP leadership. Our focus is shifted from the assumed hegemony of the CCP to the two-way interaction between the rural poor and the CCP in the pre-1949 revolutionary process. We shall see that to a significant extent the revolutionary process itself was the offspring of popular based rebellion, and that the origins of CCP legitimacy cannot be understood by a social scientific discourse that separates the study of the party from the whole episode of indigenous rebellion in modern China. For our purpose, that episode began with the rise of the Taipings and continued on into the 1920s and 1930s when the CCP under Mao became its political guardian. Of course Schwartz and others are correct in claiming that we cannot speak of the CCP as an exclusively peasant party, as a party that succeeded in mobilizing peasants without the help of other social classes, but, by the same token, we cannot assume that peasants rebelled from abstract ideas passed on to them by the CCP or that the ideas of the CCP eclipsed those of the popular classes once state oppression brought together the party and the common people. If revolutionary mobilization was, as Mao Zedong and Lu Xun asserted, a stage in which practice superseded ideology and *produced* a revolutionary theory, then the more relevant question is: what extra-ordinary political circumstances moved China's peasants to engage in rebel acts that only the Mao-party proved capable of joining and defending?

Imperialism, Warlordism, and Peasant Livelihood

One of the greatest problems with political mobilization theory is its assumption that the rural-based mobilization led by the CCP had little to do with foreign-induced changes in the Chinese peasant economy over the preceding century. On the one hand, political mobilization theorists rested their case for Communist mobilization of the peasantry on the widespread but questionable social scientific assumption that the indirect Western presence in China did not pose a serious threat to peasant livelihood, and so the crucial role that Western imperialism played in undermining the moral basis of China's peasant economies and in sowing the seeds of popular resistance to outside change was virtually ignored. On the other hand, the emergence of a foreign-imperialist-dominated Chinese military-state, and the role of the military-state in exploiting the peasantry and thereby creating massive suffering and anger in the countryside, was seldom focused on in a systematic fashion. There is little doubt, however, that the forceful intrusion of modern Western capitalist markets and the forceful development of a modern Chinese military government created the conditions that fostered widespread riots and rebellions in the Chinese countryside before the founding of the Chinese Communist Party in 1921.

In the century following the British defeat of China in the first Opium War of 1840–42 the world market position Chinese exports had enjoyed in the eighteenth century was damaged and the basic means of peasant subsistence and income security was threatened by a host of unprecedented international economic and political demands.

Although Chinese peasants were not strangers to production for exchange and trade in their own district, county, and regional markets, they hardly were prepared to produce for the world markets into which they were drawn in the years between 1870 and 1930. During this period the sporadic price rises in opium, tobacco, and cotton beckoned peasants to convert land traditionally reserved for subsistence cereals to cash crops, and the resulting monetization of agriculture led to a significant decline in peasant grain production and local self-sufficiency in foodstuffs (Chesneaux, 1976: 216–218; Thaxton, 1982: ch. 3). Naturally, with less grain available in local markets the price of grain shot up to barely affordable levels for peasant consumers—especially for the landless poor. When the international market price of cash crops declined as it did in the 1880s and 1890s and in the depression-ridden 1930s the peasants who could not garner enough income for their own family consumption invariably retreated from cash crops to production for grain self-sufficiency. By the 1920s, however, this peasant strategy of survival was proving increasingly difficult, primarily because it flew in the face of warlord attempts to rule and tax local territory. The revenue base of provincial military regimes like those in Shanxi, Yunnan, and Sichuan was literally founded on cash-crop production, so that nearly every warlord governorship depended heavily on an opium bureau whose officials collected millions of dollars on opium crops cultivated by peasants who were forced by government order to grow the poppy on lands traditionally planted to subsistence rice and millet. For much of the peasantry, therefore, the retreat back to subsistence crops could not be undertaken without a political struggle with the warlord-state.

Western imperialism also fostered the growth of a Chinese military-state whose foreign-engendered financial crisis had a decidedly negative impact on peasant welfare. Owing to the defeats China suffered in the Opium War of 1840–42, the Sino-Japanese War of 1894–95, and the Anti-Boxer War of 1900 the Qing government was compelled to finance a staggering indemnity payment to the great powers. To pay the indemnity, the Qing officials placed a host of new surtaxes on local production and pledged the revenue gotten from additional salt taxes. The Qing surtaxes taken for indemnity reparations fell directly on the shoulders of the country people and threatened local production of persimmon wine, indigo, and other items on which peasants relied to supplement variable crop income and to keep up with rising grain prices. Similarly, the late Qing surtaxes on salt threatened both the income and identity of the small peasants and peddlers involved in clandestine salt production and trade. The surtaxes on crops like indigo were suspended with the overthrow of the Qing, but they were brought back by the new Beiyang warlord regime of Yuan Shikai, and there is considerable agreement that Yuan Shikai and his warlord successors tightened control over the British-administered salt gabelle and improved the efficiency of the salt revenue system from 1912 to 1937 (Feuerwerker, 1977: 77–79; Thaxton, 1982: ch. 2).

The rising wave of peasant resistance in the early twentieth century was a response to the new taxes imposed by Qing officials. From 1901–05 there was an outbreak of antisurtax struggles in Jiangsu, Shandong, Fujian, Hubei, Hunan, and Jiangxi, and the following decade saw a spate of local uprisings against salt tax officials in South, Central, and North China. At bottom this popular resistance was undertaken to get local officials to reconsider their rigid and rigorous tax practices. The authorities, however, displayed an insatiable appetite for the new taxes. Consequently, at the county level the leaders of antitax crowds often turned the gathering storm of peasant frustration against the government. In 1904, for example, a crowd of 3,000 hungry people rose up to protest the surtax imposed on indigo by the officials in Jiangxi's Tongping county. This crowd stormed the Tax Bureau, broke open the *yamen* gates, and then released all the prisoners (Zhang and Lin, 1980: 276). The antigovernment salt tax rebels in Guangdong's Zijin county pursued a similar line of collective action in the years before the 1911 revolution (Hsieh, 1972: 147–151, 164). Nearly all of these antitax struggles brought together poor peasants, salt smugglers, and small merchants who shared an interest in stopping government tax squeeze. They persisted in more violent form in the decades following the fall of the Qing dynasty because the warlords who betrayed Sun Yat-sen and took over the Republic of China left their rebel participants no other choice if they were to survive.

The Replacement of the Traditional Negotiationist Political Order and the Radicalization of Peasant Protest

For mobilization theorists, the revolutionary potential of the peasantry was attributable to the appearance of the CCP, for it was the party cadre who turned an otherwise conservative and backward peasant world against legitimate republican authority. In their view, what gave the peasant movement its radical thrust was the ideological work of outside Communist party agitators who were said to be a great deal more radical than the peasants. The proponents of this view, however, skimmed over the avoidance and remedialist protests which sprang up in the early twentieth-century countryside, and therefore misunderstood the relationship of the emergent republican political system to the radicalization of the peasantry.

Since much of the peasantry treasured its social isolation from the premodern Chinese state, it is not surprising that peasants in different parts of China attempted to preserve this isolation by engaging in forms of avoidance protest, that is, protest to avoid the demands of the military-aristocrats who took over the republic and ruled the countryside by violence. As Michael Adas has pointed out in reference to precolonial Southeast Asia (1981: 217–225), it was possible for peasants living under traditional empires to circumvent many of the demands placed on production and labor by the small number of officials who administered taxation on behalf of the urban-based imperial court. Although there is little doubt that the Chinese magistrate and *yamen* officials engaged in institutionalized corruption and embezzled tax grains traditionally, it is nonetheless true that peasants customarily practiced a number of Little Tradition defenses against state taxation. These practices were possible because peasants were able to take advantage of the low level of efficiency in tax assessment methods and to talk the better-off members of the village into protecting the community from the unjust tax and labor demands put forth by local officials. It is well known, for example, that peasants in China had avoided taxes by underreporting harvests and by insisting that those with more land and grain, usually the rich peasants, landlords, and gentry, pay a proportion of the village grain tax commensurate with their wealth. To evade the corvee, peasants sent their sons to neighboring villages or districts. To evade military conscription, they counted on the local headmen or landlord patron to list them as injured or, better yet, to keep their names off the village rolls. Since peasants and local village leaders who bargained on their behalf had the option of withholding taxes and labor altogether, either by hiding or by fleeing the village, local officials generally found it less troublesome to negotiate deals that, in essence, sanctioned many of the shadowlike avoidance protests of the country people.

The rise of the imperialist-backed warlord republic, however, challenged the very right of peasants to pursue their older avoidance protests, and replaced the "local bargaining leadership" of many villages with a criminal minority of landlord officials and retainers who spoke for the increased tax demands of new militarists and who took advantage of the leverage afforded them by warlord forces to shift the burden of village taxation to the discontented majority of peasant landowners, tenants, and hired hands (Thaxton, 1981: 3–35).

By the 1920s many landlords were collaborating with the warlord attempt to impose surtaxes on the autumn harvest, on homemade fruit wine, and on fish taken from local streams and lakes. In both North and South China landlords often assisted warlords in their attempt to replace the village as the unit of village tax assessment and payment with a head-tax system wherein every peasant, merchant, and landlord paid a tax of one or two silver dollars for each member of the family. This head tax, or tax levied on each head within an identifiable household, had nothing in common with the size of landholdings or harvest income, so that merchants and landlords with substantial land and grain were inclined to help enforce it locally.

The Republican warlord polity also relied on landlords for assistance with corvee and military recruitment. In Guangdong the landlords complied with warlord orders to round up peasants for road building duty. Not only was there no pay for this labor, the peasants who could not afford to abandon their family fields were compelled to pay a corvee exemption fee, a fee that was beyond the means of poor smallholders (Chen, 1936: 78–79). The landlords of Shaanxi cooperated with warlord campaigns to recruit peasants for army service. In addition to knowing the settled peasants, landlords were in a position to draw up a list of unemployed local people who were vulnerable to military press-ganging, either because they were without family, lacked a strong patron locally, or were without the secret society connections needed to protect them from warlord commands.

To be sure, Chinese peasants were no less conservative than the French small-holders of whom Marx wrote in the *Eighteenth Brumaire of Louis Bonaparte* (Marx, 1973b) and so they initially appealed for protection from the strongly-armed military republic. This appeal was reflected in their attempts to renegotiate a return to the status quo in taxation with Republican officials. What turned peasants against the Republic of China after 1912 was not the CCP but the adamant refusal of the warlords who ran the Republic to return to subsistence-first tax deals with the village world. Beginning with Yuan Shikai, the warlords who took over provincial and county government refused to tolerate peasant attempts to pursue remedialist protests and this intransigence left the country people with little choice but to engage in oppositionist revolts aimed at ending war-lord rule. In the most fundamental sense, it was the repression mobilization by the nonnegotiationist republican warlord regime that heightened peasant anger over taxes and turned peasants whose rebellions started out as defensive acts for tax fairness toward an offensive mobilization directed against government itself.

Few peasants could bear the terrible burdens of the new Tax Republic, but those who led early Republican protests and demonstrations were resisting war-lord attempts at arbitrary taxation, not taxation per se. Their *qingyuan* or peti-tionist protests were initiated to persuade republican officials to respect the Qing regulation that taxes not exceed 30 percent of the actual harvest yield and to sus-pend or scale down the new surtaxes after a bad harvest. The warlords, being desperate to finance indemnity payments and build up personal armies, would not honor the older deferential modes of protest. They defined the remedialist initia-tives of the country people as criminal (*fei*). With the republican military-elite redefining the remedialist protests of the peasants as illegitimate, peasants were even more prone to participate in tax revolts aimed at eliminating the warlord tax regime altogether. Though it is seldom mentioned, the Hunan peasant movement with which Mao Zedong became associated in the years 1924–27 had its origins in peasant struggles to avoid the militarist collection of surtaxes on opium during the terrible drought of 1918—taxes that were being collected for the year 1937 (Shaoshan Fengyun, 1979: 8)! In an important sense, the great popular upheavals of 1925–1927 signaled the end, not the outbreak, of peasant attempts to deal with the warlord tax regime by deferential nonconfrontationist modes of protest. The first great revolution of 1925–1927 expressed the peasant demand to do away with the Tax Republic per se, and it was Mao Zedong's inclusion of this popular de-mand in the Communist Party's definition of revolution that made Mao so very hated by Chiang Kai-shek's military junta.

The CCP and the Moral Basis of Peasant Rebellion in Early Republican China

The men who became the leaders of the Mao Zedong CCP were neither peas-ants nor proletarians but rather lumpen poor in close touch with the mood of the popular countryside. In some cases, they had established a permanent bond with the rebellious poor a decade before they were recruited by the intellectual brain trust of the CCP in the late 1920s. Prominent national figures like Peng Dehuai and He Long launched their careers by leading the rural poor in rebellions directed at redressing injustices perpetrated by the warlord-landlord regime that took over the Republic of China in 1912. Public hostility to this regime grew fierce in the post-Qing decade, and for many future CCP leaders this decade proved to be the critical formative phase in their dealings with the elemental survival demands of the country people.

Most of the peasant movements of this early republican era started out as protests petitioning redress for local subsistence grievances. Generally speaking, these protests were led by respected local people who were reacting to the rising price of grain in local markets, which had fallen under landlord domination, and to the new wave of warlord taxes on local salt supplies and sales. Many a future CCP leader entered the political life of the nation by embracing the peasant demands that defined these protests locally. In an important sense, CCP leaders like Peng Dehuai and He Long got their start in politics by leading the poor in actions to contest the unwarranted landlord and warlord interventions into the moral economy of peasant localities.

Peng Dehuai. Peng Dehuai was born into a prosperous Hunan peasant family whose fortunes turned sour in late Qing years. Peng's mother died when he was six in 1903, and thereafter he was treated with contempt by his feudal stepmother. At the age of nine, he was forced to flee his family household and take up a series of odd jobs in the Hunan countryside. He worked as a cowherder, a coal miner, and a shoemaker's apprentice over the next four years. As an apprentice he was paid wages in meals only, and so he set out for better salary and security. At first he found work in a sodium mine, but the mine soon closed. Then, after obtaining work on a dyke-building project, which stopped when the local warlord made payment in worthless currency, Peng returned to his native Xiang Pan (Snow, 1938: 267–268).

Back on home ground, Peng Dehuai did field work until the crop failure and rice famine of 1912 spread panic through Hunan. The landlords of the province were unwilling to negotiate any compromise for peasant-crop rent payments, and they were taking advantage of the dearth to raise the price of rice they were importing. In many localities they staunchly refused to heed the requests of peasant and handicraft workers to sell the rice at a just price (Zhongguo Jianshi, 1980: 472). Their refusal brought on the fireworks of full-scale food rioting. Recalling why he joined the peasants in one of these riots against a notoriously wealthy landlord rice dealer, Peng Dehuai touched on the moral basis of his early involvement with the rebellious poor: "I was passing his place, and paused to watch the demonstration. I saw that many of the men were half starved, and I knew this man had over 10,000 *dan* of rice in his bins, and that he had refused to help the starving at all. I became infuriated, and led the peasants to attack and invade his house. They carted off most of his stores. Thinking of it afterwards, I did not know exactly why I had done that. I only knew that he should have sold rice to the poor, and that it was right for them to take it from him if he did not" (Snow, 1938: 269).

He Long. The early activities of He Long also served as a bridge to later CCP involvement with the moral economy of peasant rebellion, and anticipated the party's attempt to spread its antiimperialist propaganda into the popular countryside. Born into a poor migrant family in northwestern Hunan in 1896 He Long spent much of his youth with his father, He Shidao. The latter had been a customs guard, a local tailor, a traveling salesman, and, at one point, a beggar in order to supplement the meager income derived from an extremely small and poor family field. From time to time He Shidao was involved in the clandestine opium and salt smuggling operations of the Elder Brothers Society lodges in the Hunan-Hubei– river-lakes region (Garavente, 1978: 31–34). Thus it is not surprising that by 1915, at the age of nineteen, He Long had become the head of a small group of salt smugglers who travelled the mountainous trails near his native Zhong Jiaguan. These smugglers peddled salt in free markets at prices below those of the gabellers, and so their activities inevitably brought them to contest the attempt of warlord Yuan Shikai to increase his revenue base by establishing *new* salt tax stations in the interior of China after 1912. Prior to 1915 He Long and his friends had driven their salt carts past Bao Maoqi without paying any tax, but in that year the Ba Maoqi Salt Tax Bureau stationed police to collect taxes at various points along the road. This was the trigger to local rebellion (Zhang, 1979: 73–87).

Faced with the new taxes, He Long and ten other salt carriers decided to attack the Salt Tax Bureau at Ba Maoqi. In February 1916, during the spring hunger, they stormed and then set fire to the Salt Bureau. In this midnight attack, which became popularized as the Two Kitchen Knives Rebellion, He Long killed one tax policeman with a knife and then shot the infamous Salt Bureau director. Within a matter of hours the story of He Long's actions spread throughout the county, and peasants from surrounding villages began to celebrate the righting of official wrongdoings. The morning following the rebellion He Long called on peasants to come to Ba Maoqi to participate in the burning of the official records which showed how much each peasant household owed the Salt Tax Bureau— this was to become an increasingly popular means of writing off tax debts to the warlord republic. As the story goes, He Long and the leaders of the rebellion were even more appreciated for dividing up the ninety *jin* of salt and redistributing the property of the Salt Bureau to the neediest people in the vicinity (Zhang, 1979: 73-87).

From 1916 until 1924 He Long drew on the anger of a floating population of landless peasants, salt smugglers, and beggars to keep alive the hope of holding off the domination of the warlord-landlord regime of Yuan Shikai. These people made up He Long's so-called Peasant Army. It was an army which offered peasants an alternative means to settle grievances with local powerholders. The

Peasant Army, which started out as the Anti-Yuan Army (*Taoyuan jun*), held out the promise of a return to just rule. Its rule was characterized by relief, redistribution, and revenge which the local elite took as radical. One can understand why (Zhang, 1979: 66–102).

In the Shangzhi Uprising of 1916, for example, He Long and a band of twenty men armed with nearly a dozen rifles captured in the Kitchen Knives Rebellion relieved the county magistrate of his head and then opened up the county granary to let hungry peasants carry off the food grain they needed to save their villages from spring hunger. From 1918 to 1924 He Long was a minor Hunan military officer, but he did not give up his commitment to redistribute the grain of wealthy landlords who refused to sell or lend rice to the poor. In one instance he personally led starving peasants to open up a landlord grain bin for "hunger loans." By August 1924 He Long had begun to challenge the landlord and warlord despots of the Changde-Taoyuan area. The peasants there sought him out to ask his army to avenge the rape of their daughters by Tang Rongyuan, an officer in the warlord Wu Peifu's army. He Long responded to these requests by disguising himself as a fisherman and going into the villages to investigate complaints first hand, after which he personally apprehended the landlord or warlord assailant (Zhang, 1979: 88–94).

To be sure, revolution in the rural world becomes possible only when there is an iron determination in the minds of popular leaders to resist to the death the landlord-military state intrusion into the moral economy of the peasantry. By their tendency to focus on the assumed CCP ideological link to Moscow or the ideology that arose as a result of some empirically observed CCP relationship to the peasantry, political mobilization theorists have failed to ask, let alone explain, why men like Peng Dehuai and He Long were moved to uphold the peasants' struggles for sustenance, that is, to fight for the moral economic concerns of the rebellious poor. We can be certain that in 1912 these poor ragged nobodies had never heard of Karl Marx. Nor were they motivated solely by the protests of the peasants themselves. A major source of the moral vision which moved Peng Dehuai, and his future CCP comrades, to challenge the political and economic causes of peasant suffering seems to have been the conception of social obligation and political purpose derived from stories about the Taiping Rebellion. The Taiping epic had become part of the folk memory of China's poor. This epic provided an independent ideological tradition that encouraged peasant youths to take up the banners of rebellion. This was true for Peng Dehuai, He Long, and Zhu De, soon to become the three great commanders of the CCP-led rural revolution.

The moral outrage that moved Peng to defend the right of the hungry poor to riot and rebel was linked to the sense of injustice imparted to him through stories told by his great uncle, Wushi Laoguan, an old village storyteller who had taken part in the Taiping Rebellion. The stories presupposed a moral obligation to help the poor by beating down or leveling the rich (Huang, 1980: 1). They also tended to encourage dissent from the dominant Confucian ideology, as He Long's early socialization demonstrates. He Long had been close to the storyteller in his home village. At the age of 70, in 1906, the storyteller had gathered the village youths to criticize the gentry notion that Confucius was a saint, and to detail how the local poor had welcomed the Taiping desecration of the Confucian temples that symbolized the power of the nonworking landlord class over the tilling peasantry (*He Long Tongzhi*, 1978: 26–27). Zhu De, himself from a family of immigrant social outcasts, had grown up in Sichuan on tales of the Taipings passed on by itinerant artisans. One of these artisans, known to the peasants as the Old Weaver, had served in the Taiping Army under Shi Dagai. The Old Weaver had taught Zhu De and the villagers about the international causes of their poverty, for it was from these wandering artisans that peasants learned that the endless Qing surtaxes went to foreigners to pay indemnities (Smedley, 1956: 22–29). The Taipings had fought to level the rich and stop the taxes. They had been slaughtered. Their moral purpose, however, had been kept alive in the stories of these wandering artisans, stories which for Peng, He, and Zhu illuminated the values underlying peasant mobilization. Such values created the need for the folk-hero role the Mao-Zhu Red Army would assume in the decades ahead. Here was an ideological tradition that was to distinguish the CCP armed forces in peasant minds from the ruling military predators, and here was the ideological thread that was to connect CCP commanders to a political commitment to capture the nation in order that it be recreated in the image of popular justice. For the brief orthodox phase of Chinese Communism, roughly 1921 to 1927, this older thread of antistate history was nearly lost. It would be left to Mao Zedong to connect it back to its political promise.

The CCP and Early Revolutionary Failures: Proletarian and Peasant Connections

The Chinese Communist Party was founded in Shanghai in 1921, a time of warlord civil war, famine, peasant uprisings, and banditry throughout China. In the next three decades the victory of the CCP would become dependent on its relationship to the rise of fringe movements involving underemployed peasants, vagrants, and bandits who existed in between the old settled world in the villages and the new rootless world of the treaty port cities. Early CCP doctrine, however, was mainly the product of an intellectual revolution that led to failed experiments in proletarian and peasant-based revolutions.

The May Fourth Movement had marked the end of Western liberalism, the death knell of any hope that Western-style democratic parties could put an end to imperialism, war, and plunder in China. Thus it is not surprising that the intellectual cofounders of the CCP, Chen Duxiu and Li Dazhao, were attracted to the Russian Bolshevik Revolution of 1917 as the harbinger of a new wave of antiimperialist revolution in China and the colonial world. By 1921 the Society for the Advancement of Marxism, founded by Chen Duxiu and Li Dazhao in the spring of 1918, was making available translations of Marx, Kautsky, and Lenin (Ch'en, 1967: 76–77). These works addressed the live issues of class exploitation, government injustice, and imperialist plunder, and they understandably fired the political imaginations of the insurrectionary theorists of the CCP. The party cofounders drew from them to create a Marxist-Leninist doctrine with revolutionary implications for China, or so it seemed.

The early CCP years saw the emergence of a subtle rivalry between two schools of intellectual thought about a number of issues, including, significantly, the central question of which social groups could be galvanized for revolution and anti-imperialist struggle in China. Most interestingly, the controversy originally did not reach back to focus on what might be the role of the lumpen poor in the Chinese revolution. Rather the early focus was on classical Marxism and Leninism, that is, on Marx's proposition that the urban workers were the vanguard of revolution, and on Lenin's version of a revolutionary proletarian-peasant alliance. The orthodox phase of the CCP encompassed a proletarian stage that lasted from 1921 to 1927 and a peasant stage that lasted from 1927 until 1935. The first stage led to the destruction of the labor movement and to the decimation of the CCP, while the second led the party through a series of false starts in the village world and backward away from the classical Marxist-Leninist ideas that precluded a linkup with the militant flowering taking place in the world of the lumpen poor—a world that was neither proletarian nor peasant.

Under the early leadership of Chen Duxiu the CCP presented itself as the party of the proletariat, and it set out to establish a working class base in China's modernizing cities—Shanghai, Wuhan, and Beijing. The experiment was a failure from the start, for the proletariat was outnumbered, strategically in the wrong place, and politically inexperienced.

Precisely because Western imperialism had stunted the growth of an independent capitalist bourgeois, China remained a peasant country without a broad social base for proletarian revolution. The industrial proletariat never occupied more than 1 percent of the entire working class, whereas the peasantry still made up 90 percent of the laboring population in the 1920s. By working with the tiny proletariat, the CCP cut itself off from the numerically superior popular base it needed to outnumber and outlast the urban-based warlord regime.

Located within the heavily garrisoned cities like Shanghai, the early CCP intellectual and labor leaders became an easily identifiable and accessible target for warlord repression. The work of the CCP was by and large conducted without any territorial security, and hence the worker uprisings were subjected continuously to government surveillance and terror.

The early proletarian upsurge was, moreover, tempered by a style of politics that did not contend for political power. The industrial proletariat, in comparison to the semiproletarians whom Mao Zedong called the "city coolies" (Meisner, 1977: 28), was involved in guilds whose activities were characterized by labor racketeering and corruption; its strikes over wages and working conditions were seldom launched to establish a politically autonomous working-class order (cf.

McDonald, 1978: ch. 4). In contrast to the peasant movements that had gained momentum and security under men like He Long, the proletariat was not experienced in armed struggle. The militia leaders of the Shanghai trade unions, for example, did not know how to go about seizing a modern city, and they let their guard down to welcome the very warlord general (Chiang Kai-shek) who massacred them in the 12–13 April 1927 coup d'etat (Snow, 1938: 75; Bianco, 1971: 56).

Li Dazhao did not share Chen Duxiu's faith in urban-based proletarian insurrection. As Maurice Meisner has pointed out, Li looked to the peasantry as the main social force of the revolution, for the peasants made up the overwhelming majority of humanity in China (Meisner, 1967: 201). By its sheer existence alone, the peasantry presented a massive, though not necessarily immovable, obstacle to the criminal minority of landlords and warlords, and hence was less vulnerable to the rapid decimation experienced by the proletariat. In 1924, when Li was adapting Marxism to the conditions of China, one of his students, Mao Zedong, told the peasants of his native Shaoshan of the advantages to be gained from acting on Li Dazhao's premise that the peasant masses constituted a raw material force with great political potential: "There are 400 million people in China, but the rich people are a small minority (a gesture with the little finger indicated the weakness of the rich). The poor majority stand at 90 percent. If all of the poor people under Heaven get organized, then the poor can put down the rich. Everyone knows the thumb (the poor majority) can put down the weak small finger" (*Shaoshan Fengyun*, 1979: 22).

The warlord repression of the previous year had reinforced Li Dazhao's pessimism about the possibility of a working class revolution. The suppression of the Beijing-Hankow Railway strike in 1923 and the subsequent ebb of proletarian activity in North China underscored the logic of looking to the countryside. Not only was the peasantry a long distance away from the main force of warlord-controlled government, but also the dominance of the warlords was uneven throughout the countryside and the violent warlord contests for prized territory weakened their domination in peripheral mountainous areas. In fact the highland periphery composed nearly two-thirds of China's landscape and the cadres of the CCP could find sanctuary from warlord repression and reach out to the rural poor from this periphery.

The peasant strategy seemed to make sense for yet another reason: with the 1925–1927 upsurge of peasant mobilization, the countryside had replaced the city as the setting of popular resistance against the warlord tax machinery of the Republic of China. Unlike Marx's proletariat, the peasantry appeared to be able to draw on its own independent tradition of struggle against the ruling groups, and Li Dazhao and Mao Zedong no doubt were attracted to this tradition.

The proletariat was literally brought into being by capitalism and was consumed by its struggle to gain new rights in an alien city-state environment. The peasantry however, was an old class whose endeavors in agricultural production and exchange had created the basis for the national economy from which China's ruling class drew its sustenance. Thus the peasants did not need to be taught that the Confucian state stood on their shoulders. Their militant antiforeign protests were in opposition to the weight that mandarins, warlords, and foreign mercenaries had added to imperial state domination. Moreover, the peasantry was conscious of its longstanding rights to landownership and free market participation, so that its struggles against landlord usury and land usurpation and the warlord taxation of trade were based on practices to resist elite interference in local measures of survival. These would not be given up without a fight to the death, and the fight was being waged on familiar terrain and within supportive family and village environments.

By the 1920s it had become clear that the peasants of North and South China were capable of creating their own self-defense groups. Li Dazhao was enthusiastic about placing these in the service of local struggles against the intruding Bonapartists who were bleeding the countryside. In Hebei, Shandong, and Henan these peasant-armed−self-protection associations had sprung up everywhere, and their spontaneous struggles had begun to pose a threat to the very basis of warlord power. These struggles expressed the peasants' deep-seated determination to cut the urban-warlord polity off from village food grains and from the iron ores necessary for military growth. To Li Dazhao, this spontaneous armed retreat was in fact the tuneup for a massive popular struggle to sweep away the corrupt world of the city, which was the expression of the age of Western capitalism and imperialism, and to renovate China on a national scale in the image of the self-governing village.

Noting that the peasant self-protection associations were founded on the organizational grid of older antistate secret societies such as the Elder Brothers Society and the Red Spear Society, and not on the organizational form of the Communist Party, Li hailed these associations as the vanguard of the peasant movement (Meisner, 1967:246–247). Indeed, it was a time of promise for the peasant movement, for in the Great Revolution of 1925–27 the Red Spears had driven the Beiyang warlord Pang Bingxun out of southern Henan and dealt a severe blow to the warlord Liu Zhenhua in Shaanxi (Pang, 1980; Meisner 1967: 249).

There were however, several obstacles to the sustained political success of the peasant movement. These partly explain why the movement met with failure in the pre-1935 period.

To begin with, the peasant self-defense units were armed with primitive weapons and fought only their own local wars. They were not capable of combining into a peasant army. For the most part, the peasants were unable to leave their home fields and markets to assist their counterparts fight warlords elsewhere, and when they did cross over county lines, they took leave from their self-defense units for family-related agricultural duties rather than for military reasons. On close inspection, the peasant Red Spear victories in Henan were local county-level affairs, and at best achieved temporary regional unity. The guerilla warfare associated with the mass movements was not interconnected, provincially or nationally, and the centrifugal forces of the rebelling peasantry were, in the final analysis, vulnerable to central authority. This fact became painfully obvious to Mao Zedong once Chiang Kai-shek's Soviet-built central army moved to liquidate the peasant movement in Hunan, Jiangxi, and elsewhere shortly after the Shanghai coup of 12–13 April 1927.

A second major obstacle to revolutionary success originated in the attempt of the CCP to place the peasant movement under the hegemony of the proletariat and to use the peasants to spark working class revolution in the cities of China. The attempt found expression in the Autumn Harvest Uprising, which occurred shortly after Mao penned his investigation of the Hunan peasant movement. Under the direction of Qu Quibai, the successor to Chen Duxiu in the Shanghai-based central committee, Mao returned to Hunan to organize a peasant army for an assault on the provincial capital. The CCP leadership assumed that thousands of workers would rise up to join the peasants in a revolutionary mardi gras which would place the city under the CCP (Schram, 1966: 122–123). The uprising, which Mao started with the help of a motley band of peasants, miners, and army deserters, was doomed from the beginning. The dogma of the central committee notwithstanding, Guomindang repression had grown stronger in Changsha since the Chiang Kai-shek coup. Deprived of assistance by a substantial number of CCP cadres, the workers of the city stood by to watch the superior warlord forces cut Mao's peasant army to pieces. The city held against the countryside, and Mao's bloodied peasants beat a retreat to the remote Hunan wilderness where they began to reconsider the value of the proletarian connection.

Mao Zedong, Red *Misérables*, and the Moral Economy of Peasant Rebellion

When Mao Zedong reflected on the CCP success in the Hunan-Jiangxi wilderness he made it clear that the CCP and the peasant movement were destined to defeat without an independent revolutionary army, and he stressed that such an army could not come from the proletariat or the peasantry. In *Struggle in the Jinggang Mountains*, written 5 October 1928, Mao drew attention to the increasing participation of the wretched poor in the fighting force: "As to class origins, the Red Army consists partly of workers and peasants and partly of *lumpenproletarians*. Of course, it is inadvisable to have too many of the latter. But they are able to fight, and as fighting is going on every day with mounting casualities, it is already no easy matter to get replacements even for them" (Mao, 1965–1967, 1: 81). In suggesting the wretched poor were to play a decisive part in the antiforeign-antiwarlord struggle, Mao was commenting on the travesty of what the Chinese revolution would have been if the CCP had followed the line of struggle set forth by Chen Duxiu, a line that ran straight away from the free-floating population that was to become the vanguard of revolutionary politics.

The social interpretation of the Chinese revolution articulated by Mao, specifically his idea that the destitute existing outside of state and society could play a vanguard role, struck a sympathetic chord even in the more skeptical intellectual leaders of the CCP. The term lumpenproletariat was not a Marxian fabrication, but a living sociological category they had encountered in the wreckage of humanity strewn across the landscape of the China in which they had grown to maturity. To the radical intellectuals who had come from the peasant villages to centers of learning in urban China, the homeless vagabonds and horrible beggars who combed the countryside and who fell sick and dead on the streets of Beijing, Nanjing, and Shanghai were a shocking reminder of national backwardness and stagnation (cf. Spence, 1981: 2).

Even Chen Duxiu, the chief theoretician of these young intellectuals, originally empathized with the wretched marginal people so much that he began translating Victor Hugo's *Les Misérables* out of the hope that this classic on the plight of France's common people would provide a key to revolution in China. Not long afterwards, Lu Xun, China's Mark Twain, wrote *The True Story of Ah Q*, a potent literary story about an unemployed peasant vagabond Ah Q who, having been banished from his native village and brutalized in the towns, was in the process of losing his cultural identity (*Selected Stories*, 1972). *The True Story of Ah Q* stressed the pitfalls of the psychology that developed from the subordinate existence of this pitiable vagabond, namely, Ah Q's tendency to accept mental and physical abuse by the ruling groups, a habit that held him back from giving free reign to whatever revolutionary genius lay within his soul once he did in fact commit to the 1911 revolution. Ah Q was a symbol for the soul of an uprooted peasant China, a China too easily suppressed by class domination and too easily defeated by imperialist-backed warlords. Thus it is easy to understand why Chen Duxiu, and other early CCP intellectuals, eventually came to look upon the lumpenproletariat as an unorganized and unproductive army of Ah Qs, an army of beggars and thieves who were not capable of the Marxist class loyalty and Leninist party discipline required of true revolutionaries. By 1930 Chen was brandishing Mao Zedong's attempt to place the lumpen poor (bandits, outlaws, and warlord army deserters) at the helm of the peasant movement as a betrayal of the proletarian revolution (Feigon, 1982: 108, 113, 168–69), even though Mao was moving toward a heterodox theory of revolution that would save peasant China.

From the moment Mao Zedong entered the Jinggang Mountains he was committed to creating an independent army which could protect the peasant movement from the Guomindang warlord regime. It is no historical accident that Mao looked to the vagabond troops of Peng Dehuai and He Long to help create the beginnings of the CCP's antiwarlord army in the years 1927 to 1935. Without the assistance of their forces, Mao could not have held on in the Hunan-Jiangxi border area that made up the Jinggang base from 1928–1931. He Long, in particular, was important because he already held the answer to Mao's question: "Why is it that red political power can exist in China?" China, according to Mao, was a semicolonial agrarian country where direct foreign domination was limited to the cities and where the power of the warlord regime was not only not total but also weakened by incessant internal wars for control of the countryside. To Mao, He Long's experience in the Xiangexi area was proof that revolutionary survival was possible in the remote noncolonized rural areas plagued by the divisive wars of the Guomindang warlord regime. He Long's peasant army, and later his "official army" of outlaws, orphaned village runaways, and mutinous warlord army deserters, had gotten its start beyond the reach of foreign rule and had survived by taking advantage of warlord divisions. Most interestingly, He Long had anticipated the Maoist practice of locating his vagabond army in a Hunan-Hubei border zone where warlord power was not consolidated, and he had survived by aligning with a relatively powerful Hunan warlord who was attempting to use his outlaw-bandit force to defeat a rival warlord. Thus, in 1927, when the unofficial, centrifugal Mao party secretly asked He Long to bring his troops to serve the CCP-led peasant movement, its leadership was, in a fundamental sense, moving the party backward toward a revolutionary paradigm in keeping with the bandit instincts of the 1910s. These instincts were closely connected with the traditional moral world of the peasantry and miles ahead of orthodox Communist party ideologies in the race to discover the wellsprings of popular resistance to the warlord-state and imperialism.

The massive contradictions built into the changed nature of class dominance in rural China made it possible for the Red Army to interact with peasant interests. The landlords who occupied the market villages of the rich plains and river valleys had begun to collect exorbitant land rent and charge outrageous interest on grain and money loans, and the pressure they brought for these payments drove tenants and land-hungry smallholders to bankruptcy (Selden, 1971; Thaxton, 1981). As peasants lost their means of livelihood they increasingly left their lowland villages to become migrants, herdsmen, beggars, and part-time bandits in the hills and highlands of the mountainous periphery. These hill squatters and desperados deeply resented the landlords who had excluded them from lowland village economies where grain yields generally were greatest. When dearth, landlord usury, and government taxation made for perilous hardship the poor uplanders were known to undertake concerted reprisals against the grain-lending minority of landlords who were responsible for unjust food prices (cf. Polachek, 1982: 17–32). It was possible for these disgruntled hill peasants to linkup with friends and relatives to ignite rebellion in their old home localities, and Mao brought this possibility to the attention of the CCP in the Autumn Harvest Uprising and the Jinggang Mountain experiment to follow. The Mao-party group was able to survive and grow in part by resonating with itinerant hill-peasant fraternities joined by unemployed antimony miners and mill workers whose spring hunger protests were directed against unjust grain prices rigged by wealthy landlord and gentry figures in the towns of Hunan and Jiangxi (Smedley 1956: 224; Polachek, 1982: 27–28). Measured against the interests of landlords, this Mao-party interaction with China's poor came to be called "predatory mobilization" by Western experts of "Communist Party mobilization" (cf. Perry, 1980: 167–174, 246–247; Polachek, 1982: 28, 40–42). But such a category ignores the intense landlord-warlord pressures that produced the volcanic hill-peasant eruptions and obscured the fact that CCP "bandits" such as Peng Dehuai could recruit the poor uplanders because they conducted their primitive guerrilla campaigns to realize a popular idea of redistributive justice, which the landlord-warlord regime of Chiang Kai-shek did not recognize at all.

The hill lands of South China offered yet another potential advantage for revolutionary survival and growth: the uneven distribution of landlords. In the highlands of Jiangxi one could find whole districts where few if any landlords existed, so that class dominance was relatively weak (Ch'en et al, 1980: 118, 150, 162). Whatever the reason for this phenomenon, whether bigger landlords were not inclined to supervise high-risk capital investments in the impoverished mountains or bigger Confucian gentry were drawn to the developing world of the towns and treaty-port cities rather than the backward periphery, it was possible for the CCP to seek out peasants in hundreds of villages where landlords were no longer on hand to personally administer politics or where only a few minor landlords were unable to hold down massive peasant majorities. Thus Mao's party could begin to do political work in villages where there was a local power vacuum. The CCP first resorted to this practice in South China and then perfected it during the war of resistance in North China, where big landlords were less prevalent and small landlords did not have the direct and continuous backing of a consolidated Guomindang central army (Thaxton, 1982: Conclusion).

The Mao CCP also had advantage of terrain, and the Red Army leadership made use of the topography in building up base areas throughout the country. Again, nearly two-thirds of China is mountainous. The Guomindang warlord regime, having concentrated its technology and troop strength in the lowland city-world, underestimated the difficulty of eliminating the tiny highland base areas that sprouted in places like the Hunan-Jiangxi border. Thus the ragged dissident forces of the Mao-Zhu army were able to establish military footholds in the mountain redoubts of South, North, and Northeast China. The fact the Guomindang had failed to utilize Western financial assistance to develop a coordinated modern communication and transportation system in the treacherous mountain terrain, in support of its so-called pacification campaign, redounded to the favor of the evasive CCP forces. The Red Army was able to exist and expand because territorial security was coupled with food security. The Jinggang, Taihang, and Changbai mountains, three important bastions of CCP power, all contained vast stretches of virgin land on which the Red Army soldiers could plant enough crops to supply themselves, though of course fighting the Guomindang warlords and provisioning themselves at the same time made for a dangerous and miserable existence (Ricardo, 1982: 62; Mao, 1965–1967, 1: 68–69).

The creative organizational urges of the CCP notwithstanding, the Mao-Zhu forces owed much of their organizational prowess to the ancient, popular secret societies whose independent traditions of antistate resistance had been recognized by Li Dazhao. Secret societies like the Elder Brothers Society, the Red Spear Society, and the Big Sword Society were made up of bankrupt peasants, unemployed craftsmen, and bandits. They constituted an incipient brotherhood of lumpenproletarians whose antihunger struggles brought them into armed confrontation with landlords and local government. The Elder Brothers Society, for example, had been in the thick of the 1911 Revolution against the Qing dynasty (Wu, 1981: 19, 21, 25, 90–94). This society drew men like He Long and Zhu De into its membership in the post-Qing period, and much of the military leadership of the CCP was in fact connected to its cause. Zhu De, the commander in chief of the Red Army, had become an Elder Brother during his stint in the Sichuan Regiment, and his commitment to the society's principles of brotherhood, egalitarianism, and mutuality afforded him the invisible bond of fraternity-based protection he needed to agitate for the social rights of the common soldier within the warlord armies of southwest China up until the founding of the CCP (Smedley, 1956: 87–88, 94–96). The Society was a portal to the world of popular bandit armies and ramshackle warlord forces, and it was from this world that Zhu De and He Long drew massive numbers of poor undesirables for the Red Army before and during the wars of resistance and liberation.

While there is little doubt that the intellectual leadership of the CCP was inspired by the Bolshevik victory in Russia, the blood of these popular secret societies ran through the veins of CCP leadership and formed the template of party organization. As Zhu De once pointed out, the decentralized political cell system of the CCP was in fact copied from the small discussion groups of the Revolutionary League, which had taken it over from the Elder Brothers Society, not from the Russian Bolsheviks (Smedley, 1956: 87). Moreover, the oppositionist activity of the secret societies, not the outside CCP organizational apparatus formed in places like Shanghai, more often than not provided the impetus to peasant mobilization. The living autonomous legacy of these opposition societies was all the more important for the success of the CCP's enterprise, once Chiang Kai-shek struck to liquidate the emergent Mao-party group after 1927. Zheng Weisan, a veteran of the Jiangxi peasant movement, made this clear in his reflections on the CCP relationship with the Big Sword Society during the long march from Jiangxi to Northwest China. "It is not necessary," wrote Zheng, "to first have the organization of the Communist Party. A lot of places where the peasant movement has developed in the past have not had it. In the Long March our comrades led the Big Swords in guerilla warfare. There were no CCP cadres in this mobilization and no revolutionary organization was present. Yet the power of the movement was still great." (Zheng, 1941: 20–21).

Mao Zedong once acknowledged that the CCP suffered a "great historic punishment" (Mao, 1954: 193) at the hands of the Guomindang in Jiangxi, and Chiang Kai-shek's counterrevolution did in fact reduce the strength and scope of the revolutionary-party army to a hardly perceptible influence. It is, however, a mistake to claim, as have several mobilization theorists, that the radical leveling practices of the Mao party and the Guomindang restoration of law and order led the Jiangxi peasant movement to a dead-end road (cf. Polachek, 1982: 1–42).

The period known as the Jiangxi Soviet marked the beginning of an agrarian revolutionary experiment that was not eliminated by the Guomidang and that was not abandoned by the Mao-party group in the years approaching liberation. To be sure, the initial Mao-Zhu experiment in building a revolutionary base was defeated militarily. The main force of the Red Army, however, escaped Chiang Kai-shek's military encirclement and survived the long march into the barren loess backlands of Northwest China, where Shaanxi meets Gansu.

Jiangxi, and the long march that followed, produced an alternative historical promise for China's poorest rural people, and the Mao-Zhu forces legimated their purpose by helping to fulfill this promise. For the masterless people who were no longer rooted in village economies, Mao-Zhu embodied the promise of Moses. The Red Army was to be the instrument whereby the brotherhood of the poor would escape from Chiang Kai-shek's "regime of bondage". Thus it is not at all surprising that the weary Mao-Zhu vanguard was received and replenished in Shaanxi by Liu Zhidan, an Elder Brother Society chieftain in command of a roving band of several thousand poor men (Snow, 1938: 209–210). This Robin Hood force helped forge the crucible out of which the CCP Red Army re-emerged in Northwest China, and many of its practices, such as abolishing surtaxes and arming peasants to defend themselves against wicked landlords, were taken up by the CCP during the war of resistance.

Jiangxi was also the experience from which there emerged the great covenant of friendship between the CCP and the peasantry, that is, Mao Zedong's morally binding promise that the Red Army would enforce the efforts of peasants to reclaim family household economies and eliminate the landlord and warlord usurpers of village-produced resources. This promise was embodied in Mao Zedong's *Jiangxi Village Investigations*, a document taken from his own firsthand talks with bankrupt peasant families. Implicit in the *Village Investigations* was the message that the CCP Red Army had raised the standard of revolt on behalf of the moral economy of the peasantry, that is, of each little family. From the moment the Red Army put this message in practice, and survived the Guomindang mobilization of massive repression against it, the idea that there was a counterforce with a peasant interest in mind spread like wildfire across China. Desperate village people whose families were about to be wiped out were so intoxicated by this idea that they sometimes pooled all their worldly belongings to secretly dispatch small delegations of friends and relatives to fan out in the direction of distant mountains to find the Red Army and invite its commanders to follow them back to their villages to settle blood debts with landlords and put an end to Guomindang plunder. Thus the momentous arrival of the CCP was, in many cases, little more than a brief encounter between ragged poor people who had left their hovels to place themselves and their villages under the protection of the Mao-Zhu forces (Myrdal, 1965: 78–79; cf. Thaxton, 1981: 24–25).

For Mao the key to revolutionary success lay in the twenty million landless and uprooted human scarecrows who made up the available recruits for a popular army of the poor (Friedman, 1975: 17–23). Joined by uprooted CCP dissident intellectuals, who once had close ties to the village world, these rootless victims of imperialism and militarism would form a revolutionary force to save peasant China. Mao, unlike Engels and Marx, did not have much of a choice in this matter. Engels had characterized these "gutter proletarians" as having no loyalties to any class and labeled them the worst of all possible revolutionary allies (Engels, 1967: 9). Similarly, Marx had feared them as a potential source of support for reactionary military regimes whose Bonapartist leadership did not uphold the interests of the progressive bourgeoisie or the proletariat (Marx, 1964: 50). The centrifugal Mao party, however, turned to the lumpen elements out of the sheer necessity to survive politically in an agrarian country that had already seen the abortion of bourgeois (1911) and proletarian (1927) revolutions. Moreover, as we have seen, men like Peng Dehuai and He Long themselves belonged to the world that Marx had referred to as the "rootless proletariat in rags" and they literally had entered national politics by enforcing the elementary demands of the desperate poor during their youthful years. They were, therefore, prepared by their formative experience actively to endorse Mao Zedong's proposal to organize and lead a lumpen armed counterforce both to support the peasant movement and to liberate the nation.

The first task of this armed lumpen counterforce was to serve the peasants in the villages, and thereby demonstrate the loyalty of the rootless poor to the rooted village people. The raison d' être of the Red Army (later called the Eighth Army and the People's Liberation Army) was to strengthen the peasant movement so as to enforce the subsistence demands of the tillers. This meant the Red Army was to join in the peasant attack on landlords and warlords. Usury-based debts that had placed peasants in perpetual servitude to landlords were declared a criminal offense, and under the shield of the army, peasants conducted their own campaigns to recover the grain-producing lands they had lost to landlord usurers in the previous decades. At the same time, Mao and Zhu combined their ragged and miserable troops into regular battalion- and division-level units that supported the Peasant Self-Defense Corps against the Guomindang warlords whose tax drives had driven tillers to vagrancy and vagabondage. Under the Guomindang, the heads of peasants who had led the autumn harvest uprisings and spring hunger revolts against landlord price hikes and warlord tax squeeze had been mounted on poles. Hence the Guomindang had become the "white bandit regime" to the peasantry, white being the color of death in folk memory. By its deeds alone, the restoration of land to the tiller, the abolishment of surtaxes, and the protection of peasants against brutal landlord-warlord violence, Mao's lumpen army of "Red *Misérables*" identified itself with the peasant hope for life. China's peasants had always used the color red to describe the treasured meanings of life—the red blood that gave good health, the reddish-brown fields that gave up the grains for sustenance, the red dawn that gave another day of hope, and the red faces of the folk-opera rebels who gave courage to the powerless. The Red Army resonated with all these celebrated aspects of peasant life and more, and it won the loyalties of the peasant folk by embracing their struggles for survival in the village world. With this accomplished, the peasants looked upon the revolutionary soldiers as protectors rather than predators, and the Red Army proceeded to create a revolution within its own emergent countersociety.

For Mao Zedong and Zhu De the central questions of revolutionary survival were: how to find the massive numbers of rootless recruits needed to build a regular Red Army force and how to hold these desperate people in the army? Indeed, how could such an army possibly form and attain the staying power needed to wage a life-or-death struggle against the Guomindang, and the Japanese after 1937?

The unemployment in China's villages and the unhealthy state of warlord-army finances, not the subversive acts of the CCP, ensured a constant stream of defections from the Guomindang warlord armies to the Mao-Zhu counterforce. The market disorders fostered by the militarists made for unemployment in the villages, depriving peasants of side-occupation income needed to supplement failing harvests. The peasant carpenters of Sichuan's Heavenly Gate Village, which I visited in July 1979, tell us that warlords there had usurped their rights to obtain lumber from the tributaries of the Min Jiang River in the 1940s. With these timber warlords neglecting the Min Water Works, which were to irrigate the Chengdu rice plain, grain production fell to intolerable levels and peasants turned to migratory labor and wandering. Some of them wandered into the People's Liberation Army when it rushed into their province in 1949. (cf. *Zhandou Yingxiong*, 1978: 301–306). The changed world-market demand for antimony and coal also fostered unemployment in the Chinese countryside, and so it is not surprising that the Mao-Zhu forces were constantly joined by poor miners whose local struggles were triggered by the pinch of rising warlord mine taxes and falling global market prices for the minerals they were mining (Smedley, 1956: 224; McDonald, 1978: 77–79). The World Depression and the Japanese invasion intensified this phenomenon throughout much of China.

By far the most massive source of Red Army recruits came from the defecting troops of the new provincial and national level warlord regimes. The Red Army literally got its start from the defections led by Peng Dehuai and He Long shortly after Chiang Kai-shek's April 1927 coup d'etat. The army was replenished over the next two decades by other state-army defections, as when 15,000 Nationalist troops defected to the Red Army in Jiangxi in 1931 (Donovan, 1976: 32–33, 41–42) and thousands of Guomindang warlord troops did the same thing several years later in Shanxi (cf. Klein and Clark, 1971: 250). The fundamental reason for these defections lay in the financial crisis of the Republic of China. The central government was bankrupt and the funds that were allocated for army building did not reach the peasant vagabonds and vagrants who had been press-ganged into the army of the dominant class. On the one hand, Chiang Kai-shek did not insulate the press-ganged recruits to his soldier-state from the rampaging monetary inflation that was ruining the civilian sector—inflation that was fueled by the financial practices of the central government. On the other hand, Chiang Kai-shek's high ranking officer corps defined national security in terms of their own greedy dreams to get rich, and they continued the warlord practice of withholding pay from the regular troops. As a result, there were rebellions and desertions en masse from the Guomindang warlord armies. The uprooted, miserable ex-peasants and ex-miners who carried out these actions went over to the Red Army out of a desperate need for survival and a deep hatred for the aristocratic and arrogant Guomindang officers, most of whom hailed from landlord backgrounds.

If the CCP was to raise its Red Army above the context of localized peasant movements and wage a war for national power then it had to inspire its recruits to lay down their lives for the idea of an independent China capable of pursuing national self-determination. To do this, the Red Army had to prove by its actions that it was an instrument of security and salvation for its wretched participants as well as the peasantry.

The promise of security and subsistence was an important reason why the rootless poor came to and stayed in the Red Army. This promise was, in a crucial sense, personified by the very presence of Peng Dehuai, the Deputy Commander of the Eighth Route Army during the Anti-Japanese War. As early as 1919, when the early CCP leaders were seeking salvation in Marxist slogans, Peng Dehuai had been creating "Poor People's Salvation Societies" (*jiupinghui*) within the Hunan warlord army in which he had taken refuge from the law. These poor people's societies declared their opposition to indemnity payments and to the withholding of troop pay, by then a widespread practice among high ranking warlord officers. The societies began as secret-discussion groups of six and seven men. By 1927 Peng had expanded them to include 17 members. Their primary purpose was to guarantee the livelihood of the troops, but they also guaranteed land to peasants in the localities of their encampments and punished the misanthrophic landlords (Huang, 1980: 2–3).

The major reason why the declassé elements stayed with the Red Army, however, was that the Mao party changed the quality of life and death for the common soldier, even though life in the Red Army remained miserable and extremely spartan. The Mao-party cadres, however, broke away from the Marxist tendency to treat the rootless poor as less than human and personally restored to them the sense of self-respect and dignity they had all but lost in the brutal years without family protection. In the same decade that Chiang Kai-shek's officers brought back the feudal death penalty for Guomindang soldiers, Zhu De and Peng Dehuai were sanctioning the right of Red Army soldiers to organize themselves to prevent officers from beating poor recruits. The promise of an egalitarian fraternity of commanders and troops was guaranteed by democratizing company-level soldier meetings, and by empowering the common soldiers to dismiss officers who refused to abide by majoritarian decisions on internal army issues, such as equal access to the unit's budget books. Thus it became an open secret within both Guomindang and Communist armies as to which party stood for the dignity of the common soldier.

Ah Q and China's miserable vagabonds had experienced death without dignity, a death so lonely and horrible and empty that the inauspicious moment deprived them of the here-and-now dignity of dying and compromised any claim to martyrdom. The Mao-party revolutionized Red Army life for China's uprooted have-nots by holding funeral ceremonies and conducting memorial services in honor of the soldiers who died at the hands of the Guomindang warlord regime and the Japanese Imperial Army (Mao, 1965–67, 3: 177). The memorial meetings dignified the wait for death and strengthened the will of Red Army soldiers to change the order of political oppression by sacrificing themselves on the battle field. The meetings also helped the wronged, the angry, and the forgotten poor to reconcile themselves to the certainty of death, for now they were assured a place in a mighty national community of martyrs.

In his work on *Man's Concern with Death*, Arnold Toynbee implied that the Jews who risked martyrdom in resisting the Seleucid emperor's effort to subordinate them to Greek-Syrian rule were inspired by the prospect of becoming participants in a forthcoming messianic kingdom (Toynbee et al, 1968: 18–19). Mao was not yet Yahweh. But the Red Army, like the Taiping Army before it, did embrace the millennial vision of a poor people's kingdom, and its commanders and commissars expressed the hope that their egalitarian fraternity would be extended across the generations to come. To the Red Army soldier who knew his family line would not be continued by offspring, the act of dying in the service of the nation, defined as the armed interest of the popular classes, fulfilled a very personal need for an alternative historical link to immortality.

8. What Makes Peasants Revolutionary?

Theda Skocpol

The centrality of peasants in modern revolutions was underscored for the first time in contemporary North American scholarship by Barrington Moore, Jr., in *Social Origins of Dictatorship and Democracy: Lord and Peasant in the Making of the Modern World.* Eloquently, the opening sentences of Moore's chapter on "The Peasants and Revolution" declared that the "process of modernization begins with peasant revolutions that fail. It culminates during the twentieth century with peasant revolutions that succeed" (Moore, 1966: 453). *Social Origins* in fact proved uncannily prescient and timely in its emphasis on the revolutionary potential of the peasantry. When Moore's great opus was in preparation during the 1950s and early 1960s, neither Marxism nor orthodox social science paid much heed to the roles of agrarian classes in "the making of the modern world." The peasantry, especially, was spurned as the repository of conservatism and tradition, of all that needed to be overcome by a revolutionary bourgeoisie or proletariat, or by a modernizing elite. But once the United States became tragically engaged from the mid-1960s in a military effort to stymie the Vietnamese Revolution, U.S. scholars quite understandably became fascinated with the revolutionary potential of the peasantry—especially in the Third World. The questions addressed by Moore's chapter on peasants in *Social Origins*—"what kinds of social structures and historical situations produce peasant revolutions and which ones inhibit or prevent them" (Moore, 1966: 453)—were immediately relevant for an entire nascent genre of research and theorizing on peasants and revolution.

The first major contribution to this new literature, written in the heat of the movement against U.S. involvement in Vietnam, was Eric R. Wolf's 1969 book *Peasant Wars of the Twentieth Century.* Studies undertaken by younger scholars emerged during the 1970s: Joel S. Migdal's *Peasants, Politics, and Revolutions: Pressures toward Political and Social Change in the Third World* (1974); Jeffery M. Paige's *Agrarian Revolution: Social Movements and Export Agriculture in the Underdeveloped World* (1975); and James C. Scott's *The Moral Economy of the Peasant* (1976), the last of which was extended into a theory of peasant-based revolutions in a recent article (1977a) "Hegemony and the Peasantry."[1] In contrast to the Old World frame of reference predominant in Moore's *Social Origins*, the works of Wolf, Migdal, Paige, and Scott share a principal focus on Third World revolutions, the natural result of the Vietnam-era preoccupations out of which they developed.[2] Nevertheless, variations of method and substantive focus are immediately noticeable. Eric Wolf seeks to generalize inductively about peasant-based revolutions on the basis of in-depth histories of six twentieth-century cases: Mexico, Russia, China, Vietnam, Algeria, and Cuba. Joel Migdal elaborates a systematic theory of how imperialistic modernizing forces impinge on peasant villages and how peasants, in turn, are likely to respond economically and politically. This theory is illustrated with bits and pieces of secondary evidence gleaned from fifty-one published village studies in Asia and Latin America, as well as with primary evidence from Migdal's own field experiences in Mexico and India. James Scott's ideas on peasant revolutions are widely but impressionistically based, illustrated by examples from publications on revolutions ranging from the seventeenth-century English case to the recent Chinese and Vietnamese Revolutions. Finally, Jeffery Paige's study is the most methodologically elaborate. It combines a quantitative analysis of agrarian movements between 1948 and 1970 in 135 agricultural export sectors, with in-depth historical accounts of agrarian movements in three countries—Peru, Angola, and Vietnam. All of this evidence is used to test an explicit formal theory of rural class conflict in the contemporary underdeveloped world.

The works of Wolf (1969a), Migdal (1974), Paige (1975), and Scott (1977a) cry out for discussion as a set. By looking at these works together, and by weighing the relative merits and common limits of their arguments, we can readily lay bare the state of current knowledge on peasants and revolution and indicate unresolved issues and potentially fruitful paths for future research. I shall review and evaluate what these scholars have to say in answer to three major questions: (1) which peasants are most prone to revolution and why? (2) what roles do political and military organizations play in peasant-based revolutions? (3) does capitalist imperialism create conditions for peasant-based revolutions—and, if so, how? These organizing questions will take us to the heart of the basic arguments of the four authors—and into the thick of the often sharp differences among them.

What is more, these questions will focus our attention on historical and cross-societal variations in the social and political factors that contribute to peasant-based revolutions, rather than prompt us to dwell on ahistorical conceptions of the nature of "the peasant" as a supposedly general human type. Some of the recent debates between those who see peasants as inherently moral communitarians (e.g., Scott, 1976) versus those who insist that they are inherently individualistic and competitive rational individuals (e.g., Popkin, 1979) have had the unfortunate effect of drawing attention away from the *sharply varying* social structures and political situations within which peasants and potential revolutionary organizers or allies of peasants have actually found themselves. As our joint interrogation of Wolf, Migdal, Paige, and Scott will underline, it is quite fruitless to predict peasant behavior or its revolutionary (or nonrevolutionary) effects on the basis of *any* broad speculation about the nature of the peasantry. Varying social structures, political configurations, and historical conjunctures constitute much more appropriate terms of analysis and explanation.

Which Peasants Are Most Prone to Revolution, and Why?

Our excursus through the recent literature on peasants and revolution starts with a question that will eventually reveal itself to be too narrowly framed. All the same, it is a revealing place to begin because three of our authors split sharply in their answers.[3] Eric Wolf and James Scott argue different variants of one polar position—that the peasants most prone to revolution are village dwellers who possess landed property. In contrast, Jeffery Paige argues that smallholding peasants are normally conservative and quiescent, whereas *propertyless* laborers or sharecroppers, cultivators who earn income from wages not land, are more likely to become revolutionary.

The key issue in explaining revolutions for James Scott (1977a) is whether or not a lower class has the cultural and social-organizational autonomy to resist "the impact of hegemony ruling elites normally exercise" (Scott, 1977a: 271). Despite their localism and traditionalism, precapitalist peasant smallholders, sharecroppers, or tenants are in Scott's view unusually likely to enjoy such autonomy. Their village-and kin-based social networks promote local communal solidarity, even as their worldviews and values are inherently in tension with dominant-class culture. Moreover, the immediate processes of economic production are directly controlled by the peasants themselves. "If this analysis is accurate," Scott concludes:

> it implies that we are often likely to find the strongest resistance to capitalism and to an intrusive state among the more isolated peasantries with entrenched precapitalist values. While the values that motivate such peasantries are thus hardly socialist values in the strict, modern use of that world, their tenacity and the social organization from which they arise may provide the social dynamite for radical change. The situation of immigrant workers and landless day laborers . . . may well seem more appropriate to strictly socialist ideas, but their social organization makes them less culturally cohesive and hence less resistant to hegemony (Scott, 1977a: 289).

Wolf (1969a) tends to agree with Scott about the kinds of peasants most likely to become involved in revolutions, but he provides a different analysis of the reasons why. Impressed by the obstacles that poverty and vulnerability to repression can place in the way of political involvement by peasants, Wolf argues that most poor peasants and landless laborers are unlikely initiators of rebellion. They are usually closely tied to or dependent upon landlords, and cannot rebel unless outside forces intervene to mobilize and shield them. In contrast, says Wolf, much greater "tactical leverage" to engage in rebellion is normally possessed by smallholders or tenants who live in communal villages outside direct landlord control, and by peasants (even poor ones) who live in geographically marginal areas relatively inaccessible to governmental authorities. As Wolf concludes: "ultimately, the decisive factor in making a peasant rebellion possible lies in the relation of the peasantry to the field of power which surrounds it. A rebellion cannot start from a situation of complete impotence" (Wolf, 1969a: 290). Thus, for Wolf, the crucial insurrectionary capacities possessed by communal, property-holding peasants are not cultural as Scott would have it, but lie instead in the material and organizational advantages their situation offers for collective resistance against outside oppressors.

The way Jeffery Paige (1975) approaches the issue of which sorts of peasants are most prone to revolution differs considerably from the approaches of Scott and Wolf. Instead of speaking of peasant villages facing outside forces, Paige organizes his argument strictly around class relations between lower-class laboring "cultivators" and upper-class "noncultivators" who appropriate surplus income from agricultural production in established capitalist enclaves of underdeveloped countries. Paige hypothesizes about the political effects of different sources of income from export-zone agricultural production. His basic model (see Figure 1) is a fourfold box which holds that certain organizational forms of agricultural production are typically associated with alternative combinations of cultivator and noncultivator income from land or wages or capital. In turn, different kinds of agrarian politics are expected to occur for each combination of income sources.

This discussion will deal only with two out of four of Paige's theoretical boxes—namely the top two, where the "noncultivators" are landed upper classes that derive income through politically enforced ownership of large amounts of land. One of the most insightful features of Paige's argument is his insistence that patterns of agrarian class conflict are dependent not only on the characteristics and situations of the lower classes themselves, but equally on the characteristics and situations of the upper, noncultivating classes. For example, Paige argues that agrarian revolution is potentially on the agenda only when noncultivators derive their income from land rather than from capital, because only then are the upper classes forced by their structural position to refuse incremental, reformist concessions. This turns class conflicts with cultivators into a zero-sum game, in which control of property and state power are inherently at issue. Whether or not one fully accepts the substance of Paige's argument,[4] the class-relational logic of his analysis is exemplary: whether peasants become revolutionary depends as much on the interests and capacities of their class opponents as it does on the interests and capacities of the peasants themselves.

Agrarian conflict also depends in Paige's model upon the likely political behavior of different kinds of lower-class cultivators—and with respect to this matter Paige arrives at opposite conclusions from Scott and Wolf. When smallholding peasants who derive their livelihood from land ownership are dominated by a landed upper class, Paige holds that the normal result will be an absence of overt conflict. Propertyless laborers, instead, are the ones Paige deems likely to make revolutions against landed upper classes. Landholding peasants are hypothesized to be mutually isolated and economically competitive among themselves, averse to taking risks, and strongly dependent upon rich peasants and landed upper classes. Wage-earning cultivators are held to be solidary, willing to take risks, and autonomous from upper-class controls; thus they are structurally inclined to give deliberate support to revolutionary political movements. Specifically, Paige argues that migratory laborers will tend to ally with native communities to support anti-colonialist, nationalist movements, whereas sharecroppers (especially in decentralized agricultural systems such as wet-rice agriculture) will support class-conscious revolutionary socialist movements.[5]

Nothing better illustrates the contradictory lines of reasoning embodied in Eric

CULTIVATORS

	LAND	WAGES
LAND	COMMERCIAL HACIENDA No overt conflict (or Agrarian revolts)	SHARECROPPING or MIGRATORY LABOR Revolution (Socialist or Nationalist)
CAPITAL	SMALL HOLDING Reformist commodity movements	PLANTATION Reformist labor movements

NONCULTIVATORS

Figure 8.1. Paige's theory of rural class conflict: combinations of cultivator and noncultivator income, typical forms of agricultural organization, and expected forms of agrarian social movements
Source: Adapted from Paige, *Agrarian Revolution*, Figure 1.1.

Wolf's versus Jeff Paige's theories than the contrasting conclusions these authors draw from the rural social basis of the Vietnamese Revolution. Eric Wolf (1969a: ch. 4) locates the areas of strongest support for the Communist-led revolution disproportionately in northern and central Vietnam, in certain mountainous regions populated by ethnic minorities, and (during the 1960s) in those areas of southern Vietnam differentially populated by smallholding peasants. Wolf reasons that these were areas where peasants could safely provide solidary support, relatively free from French, landlord, or U.S. repressive power. In southern Vietnam, Wolf says, village communities were unstable and therefore more difficult for the Communists to organize. Moreover, landlords and their allies were quite strong in the South.

Paige, on the other hand, tries (1975: ch. 5) to make a sharp theoretical distinction between areas of Vietnam that provided strong "spontaneous" social support for revolutionary socialism and geographically marginal areas where Communist forces flourished during the military phases of the revolution. Using this distinction, Paige argues that the earliest, historically consistent agrarian support for the Communists was centered in the export-oriented, rice sharecropping areas of the Mekong delta in southern Vietnam—precisely where, according to his analysis, the cultivating lower strata consisted of workers without secure landholdings, who were paid in crop shares and condemned to common low status in an export economy dominated by large landholders, creditors, and merchants. The southern Vietnamese sharecroppers, Paige reasons, had a strong interest in, and capacity for, collective revolutionary action, whereas smallholding peasants in central and northern Vietnam were dominated by village notables and divided against one another by competition for land and village resources.

Thus, the available answers to our first organizing question—which peasants are most prone to revolution, and why?—are without doubt strikingly contradictory. Who is right? Or, to put it another way, whose way of posing the issues and developing an explanation is more valid and fruitful? If explicit, thorough reasoning and methodological sophistication were sufficient to ensure correctness in social science, our vote of confidence would automatically go to Jeffery Paige, for his *Agrarian Revolution* is an unusually meticulous piece of scholarship. Nevertheless, I believe that Paige's argument is open to serious question—especially on the issue of which peasants are most prone to revolution.

As we have already noted, Paige's model predicts that in an agrarian system where both the upper classes and the lower classes derive their incomes from land, there should normally be "little or no peasant political activity" (Paige, 1975: 41). However, Paige is quickly forced to note that although "the combined political characteristics of upper and lower classes dependent on land seem to suggest that few rebellions of any kind should take place, periodic uprisings have been a constant part of manorial economies from the German peasant wars to the Bolivian revolution of 1952" (Paige, 1975: 41–42). He admits that these historical realities "do seem to contradict the principle that peasants should lack the coherent political organization necessary to oppose the landlords" (Paige, 1975: 42). But there is no real contradiction, claims Paige, because in the cases at issue the peasants are always helped by breakdowns of state power or by outside political allies: "Peasant rebellions in commercial hacienda systems depend on the weakening of the repressive power of the landed aristocracy, the introduction of organizational strength from outside the peasant community, or both" (Paige, 1975: 42). Even when such facilitating factors intervene, the peasants still are not "truly revolutionary," Paige asserts. His explanation has several steps:

> Many peasant revolts which occur when a landed upper class has been critically weakened are little more than simultaneous land rushes by thousands of peasants bent on obtaining land that they may legally regard as theirs. . . . (Paige, 1975: 42–43).

> The land seizures, in turn, may destroy the rural class structure and end the political power of the landed upper class. . . . (Paige, 1975: 45).

> [Nevertheless,] even after the landed class has been weakened to the point that it can be liquidated by widespread peasant land seizures, the peasants themselves still lack the internal political organization to seize state power. . . . (Paige, 1975: 43).

> In fact the peasants are seldom the beneficiaries of the political changes they set in motion . . . [R]eform or socialist parties . . . [provide] the political organization and opposition to the landed elite that the peasants themselves . . . [cannot]

sustain. It is, therefore, usually those parties that fill the political vacuum left by the departure of the landlords (Paige, 1975: 45).

I have quoted at such length because it is very important to note what Paige is doing here. In the course of elaborating a theoretical category in which "little or no peasant political activity" is expected, Paige recounts evidence of revolts and (in effect) revolutionary overturns of landed upper classes and states that support them. Indeed, by the end of the discussion, Paige offers a formulation that is really quite different from the theoretical prediction of no political activity with which he began; instead Paige states that "the characteristic forms of political behavior in systems in which both the upper classes and the lower classes are dependent on income from land *are, alternatively, political apathy or agrarian revolt*" (Paige, 1975: 45, emphasis added). What is more, although he never says so explicitly, Paige surely realizes that under appropriate military conditions such "agrarian revolts" can have truly revolutionary consequences. All of this is said not to contradict theoretical expectations, because the peasants are only revolting for immediate objectives (such as driving out the landlords and taking their property!) and are not deliberately trying to reorganize national politics, and because the revolts of the peasants can only spread and achieve lasting results when military breakdowns or outside organizers intervene to help the peasantry.

Nothing said by Paige in all of this maneuvering to deal with the revolts of landed peasants is wrong historically. But it should not escape the reader's attention that Paige has now set formidably high standards for an agrarian cultivating class to qualify as truly revolutionary. Our curiosity should be thoroughly aroused: do migratory laborers and sharecroppers meet these standards in Paige's theoretical discussion and empirical accounts?

According to Paige, the "typical form of social movement in systems dependent on landed property and wage labor is revolutionary. Such movements involve not only violent conflict over landed property and direct attack on the rural stratification system, but also a coherent political effort to seize control of the state by force . . . [L]ong guerilla wars are the likely result" (Paige, 1975: 58). Yet Paige carefully distinguishes between two subtypes in this "land and wages" category. In the first subtype, where migratory labor estates are involved, the "workers themselves are too divided to provide the coherent political organization necessary for armed insurrection" (Paige, 1975: 68). Thus, "only in colonial areas where the estate system has not completely eliminated the power of the indigenous landed classes can a revolutionary nationalist movement occur" (Paige, 1975: 70). In such cases, organized nationalist parties and armies created by indigenous elites can intervene to organize the migratory laborers who, otherwise, like peasants "on a commercial hacienda . . . [are] incapable of providing the organizational strength to oppose the power of the landlords" (Paige, 1975: 70). Obviously, therefore, for the revolutionary nationalist variant of his "land and wages" category, Paige fails even to assert that there are dynamics among the cultivators themselves different from those found in the "land and land" category. A critic can justly point out that the differences in political behavior between smallholding peasants and migratory laborers seem to depend not so much on the income sources of the cultivators themselves as upon the larger societal and political contexts within which these agrarian lower classes are located.

But when we arrive in *Agrarian Revolution* at discussions of the truly revolutionary landless cultivators—sharecroppers in systems of decentralized wet-rice agriculture—then military factors and organized political parties suddenly take on very different roles from those they play in agrarian revolts or merely nationalist revolutions. *Socialist* revolutions are, for Paige, genuinely class based affairs. To be sure, organized ideological parties are also involved in these revolutions— namely, Communist parties and ideologies. But Paige baldly maintains that these parties bear a unique relationship to sharecropper tenant supporters: "... [A]reas of tenancy have shown a pronounced attraction to left-wing, particularly Communist, ideologies and a surprising potential for powerful political organization. ... *Unlike the politics of peasants dependent on individual subsistence plots, these political affiliations are internally generated, not introduced by outside urban-based parties*" (Paige, 1975: 62, emphasis added).

"In the case of decentralized sharecropping systems the organization is based on a Communist party *organized from within* the worker community" (Paige, 1975: 70, emphasis added). In short, Paige would have us believe that parties involved in organizing smallholders or migratory laborers come to them from without, whereas Communist parties organizing rice sharecroppers somehow emerge from within as pure expressions of cultivators' class interests and their conscious revolutionary determination to overthrow landlords and the state.

A moment's reflection will reveal the unbelievability of Paige's bizarre theoretical treatment of revolutionary Communism in Vietnam and in other rice sharecropping systems. Asian Communist parties, like all modern political parties from reformist to socialist to nationalist, have been created and led by urban-educated–middle-class people.[6] In no sense are they the autonomous organizational creations of agrarian lower classes. Sometimes these parties have operated in the countryside primarily as political mobilizers, without deploying their own military forces. At other times—especially during armed guerilla struggles for revolutionary power—Asian Communist parties have combined political and military mobilization of peasants and workers. Invariably, Communist parties *come to* agrarian lower classes in search of their support for national political objectives that go well beyond the immediate goals of the vast majority of the peasants, whether smallholders or sharecroppers. In Vietnam, the Communists had anti-colonial, nationalist objectives as well as the "revolutionary-socialist" goals exclusively stressed by Paige.[7] And the survival of the Vietnamese Communist party from 1930, let alone its ultimate victories in northern and then southern Vietnam, is simply incomprehensible as the product of anything less than widespread social support among many different kinds of Vietnamese peasants, not to mention Vietnamese workers and middle classes.

Paige's climactic argument about the social basis of Vietnamese Communism refers to southern Vietnam in the early- to mid-1960s— and here peculiarities and contradictions abound. For Vietnam as a whole Paige dismisses nonsharecrop-ping areas of Communist strength as indicators of military presence rather than political appeal. Yet for southern Vietnam he uses (Paige, 1975: 329–33) as his indicator of Communist political appeal an index of the geographical locations of assassinations of village notables and chiefs by the (Communist-led) National Liberation Front. But assassinations, surely, are an expression of combined politi-cal and military struggle. Even more important, assassinations would logically seem to reveal those localities where Communists were *contesting for control*, not the places where such control was already securely possessed. Indeed, Paige's own historical discussion reveals a well-known fact about politics in southern Vietnam. It was always an arena of uphill struggle for the Communists, and not only because of French and then U.S military strength. Even in those localities with Paige's theo-retically appropriate proto-revolutionary class relations, the Communists had to compete for power not only with local repressive organizations controlled by land-lords, but also with two powerful nonrevolutionary sects, the Cao Dai and the Hoa Hao.[8] The Hoa Hao, according to Paige's own data, did just as well among the rice sharecroppers as the Communists. This sect was ultimately eclipsed only after the assassination of its leader and much governmental repression; until then it was much more truly a spontaneous peasant organization than the Communists ever were. Yet Paige's theory cannot make sense of the Hoa Hao. For the theory predicts only "revolutionary socialist" politics for the rice sharecroppers of the Mekong delta.

In sum, Jeffery Paige's arguments about the political capacities of landholding versus landless peasants do not hold up in the face of critical scrutiny. Paige theoretically posits a kind of "revolutionary socialist" agrarian lower class that probably does not exist in reality. Certainly Paige provides no valid evidence that cultivators in this category can organize themselves selfconsciously to attack class relations and the state, for the presence among the sharecroppers of Communist slogans and activities is his prime empirical indicator of revolutionary socialism.[9] A close, skeptical reading of *Agrarian Revolution* suggests that *either* peasant smallholders or landless laborers can end up playing important parts in revolu-tions. This is hardly the conclusion entailed by Paige's model; thus one is forced to wonder about its fruitfullness. Income sources in the abstract are not valid predictors of the political interests and capacities of agrarian classes.

In *Social Origins*, Barrington Moore presents (1966: 475–76) a distinction between contrasting sorts of local community solidarity: "conservative solidarity," in which peasant smallholders, tenants, or laborers are dominated by rich peasants or landlords who control the resources and organizational levers of village society; versus "radical solidarity," in which peasants themselves share resources and run village organizations which can be set in opposition to landlords or the state. Paige's attempt to derive degrees of solidarity among cultivators directly from their sources of income in land versus wages blinds him analytically to the possibility of "radical solidarity" among smallholding peasants.[10] Yet in socio-historical situations where such solidarity has existed (for example, Russia and

Mexico), communities of landholding peasants have been collectively able and willing to revolt against landlords and the state. Thus, James Scott and Eric Wolf are correct to argue that communities of peasant smallholders have at times fuelled revolutionary overturns of dominant classes and the state.

This brief detour into Barrington Moore's Social Origins suggests the kind of analytic approach necessary to improve upon Paige: a social-structural approach that looks closely at institutionalized economic and political relations between landed upper classes and agrarian lower classes, on the one hand, and institutionalized relations among the peasants themselves, on the other. Much more than James Scott, Eric Wolf resembles Moore in using such a social-structural approach. Scott may be right in some of his assertions about the revolutionary potential of peasant communities, but his primarily cultural approach leads him to romantic, ahistorical assertions about the peasantry in general. To read Scott (especially 1976 and 1977b) is to get the impression that all peasant villages are basically the same: communal, subsistence-oriented, nonexploitative, culturally in tension with outside dominant classes, and economically on the defensive against encroaching capitalism or imperialism. But as demonstrated by Paige's astute and detailed analysis (1975: 285–300) of the villages of central and northern Vietnam, exploitative and competitive internal divisions and class tensions can readily exist within subsistence-oriented villages with communal resources. Imperialist pressures can exacerbate internal divisions and exploitation.[11] And as the comparative-historical investigations of both Barrington Moore and Eric Wolf document, the structural variations of class and community arrangements within agrarian societies are very great. These variations, in turn, determine different landlord and peasant responses to capitalism and different patterns of agrarian politics from case to case. James Scott's transhistorical cultural approach cannot descriptively handle— let alone explain—such variations of structures and outcomes.

Eric Wolf, however, *is* sensitive to the full range of social-structural and political issues that must be taken into account to explain peasant-based revolutions. Although there is nothing rigorous about his answers, Wolf inquires about peasants' property holdings, about their relations to one another and to landlords and—perhaps just as important—about their relations to the state and to organized political and military forces challenging state power. In these final emphases Wolf goes beyond even Barrington Moore. Wolf's notion of "tactical mobility" for the peasantry encompasses many of the same concerns addressed by Moore's discussion of conservative versus radical forms of village solidarity. Yet Wolf is alluding to more than whether peasants are collectively solidary and free from tight controls by landlords. His concept also inquires into the relative freedom of peasants from state repression, either by virtue of their marginal geopolitical location, or as a result of the intervention of armed revolutionaries to shield the peasants.

In a sense Eric Wolf's explanatory approach is too complex and vague to be more than a set of analytic pointers. It tells us to pay attention to political and military as well as socioeconomic relationships. It also suggests that we must examine more than the situation of the peasantry and the agrarian economy alone, if we are to understand peasant participation in revolutionary transformations. Taking heart from these pointers, we should now bracket the debate over which kinds of peasants are most prone to revolution and move on to examine directly how broader political and economic forces are implicated in peasant-based revolutions.

What Roles Do Political and Military Organizations Play in Peasant-based Revolutions?

Joel Migdal's *Peasants, Politics, and Revolution* (1974) has not been discussed in any detail so far, yet this is a good time to bring up some of its key arguments. By highlighting the centrality of political organizations in revolutions, Migdal achieves among our authors a unique angle of vision on the questions of how and why peasants become revolutionary.

Wolf (1969a), Scott (1977a), and Paige (1975) alike tend to envisage revolutions as (in one way or another) made by class forces—although Wolf, it is true, does begin to bring states, parties, and armies into the picture in ways alluded to above. Certainly Jeffery Paige strives mightily for pure economic and class reductionism. Reformist, socialist, nationalist, and Communist parties abound in his empirical data and illustrative historical accounts, but such parties are never there as independent variables, only as indicators of economically determined political conflicts. Agrarian income sources and class relations are supposed to explain reforms, revolts, and revolutionary movements. Despite his sharp differences with Paige, James Scott also belittles the causal importance of political organizations in peasant revolutions. Scott grants that a "revolution to be successful may . . . require a disciplined party or army in addition to an aroused peasantry" (1977a: 292) because only such extra-peasant forces can provide "the coordination and tactical vision" (1977a: 294) necessary to overcome peasant fragmentation and achieve national state power. Scott nevertheless celebrates the indispensable revolutionary force of autonomous peasant violence. He maintains that "the spontaneous action of the peasantry in many revolutionary movements . . . has forced the issue and mobilized its would-be leadership . . ." (Scott, 1977a: 295), adding that "more often than not it has been the autonomous . . . action of the peasantry that has *created* the revolutionary situations . . ." (Scott, 1977a: 295–96). Institutionalization of peasant politics, argues Scott, is very likely to undercut revolution: "There is . . . no a priori reason for assuming that the outside leadership of the peasantry will be more militant than its clientele. . . . In fact, one would expect that the more organized, the more hierarchical, and the more institutionalized a peasant . . . movement becomes . . . the more likely it will become woven into the established tapestry of power" (Scott, 1977a: 296).

In contrast, Joel Migdal asserts that the peasant revolutions of the twentieth century have been propelled by armed revolutionary parties that have directly mobilized peasant support. Such "revolutionary movements," Migdal points out, "are created by the impetus of those from outside the peasant class . . . . [T]he participation of peasants in revolutionary organizations is preceded by the development of an organizational superstructure by students, intellectuals, and disaffected members of the middle class" (Migdal, 1974: 232). To be sure, peasants must also be involved in the revolutionary process. Yet for Migdal the issue is not how agrarian class relations themselves generate revolutionary movements, nor how peasant spontaneity creates revolutionary situations and prods radical elites to make revolutions. Rather, Migdal seeks to explain how social exchanges between revolutionary parties and local peasant populations can be established— exchanges so stable and mutually rewarding as to account for sustained peasant support and "participation in institutionalized revolutionary movements" (Migdal, 1974: 228–29).

Underlying Migdal's approach to peasant revolutionary involvement is his strong belief that twentieth-century peasant revolutions differ fundamentally from revolutions and revolts in previous times: "In the last fifty years, peasants in certain areas have engaged in prolonged national struggles to change the system of government and the distribution of power. These movements have not been based on a sudden burst of violence after frustration has built as was often true of the spasmodic, anomic peasant rebellions of past centuries. Rather, peasants in these cases have engaged in long drawn-out revolutions in a variety of institutionalized ways—as political cadres, as disciplined soldiers, as loyal suppliers of food, money, and shelter, and as active and passive members of a host of revolutionary organizations and groups" (Migdal, 1974: 226). "Why," Migdal wonders, "has the character of . . . [peasant] participation changed from the more eruptive, anomic qualities of the French Revolution . . . and the Russian Revolution to the organized aspects of the Chinese and Vietnamese Revolutions?" (Migdal, 1974: 227). Migdal never answers this question very satisfactorily. His book argues at length that peasants in the twentieth-century Third World face an unprecedented economic crisis due to pressures from imperialism. Participation in organized revolutionary movements which offer programs to address local peasant problems is said to be one way that peasants can try to cope with the unprecedented crisis. But Migdal never compares, for example, prerevolutionary French and Russian peasants to Chinese and Vietnamese peasants. He does not show that the economic difficulties faced by these two sets of peasants were different in ways that could explain "anomic" versus "institutionalized" forms of revolutionary participation.

Even if Migdal fails to explain adequately why peasants have historically participated in revolutions in different ways, he still points toward a distinction that needs to be made. The distinction is *not* really between twentieth-century and pre-twentieth-century peasant-based revolutions. Migdal is mistaken to argue that peasants participated in the French and Russian Revolutions as "eruptive" masses of "anomic" frustrated individuals. On the contrary, peasants in those revolutions were well organized at local levels and pursued their goals in a very determined, sustained fashion over a period of years (see Skocpol, 1979: ch. 3).

The same can be said for the village-based supporters of Emiliano Zapata in the Mexican Revolution, which also fits the same overall pattern as the French and Russian cases (see Wolf, 1969a: ch. 1). The pattern of these revolutions has been one of the breakdown of the old-regime state, followed by widespread local peasant revolts that undercut landed upper classes and conservative political forces. Organized revolutionaries have then consolidated new state organizations, *not* by politically mobilizing the peasantry, but rather by more or less coercively imposing administrative and military controls on the countryside.

A contrasting pattern of peasant-based revolution is exemplified by the Chinese, Vietnamese (and perhaps Cuban) Revolutions, and by the revolutionary anticolonial movements of Portuguese Africa.[12] Here peasants have been directly mobilized by organized revolutionary movements, either before (Cuba; Portuguese Africa) or after (China; Vietnam) the collapse of effective state power in the preexisting regime. Because of this direct mobilization, peasant resources and manpower have ended up participating in the build up of new-regime social institutions and state organizations. Peasant participation in this revolutionary pattern is less spontaneous and autonomous than in the first pattern. But the results can be much more favorable to local peasant interests, because during the revolutionary process itself direct links are established between peasants and revolutionary political and military organizations.[13]

Once we make the distinction between these two alternative scenarios for peasant-based revolutions, many apparent disagreements among scholars about such issues as "which peasants are revolutionary" and "what roles are played by organized political forces" tend to dissolve. Basic explanatory questions can also be sorted out in terms of their applicability to one pattern or the other. It should be clear that autonomous peasant villages are more likely to play a pivotal role in the first revolutionary pattern, where widespread local revolts accelerate the downfall of the old regime and *indirectly* condition the consolidation of the new regime. Without being willing to call them revolutionary, Jeffery Paige (1975) describes instances of this pattern under his category of "agrarian revolt." Moreover, much of what Eric Wolf (1969a) has to say in his "Conclusion" and virtually all of what James Scott has to say in "Hegemony and the Peasantry" (1977a) fits this first pattern of peasant-based revolution. By contrast, Joel Migdal (1974) deals mainly with the second pattern, as does Paige (1975) in his "revolutionary nationalism" category.

When peasants are directly mobilized into revolutionary politics (according to the second pattern), then autonomous villages are not causally important. What is more, many different kinds of peasants—subsistence smallholders in marginal areas; landless laborers or tenants; even solidary villages of peasants, or else of landlords and peasants together—can potentially be mobilized by revolutionary movements. In my view, there has been too much of a tendency in the literature to suppose that the adherence of peasants to organized revolutionary movements must be explained by the economic interests and social circumstances of the peasants themselves. Even Joel Migdal succumbs to this tendency when he argues

(1974: 229–30) that peasants undergoing the most rapid, disruptive exposure to newly penetrating market forces will be the ones most likely to respond to organized political movements that offer solutions to their market-induced woes. But there is no reason at all to suppose that peasants in traditional social structures are free from experiences of poverty, class exploitation, and political insecurity.[14] There is no reason why organized revolutionary movements, once on the scene, cannot appeal to many different kinds of agrarian cultivators, including traditional ones. This certainly was what the Vietnamese Communists succeeded in doing: in mountainous areas, they mobilized minority ethnic groups, peasants and notables together, by appealing to their fears of ethnic exploitation; in northern Vietnam, they mobilized peasants by displacing the French and by shoving aside within the communal villages exploitative landlords and Confucian notables; and in southern Vietnam they mobilized peasants, including Paige's rice sharecroppers, by seizing and redistributing large land holdings and by organizing local associations to support peasant livelihood and defend their possession of the redistributed land.[15]

Insofar as the occurrence—or success—of peasant-based revolution depends upon the direct mobilization of peasants by revolutionary movements, then the sheer availability and viability of such movements becomes decisive—just as much as the condition of the peasants themselves. Migdal, in fact, correctly points out that a crucial "factor determining the probability of peasants' participation in revolutionary movements is the degree to which revolutionary leadership appears, with an organizational framework capable of absorbing peasants and then expanding power through their recruitment" (Migdal, 1974: 232). Moreover, given that "revolutionary movements are created by the impetus of those . . . outside the peasant class," Migdal admits that "exogenous factors," beyond the scope of his analysis of peasant villages per se, "determine in which countries such outside revolutionaries will appear and where they will provide a high degree of revolutionary leadership in those countries in which they do appear" (Migdal, 1974: 232, 235).

Perhaps the most important questions to ask about the emergence and growth of institutionalized revolutionary alliances between peasants, on the one hand, and political parties and armies, on the other, refer not to the peasants themselves, but to the circumstances that produce organized revolutionaries and allow them to operate effectively in the countryside. Under what social-structural and world-historical conditions have nationalist and/or Communist parties emerged *and become willing and able to address themselves to rural populations*? Have colonial situations been more amenable to this development than neocolonial situations? How have variations in colonial situations and processes of decolonization helped to produce or inhibit the formation of agrarian revolutionary alliances? What social-structural, historical, and (even) cultural factors can help us understand why Asian Communists have been more willing to attempt peasant mobilization than have, say, Latin American Communists or Communists in Moslem countries? Answers to questions such as these may turn out to explain more about the occurrence of peasant-based revolutions of the second pattern than any amount of investigation of the peasant situation as such.[16] For impoverished and exploited peasants in many places may potentially be amenable to revolutionary mobilization—if a revolutionary organization can establish itself with some minimal security in the countryside, and if its cadres can address peasant needs successfully. But this process cannot begin to get underway unless such a revolutionary leadership emerges in colonial or national politics, finds itself unable to achieve power in the cities alone, and proves militarily and politically capable of operating in the countryside.

Once a political movement is in contact with the countryside, there may be only some possible policies that will work to mobilize the peasantry, given on the one side—the constraints faced by revolutionaries—and on the other side—the specific features of local class, community, and political arrangements among the peasantry. In Joel Migdal's book (1974: chs. 9–10), reformist, conservative, and revolutionary political organizations are treated as if they make the same kinds of appeals to the peasantry—namely, the offering of selective economic incentives to individuals and small groups. To some extent this may be true. Yet, compared to nonrevolutionary politicians, revolutionaries may offer distinctive kinds of benefits to peasants, and they certainly demand more costly kinds of support from peasants in return. Nonrevolutionary politicians are well advised to offer modest, economic benefits to particular individuals and subgroups, playing them off against others *within* the peasantry. Revolutionaries must attempt to stimulate demand for, and then supply, more *collective* benefits (even if just at local levels). *Class* benefits—such as redistributed land or local political power—can tend to unite peasants against landlords. *Security* benefits—such as village defense against counterrevolutionary military forces—can also broadly unite peasants. Insofar as revolutionaries can organize and lead peasants by providing such benefits, they can, in turn, profit from the willingness of peasants to act together in defense of the collective benefits. Then, on the basis of such willingness, the revolutionaries can ask for major sacrifices of resources and manpower from the peasantry—in order to sustain the extra-local party and army organizations that are indispensable to win national state power. Thus, Joel Migdal is undoubtedly right to analyze the process of institutionalization of a peasant-based revolutionary movement as an exchange between revolutionary politicians and peasants. But he could have suggested good reasons why this revolutionary exchange—much more than reformist or conservative exchanges—probably has to take place on the basis of collective benefits for the peasants.[17]

If the above points are true, then we can understand the kind of dilemma faced by organized revolutionaries if and when they attempt to operate in the countryside. The revolutionaries must discover or create among the peasantry the demand for collective benefits. They must be able to supply the relevant benefits with great sensitivity to the specific features of local political and social arrangements. All of this must be done without getting themselves and their initial supporters killed or driven away. And not until after such delicate and dangerous political work has been completed can the revolutionaries expect to benefit greatly from widespread peasant support.

It is hard to imagine the successful institutionalization of such social exchange between peasants and revolutionaries except in places and times unusually free from counterrevolutionary state repression. Marginal, inaccessible geographical areas are the most suitable places for the process to begin, but for it to spread and succeed, no doubt exogenous events must intervene to drastically weaken the existing state power. Just as such developments in the realm of the state must occur to create a revolutionary situation in the first pattern of peasant-based revolution, so must they occur in the second pattern to facilitate the institutionalization of peasant participation in the organized revolutionary movement. In both patterns of revolution, defeats in wars and international military interventions are the most likely ways for existing state power to be disrupted—opening the way either for autonomous peasant revolts, or for appeals by organized revolutionaries to peasant support in the countryside.

Our second question—what roles do political and military organizations play in peasant-based revolutions?—has brought us far from the immediate circumstances of the peasantry. State power, it turns out, plays a decisive role in limiting the possibilities for emergence and success of such revolutions. Moreover, organized (political and military) revolutionary movements play crucial roles in peasant-based revolutions, but in alternative ways. Either they consolidate revolutionary new regimes separately from, and in necessary tension with, the peasantry, or they directly mobilize peasant support to defeat counterrevolutionaries and consolidate the new regime. Peasant participation is a pivotal arbiter of revolutionary success in both patterns, yet—ironically—peasants are politically autonomous collective actors only in the pattern where developments in the realms of the state and organized national politics go on "above their heads." In the other pattern— Joel Migdal's pattern of "institutionalized" peasant revolution—organized revolutionary movements are the key collective actors, as they struggle politically to bridge the gap between peasants and the national state.

Having come this far from the peasantry itself, we must now in a sense step back still further—into the sphere of the world political economy. For the third—and last—organizing question directs our attention to the great emphasis placed by our authors on capitalist imperialism as a world-historical impetus to peasant-based revolutions.

Does Capitalist Imperialism Cause Peasant-based Revolution—and, if so, How?

In *Social Origins of Dictatorship and Democracy*, Barrington Moore explained peasant revolts and revolutions by looking, first, at the structural vulnerability to peasant insurrections of different kinds of premodern agrarian sociopolitical orders. Then he investigated how, in "the process of modernization itself" (Moore,

1966: 459), different degrees and forms of agricultural commercialization could enhance or preclude possibilities for peasant revolts against landed upper classes. Like Moore, three out of four of the scholars under consideration here—Wolf, Migdal, and Paige—seek to generalize about the macro-structural and world-historical contexts that promote peasant-based revolutions.[18] Yet, whereas the relevant context for Moore consisted of variously structured agrarian states undergoing commercialization and industrialization in alternative possible ways, the macro-historical context for Wolf, Migdal, and Paige is envisaged in global rather than cross-national terms. In one way or another, each of these authors stresses *imperialistic Western capitalism* as the fundamental promoter of peasant revolutions. The—not insignificant—differences among them have to do with exactly how this world-historical force is conceived and the specific ways in which it influences or creates potentially revolutionary peasant forces.

For Eric Wolf (1969a) the "peasant rebellions of the twentieth century are no longer simple responses to local problems. . . . They are . . . parochial reactions to major social dislocations, set in motion by overwhelming societal changes" (Wolf, 1969a: 295). The agent of change is "a great overriding cultural phenomenon, the world-wide spread and diffusion of a particular cultural system, that of North Atlantic capitalism" (Wolf, 1969a: 276). Wolf sees the spread of North Atlantic capitalism primarily as the impingement of market economics upon precapitalist societies in which "before the advent of capitalism . . . social equilibrium depended in both the long and short run on a balance of transfers of peasant surpluses to the rulers and the provision of a minimal security to the cultivator" (Wolf, 1969a: 279). Intrusive capitalism has upset the prior balances: peasant populations have increased markedly, even as peasants have lost secure access to their lands and been transformed into "economic actors, independent of prior social commitments to kin and neighbors" (Wolf, 1969a: 279). Simultaneously, there has occurred "still another—and equally serious—repercussion . . . a crisis in the exercise of power" (Wolf, 1969a: 282). For the spreading market has created more distant and exploitative relationships between peasants and their traditional overlords, whether tribal chiefs, mandarins, or landed noblemen. And it has also created partial openings for new kinds of elites—entrepreneurs, credit merchants, political brokers, intellectuals, and professionals. Out of this disequilibrated transitional situation peasant revolutions have sometimes emerged. Specifically, they have happened when a political fusion has occurred between armed organizations of one marginal kind of new elite—the "new literati" of intellectuals and professionals—and "the dissatisfied peasants whom the market created, but for whom society made no adequate social provision" (Wolf, 1969a: 288–89). Thus peasant revolutions are for Eric Wolf one possible resolution of the profound societal disequilibria caused for preindustrial populations, elites and peasantries alike, by the worldwide expansion of North Atlantic capitalism.

Joel Migdal's (1974) vision of the forces at work to prompt potential revolutionary involvement by peasants in the Third World is not greatly different from Eric Wolf's—but there are two distinctive nuances in Migdal's approach. First, in contrast to Wolf's broad focus on society as a whole, Migdal looks more narrowly and in greater depth at peasant villages as such. Migdal's basic argument is that peasants in the twentieth-century Third World have been undergoing a disruptive economic transition from predominant "inward orientation"—marked by subsistence agriculture and strong communal and patronage controls—to greatly increased "outward orientation"—marked by the substantial involvement of individual peasants and households with extra-local "multiplier mechanisms: markets, cash, and wage labor" (Migdal, 1974: 87). According to Migdal, traditional peasant villages remained "inwardly oriented" in order to give their members assured, minimal security in the face of exploitative overlords and uncertain ecological conditions. When recurrent crises did strike, moreover, traditional peasants attempted to protect themselves through greater selfexploitation and reliance upon patrons or communal ties. Only an extraordinary crisis of unparalleled impact and continuity could push peasants into greater "outward orientation" in their economic behavior.

Like Wolf, Migdal sees the roots of this crisis in the worldwide expansion from the eighteenth century of the capitalist-industrial West. Yet—and here is the second distinctive feature in Migdal's argument—he especially highlights the *political mediation* of that expansion. Migdal speaks of "imperialism" rather than of "capitalism" or "markets" as the prime force promoting changes within and between nations. And he portrays disruptive changes—such as population growth following from public health programs, and increased market penetration due to tax impositions, transportation improvements and legalized land transfers—as resulting primarily from increases in state controls over formerly locally-autonomous peasant villages. "Imperialism," says Migdal, "caused a reorganization of societies' centers, enabling them to achieve new levels of efficiency in the transfer of wealth from the peripheries. Direct colonial rule or indirect imperial domination led to vast increases in the state's power through more effective administrative techniques. Bureaucracies were more complex and coherent and, as a result, were able to penetrate rural areas on a much broader spectrum than previously" (Migdal, 1974: 92). Because of the increasingly "outward" economic orientation that many peasants have been forced to adopt in response to the changes wrought by strengthened states, Third World peasants have found themselves at the mercy of extra-local economic conditions which leave them insecure or exploited within the national society and world economy. As a result, Migdal argues, they become potential supporters of political parties and movements, from conservative, to reformist, to revolutionary.

Predictably, Jeffery Paige (1975) understands the global forces promoting what he calls "agrarian" revolutions differently from Wolf and Migdal. What interests Paige is not the external impact of "North Atlantic capitalism" upon precapitalist agrarian societies, but the *new kinds* of economic enclaves—agricultural export zones—created within underdeveloped countries by world markets in agricultural commodities. Indeed, according to Paige, "the economy of the typical underdeveloped country can be described as an agricultural export sector and its indirect effects" (Paige, 1975: 2). In the newly formed commercial zones lie the seeds of contemporary agrarian revolutions. Without completely discounting the involvement of other social and political forces in recent revolutions, Paige maintains that the "relationship of the rural population to the new forms of class cleavage and class conflict introduced by the agricultural export economy is essential in understanding the origin of . . . agrarian unrest in the developing world" (Paige, 1975: 3). Class conflicts in export agriculture have come to the fore since World War II, because political conditions have been propitious: "The strength of colonial and imperial political controls long prevented the political expression of these conflicts, but with the decline of colonial power in the postwar era, the commercial export sectors of the underdeveloped world have become centers of revolutionary social movements" (Paige, 1975: 3).[19] In sum, whereas Wolf and Migdal see peasants in the contemporary Third World *reacting to encroaching world capitalism*, with their local revolts or attachments to national political movements sometimes producing revolutions as part of this reaction, Paige sees agrarian cultivators *reacting from within the capitalist world economy* to overthrow landed upper classes heretofore dependent upon colonial or imperial state coercion for their survival.

The differences between Wolf and Migdal, on the one side, and Paige on the other, may seem worthy of extended discussion and adjudication, but I propose to step quickly around them. For if the arguments of parts one and two of this essay are valid, then both camps may be saying partially correct things about the ways in which globally expanding capitalism (or imperialism) has helped to cause peasant-based revolutions. The historical record certainly seems to affirm that *both* peasants economically or politically threatened by newly penetrating capitalist forces, and agrarian cultivators involved in export-agricultural production have been—alternatively, or simultaneously—constituents of peasant-based revolutions. In Vietnam, for example, the revolution gained support from northern peasants resentful of French colonial controls, and also from southern peasants set in opposition to the great landlords who dominated the export-oriented rice economy. The Vietnamese Communists were able to sink roots in both groups, drawing from them resources to wage prolonged revolutionary war.

More interesting to me than the disagreements among Wolf, Migdal, and Paige are the shared features of the ways they think about the role of imperialist capitalism in promoting peasant-based revolutions. Despite their considerable differences, all three authors emphasize imperialism's *commercializing* influence upon agrarian societies and peasant life. Through this emphasis upon agrarian commercialization, the views of these primarily Third World–oriented authors end up meshing well with the more Old World–oriented analysis of Barrington Moore (1966). Capitalist commercialization either develops endogenously as Moore portrays it, or it is imposed from without as Wolf, Migdal, and Paige suggest. Commercialization promotes peasant-based revolution by creating new social strata prone to revolution (as Paige would have it). Or it arouses peasants to defensive revolts by intensifying exploitation and weakening traditional dominant strata (as Moore, Wolf, and Migdal would have it). Thus, commercialization—perhaps endogenously generated, perhaps induced by imperialist capitalism—is envisaged as promoting peasant-based revolutions, because of its effects on agrarian class relations and peasant communities.

But even if everyone seems in cozy agreement about the prime causal role (if not the exact forms and effects) of capitalist commercialization, there is still room to doubt whether such commercialization is a necessary cause—or even an essential concomitant—of peasant-based revolution. Take the Chinese Revolution, undoubtedly socially based in the peasantry. Although scholars disagree, many believe that Chinese agriculture was *not* on the whole any more commercialized in the first half of the twentieth century than it had been for centuries before (see Elvin, 1973; Perkins, 1969; Skinner 1964–65). Certainly the northern areas of China, where the Communists eventually developed their deepest ties to the peasantry, were not highly commercialized relative to other parts of China; nor had these areas experienced significant modernizing changes. The most important changes for the worse experienced by Chinese peasants between 1911 and 1949 were huge increases in taxation and violations of physical security. These woes were due to intense civil warfare followed by foreign military invasions by the Japanese. By addressing the issues of taxes and security, and by transforming longstanding local political and class relations between peasants and landlords, the Chinese Communists were able to mobilize peasant support for their revolutionary acquisition of state power. In all of this there is no indication that increased agrarian commercialization—whether endogenously generated or due to imperialist penetration—was the decisive cause of peasant involvement in the Chinese Revolution.

With the strong emphasis on capitalist imperialism as a promoter of increased agrarian commercialization, another aspect of imperialism has been relatively neglected. Expanding North Atlantic capitalism has, since its inception, had enormous impact upon inter-state relations and the politics of lagging countries. In the second section of this essay, we established that suspensions of state coercive power have been necessary to every successful peasant-based revolution, and that revolutionary political parties willing and able to mobilize the peasantry have been central to many such revolutions. Therefore, it obviously stands to reason that imperialism may have helped to promote peasant-based revolutions not simply because of its economic effects on peasants but also because of its effects on states and organized politics.

What sorts of effects on states and politics? Both the Chinese and the Vietnamese Revolutions point to relevant ones. In the Chinese case, defeats in wars and steady encroachments on Chinese sovereignty by Western capitalist nations and by Japan pushed the Manchu rulers into reforms that led to conflicts with the landed gentry. Out of these conflicts grew the Revolution of 1911 and the subsequent dissolution of the imperial state. In turn, foreign ideologies and models of party organization facilitated the emergence of revolutionary movements among educated urban Chinese. And finally, during World War II, military conflicts between the Chinese Guomindang government and the Japanese, and between the United States and Japan, opened the geopolitical space needed by the Communists to mobilize the peasants of North China for social revolution and military victory (see Skocpol, 1979: 67–80, 147–54, and ch. 7).

In Vietnam, French imperialism conquered and colonized the country. The direct effects on the peasantry were very great—mediated in the North especially by colonial tax exactions (as Joel Migdal's theory would emphasize) and mediated in the South especially by export-oriented agriculture (as Jeffery Paige's theory would emphasize). Yet the Vietnamese Revolution also grew out of the impact of colonialism upon the politics of indigenous middle-class Vietnamese who received modern educations yet were denied important elite posts in the French-dominated colonial state. Nationalist and revolutionary political movements were the predictable result. Still, the progress, even survival, of these movements depended upon a weakening of French power—and that came only with the inter-imperialist military rivalries of World War II. The Japanese captured colonial Vietnam and in 1945 displaced the Vichy French administrators, only themselves to face defeat soon thereafter at the hands of the United States and Britain. The disruptions—and ultimate vacuum—of state power during World War II gave the Vietnamese Communists an ideal opportunity to claim the nationalist mantle, to assert sovereignty on the heels of the departing Japanese, and finally to mobilize Vietnamese peasants (especially in the North) to resist France's attempt to reimpose colonial control (see McAlister, 1971: pts. 4–8; Dunn, 1972: ch. 5).

Thus, the *military and political reverberations* of imperialist expansion contributed crucially to the emergence and success of the Chinese and Vietnamese Revolutions. Without the breakdown of the imperial and colonial regimes, without the emergence of organized revolutionary parties, and without the openings created for them by inter-imperialist military rivalries, the peasants of China and Vietnam could not have been mobilized for revolution. And given the local agrarian structures of China and Vietnam, the peasants could not have become revolutionary in the absence of direct mobilization.

In *States and Social Revolutions* (1979), I analyzed the causes and outcomes of three revolutions—the French, Russian, and Chinese—also discussed by Barrington Moore in *Social Origins* (1966). My approach placed much greater emphasis than Moore's on the relationships among states, and on relationships between state organizations and social classes, including the peasantry. Capitalist development figured in my analysis more as a motor of inter-state competition, and as a propellant of changing relations between states and classes, than it did as an agent of commercialization and market penetration. Imperialism has been seen as promoting peasant-based revolutions primarily through the effects of agrarian commercialization in Third World countries. Yet the impacts of globally expanding capitalism on states and politics in the Third World may have been equally or more important—the touchstone case of Vietnam suggests as much. Perhaps, therefore, future analyses of the role of capitalist imperialism in causing and shaping peasant-based revolutions in the Third World could profit from taking the kind of state-centered approach used in *States and Social Revolutions*.

Capitalism's global expansion has, to be sure, encroached upon and remade traditional agrarian class relations. Yet that expansion has also been accompanied by colonization and decolonization, and by a continuation of the inter-state military rivalries that marked capitalism's European birthplace, even in feudal times. Peasant-based revolutions—in which peasant revolts or mobilization become pivotal in intertwined class and national-state transformations—have grown not only out of capitalist agrarian commercialization. Such revolutions have emerged more invariably out of occasionally favorable political situations shaped in large part by the inter-state dynamics of the modern world-capitalist era. For these dynamics have, at crucial conjunctures, weakened indigenous or colonial state controls over the peasantry. Moreover, they have often allowed, even impelled, revolutionary political movements to forge new relationships with the mass of the peasantry. Only in favorable political circumstances such as these, has the insurrectionary potential of peasants—whether traditionalist or commercializing, landed or landless—actually been able to propel revolutionary transformations.

Conclusion

"Before looking at the peasant," Barrington Moore wrote in *Social Origins*, "it is necessary to look at the whole society" (Moore, 1966: 457). His point is amplified by Michael Adas in the Introduction to *Prophets of Rebellion*, a recent comparative investigation of millenarian peasant-based protests against European colonialism: "When I first conceived this study," writes Adas, "I intended to focus specifically on peasant protest, but as I gathered evidence it became clear that elite groups played key roles in the genesis and development of these movements" (Adas, 1979: xxv). The burden of this review of recent scholarship on peasant-based revolution has been that, here as well, peasants are only part of the story. Too close a focus on peasants themselves, even on peasants within local agrarian class and community structures, cannot allow us to understand peasant-based revolutions.

A holistic frame of reference is indispensable, one that includes states, class structures, and transnational economic and military relations. Ironically, of the four students of peasants and revolutions whose works have been reviewed here, only Eric Wolf (1969a)—the one who wrote earliest and least theoretically—comes close to a suitably holistic analysis. Since Wolf—and since Barrington Moore's *Social Origins* (1966)—the tendency among scholars has been to look more narrowly (if also often more systematically) at peasants and agrarian economies, seeking broad theoretical generalizations about peasant politics from that level of analysis alone. Much of value has been learned about agrarian class relations and peasant communities. But an integrated explanation of peasant involvement in revolutions, from the eighteenth-century French Revolution to the anticolonial revolutions of the mid-twentieth century, has not yet been achieved.

No doubt such an explanation can only be developed in conjunction with explanations of other forms of peasant-based political protest (and its absence or failure) in various epochs of world history. Yet as we move forward, we will do well to keep in mind a basic truth: during all the centuries of peasant existence from ancient to modern times, the forms of revolt open to peasants, as well as the political results conceivably achievable by peasant protests, have been powerfully shaped by the stakes of political struggles, domestic and intersocietal, going on within the ranks of the dominant strata. Peasant revolutions are not at all an exception to this enduring truth. They are, indeed, its fullest and most modern expression.

Acknowledgment

This essay is an extended and modified version of an article that originally appeared in *Comparative Politics*, 14, 3 (1982).

9. Afterword: Peasantries and the Rural Sector— Notes on a Discovery

Sidney W. Mintz

The papers in this volume suggest the benefits of a cooperative undertaking as wide-ranging in academic discipline as it is in historical epoch and in geography. Among fields of inquiry which might benefit from interdisciplinary effort, the study of the peasantry should stand high. It was the peasantry—and, in particular, its capacity to initiate radical political transformations—that brought together so many different specialists to exchange insights and to seek common analytical ground. Perhaps it is worth taking note where anthropology, which proposes to be the study of all humankind, fits in.

It has been the changing field of vision of modern anthropology that has gradually allowed the rural sector of certain countries—even those not usually studied by social scientists—to come into view, and hence, figuratively at least, to be discovered. Thus, for instance, in good measure it was Robert Redfield's *Tepoztlán* (1930) which brought anthropology into the Mexican countryside. Redfield was not dealing with people who were "tribal" in any convincing sense; yet they were those villagers among whom Mexico's "tribal" peoples lived and worked. It is important, I believe, that *Tepoztlán*, in spite of its many limitations, was published more than half a century ago, thereby documenting a recognition by anthropologists of "rural people," or "the folk," or "the peasantry," at a relatively early point in the discipline's history.

At the same time, however, anthropology has never made the study of the world's peasantries part of its platform as a field-oriented profession. It has instead continued to stress our continuing lack of sufficient information about "simpler" peoples, our original commitment to the study of "primitives," and— justifiably, I believe—the urgency of these tasks in a world being homogenized and scourged of primitive peoples with frightening speed (see, for instance, Lévi-Strauss, 1966). But that the rural sectors the existence of which was signalled by studies like Redfield's have remained in some degree still unremarked, as well as unstudied, is also anthropology's problem.

Silverman (1979) has called attention to anthropologists' lack of interest in the study of peasantries until the 1930s in the United States, and even later elsewhere. In the encounter between anthropologists and rural people living within the reach of big, old civilizations (usually of the sort commonly referred to during the Victorian era as decaying—like China, India, Burma, etc.), anthropological studies of the peasantry seemed for long to have been almost accidental in character. To study tribal people—like the Karen or the Kachin, rather than nontribal villagers in Burma, or tribal people like the Huichols or Tarahumaras in Mexico, rather than nontribal villagers there—must have been clear (if not always wholly conscious) choices. They were choices consistent with anthropology's older objectives, and entirely defensible. But if they have become less so, I would contend it is not only because the world is changing.

Anthropology commonly drew distinctions between "primitive" peoples on the one hand, and the rural poor—the "folk" in contrast to the elite—of European national states, on the other. This contrast (expressed in German, for instance, in the contrasting terms *Völkerkunde* and *Volkskunde*) tended to separate the West, with its own state structures and classes, and its histories of itself, from the non-Western world. "Primitive" peoples inhabited niches or zones within that non-Western world, and were to be both anthropology's sole concern, and her monopoly—or so the contrast between "primitive" peoples and their neighbors seemed to imply. But I suspect that this view beclouded the important fact that "villagers" and "primitives" often shared the same space, both geographically and, in some regards, in their relationships to outside forces—such as state power and international interests—as well. Of course this has not always been nor is it always the case; the degree to which "villagers" and "primitives" might be exposed to such forces and the nature of these controls and influence have varied greatly. But whether one has in mind the villagers and "Montagnards" of Vietnam, or the villagers and "tribal nomads" (e.g., Qaeshqai, Turkoman, Bakhtiari, etc.) of Iran, the lines between these groups have sometimes been drawn with misleading firmness.

This is not to argue that the villager-primitive distinction is fundamentally erroneous. No useful purpose is served by merging categories which distinguish genuine cultural or structural differences, in relation to outside forces as in all else. But what we know of the ways in which ethnic categories can both take shape and dissolve; of the ways groups can attach themselves to each other, thereby becoming what thay were not before; of the consequences of prior relationships, real or contrived, for group self-consciousness—what we know of these matters should warn us against prior assumptions about contact or its absence.

Barth and his students argue that ethnicity inheres more in structural than in cultural features (Barth, 1970). Other observers (Gregory, 1976; Mintz, 1968; Nagata, 1974; Wallerstein, 1973) have pointed to the fluid, changeable nature of ethnic identity itself. This does not mean, of course, that group differences are trivial or nonexistent. How groups of rural people are defined, divided, or united is one of the principal problems that anthropological research should address. But nonhistorical assumptions about group differences are open to question, particularly if research is premised on their supposed accuracy. Cultural differences should not be allowed to obscure other sorts of relationships between groups. In fact, the intersection of culturally different rural sectors may be a critical locus for eventually understanding better the nature of different forms of peasant protest.

I am unable to provide a thorough example for this assertion; but the point may be made quite simply. During fieldwork in Iran in 1966–1967, I spent time in a

Turkic-speaking Qaeshqai village in Fars Province, the members of which had been recently settled at the behest of their khan, not far from ancient villages of Farsi-speaking non-Qaeshqai. Contact between the tribespeople and their nontribal neighbors was still limited, but growing. Qaeshqai interest in modern agriculture was more intense, the attitudes toward change seemingly more open than in the surrounding Persian villages. Whereas Qaeshqai political attitudes toward the government had previously been couched in tribal terms, I was able to collect some evidence that the complaints of these newly-settled tribespeople were taking on a rural-urban or class-based character. I would argue that, along the edge of contact between these culturally distinguishable groups, new processes of self-identification were being set in motion, largely dictated by forces emanating from outside the communities themselves. By treating Qaeshqai and Farsi-speaking villagers as two separate categories, however, counterposed and defined by contrast, one runs the risk of building into one's analysis distinctions that cloak, rather than reveal, the nature of change. But perhaps this can be said in a different way.

Almost until the eve of World War II, North American anthropology had shown itself to be quite strikingly traditional in regard to the peoples it studied, the reasons given for their study, and the role of history in such studies. A determined effort was made to recapture pasts almost entirely effaced. History meant both the succession of events in the life of a people, and their view of these events; but it only rarely meant the history of contact and destruction.

In most cases, an image of peoples who, few in numbers and simple in technology, both bound and divided by ties of blood and locality—peoples whose societies could be explained in terms of themselves—prevailed. Such were thought to be the societies whose variability of belief, custom, and behavior might give us the total spectrum of human possibilities, thereby making anthropology into a true comparative science. Of course it was recognized that even these peoples were changing, and always had been changing. Yet change usually figured very little in their study. Though North American examples of this rather static and enclosed approach are numerous, perhaps the best example is provided by Bronislaw Malinowski, by any measure one of the greatest ethnographers who ever lived. Malinowski refers quite frankly to his failure to deal with "the changing native" in his monumental studies of the Trobriand Islands, calling it "the most serious shortcoming of my whole anthropological research in Melanesia" (Malinowski, 1965 [1935], 1: 481). Yet it is not the failure to report change that seems most serious to me in this connection, so much as the failure to *see* it; and I believe that this failure largely arose from the way societies were classed and conceived of by most anthropologists.

On the traditional side of anthropology, the "primitive" side, the peoples who were studied were typified by a wide variety of recognized sociological features such as rank, gender-based distinctions, differential privilege, differential access to spouses, and widely varying statuses. Generally speaking they were not thought to have classes, and with good reason. But without classes, they could hardly have had class conflict. This is not to say, of course, that conflicts between and among groups in so-called primitive societies were unknown or unnoticed. But the processes by which such peoples become "modern"—which has often meant, among other things, becoming members of classes by virtue of economic relationships imposed upon them from outside—were not always seen for what they were. Moreover, the display of discontent by members of such groups often did not take a familiar form, and cultural differences may have helped to conceal what was happening. But commonly this discontent has been expressed in movements, ostensibly religious, led by members of such societies whose relationships to the outside were more developed, more knowing, and more sophisticated, than those of their neighbors. Wovoka, the Owens Valley Paiute called Jack Wilson, who is famous for having initiated the second Ghost Dance, spoke English, had been partly raised by a white settler, and was noticeably "acculturated" (Mooney, 1896). Evara, the inventor of the Vailala Madness, was wearing a white duck coat with a 1919 Victory Medal when F. E. Williams (1923) first saw him, and his prophecies were heavily "westernized," as Worsley's insightful study (1957) makes clear.

In many such instances, it appears to be the least "primitive" of the "primitives" who most effectively articulate politically the hidden (and misapprehended) discontent of the people. Perhaps anthropologists have not been sufficiently quick to see that such protests bridged the chasm between primitive and civilized precisely because even earlier bridges had already been laid down in the opposite direction. In other words, I am suggesting that modern forms of protest may be linked to the wrenching insertion of "primitive peoples" into the activities of bandit capitalism, though these have generally been regarded as simply other instances of "revitalization" (Wallace, 1966).

By these assertions I certainly do not mean to reduce the study of culture contact to an analysis of class formation, or the many-stranded process of change it can initiate to its economic and political elements. But the primitive/villager distinction can, I believe, conceal certain subtly changing aspects of rural life. In many of the world's societies, peoples of the sort called primitive or tribal and those of the sort called peasant stand in dynamic, ongoing relationships to each other and do not (or only variably do) form wholly separate categories. From the perspective of their daily lives—no matter what they are thought to be by their governments, or by the social scientists who study them—they may intersect in particularly important ways, not readily understood by the outside observer, and possibly not even fully understood by the peoples themselves. Accordingly, if we begin their study with categories that implicitly define their relationships to each other, we may very well be starting out just where we ought to be ending up, after our research.

My point here, then, is that rural has meant different things in different places. What it actually does mean will depend to some extent upon the kind, extent, variability, and duration of the penetration from the outside, as well as upon the preexisting groups and their cultures. To the extent that we anthropologists have conceptualized the rural sector as the countryside, inhabited by villagers or peasants, quite separate from what we think of as the bush, inhabited by primitives, we may have misled others, as well as ourselves.

Two categories of human being; two kinds or types of rural sector; two kinds of culture—and perhaps therefore two separate processes of change, of civilization, of modernization, even of protest. Yet a moment's reflection demonstrates that these are not in any pure sense two categories. There is no unilaterality or bilaterality of change, neither one high road to modernity nor two, leading from primitives and peasants to proletarians and Rotarians. And while the line between peasants and primitives may seem—and indeed be—very clear at times, on the ground and in everyday life it certainly is not always so. Such a suggestion deserves underlining, I suspect, not only because of anthropology's shortcomings. International events since World War II have brought "tribes" into view once more. Once more (as in the days when scanty clothing was enough to define the "level" of culture of their wearers), "tribal" has become a code word that confounds while supposedly describing. Once more, if a people's garb is sufficiently distinctive, their relationships to each other and to outsiders tend to be explained without any recourse to a class coefficient, or to economic differences expressed by their links to the outer world. Once more, we need to be reminded that so-called tribal peoples have been losing members by attrition for centuries, and that they commonly lose them to the peasantry—but as landless laborers. Whether in Mexico or in the Philippines, being barefoot may be explained either as being "tribal" or simply as being poor. An accurate comparative sociology of rural life will have to escape from preconceptions about the countryside; to minimize its emphasis on isolation; to suspend its judgments about the coherence, homogeneity, and solidarity of preconceived groups, tribes and communities. The "discovery" I have in mind, in other words, hinges on a readiness to be surprised by the ways rural peoples are organized with relation to each other and to the external world.

Silverman's critique of North American (and other) anthropologists' studies of peasantries notes that they began to study "settlements of small-scale agriculturalists within civilized, state societies . . . long before they treated peasants as an analytical category" (Silverman, 1979: 49). This is indeed true, and a genuine shortcoming. In referring to such early works as Redfield's *Tepoztlán* (1930), Arensberg's *The Irish Countryman* (1937), Embree's *Suye Mura* (1939), and Fei's *Village Life in China* (1939), all of which are studies of rural (but not "primitive") people within large states, she makes her point. Yet it may also be important to recognize that typological, analytical studies of peasantry are relatively new for all of the social sciences, as well as for history. Yet anthropology began to move away from its exclusive preoccupations with the so-called primitive world half a century ago. That this change in subject matter was not accompanied by a significant revision of either the objectives of research or of the place of a historical perspective in understanding the communities studied is, as I have tried to suggest, also related to anthropology's particular intellectual commitments. This may be best suggested by turning back momentarily to North American anthropology's crowning achievement: its monographic treatment of cultures of Native American peoples. That literature is marvelously rich; but studies of living Indians came tardily. Anthropology justified itself by asking live Indians what life *used to be like*—not what life was like at the time they were asked. Steward said it clearly:

> In the 1920's, anthropology in this country was still primarily concerned with gleaning remnants of native culture from the American Indians and had little interest in how modern acculturated Indians live. One of the first concessions to the importance of presentday Indians was Mead's [1932] study of the "Antler (Omaha) Tribe," a reservation group with a broken down tribal culture. . . . The adoption of the contemporary acculturated Indian as a legitimate subject for investigation was induced partly by the disappearance of native cultures, partly by new interests and needs created by the national economic and social upheavals of the 1930's (Steward, 1950: 30).

Certainly the world economic crisis of those years was intense enough so that even believers in blind tradition learned that cultures, not to mention political and economic systems, could change and were always changing.

The difficulty, however, appears to have been related not only to what categories of people were studied and to what periods in their histories were of interest, but also to the purposes for which the materials were collected. Alexander Lesser, whose *Pawnee Ghost Dance Hand Game* (1933) was ahead of its time in what it had to say about the culture of living Indians, makes this part of the argument in an important paper (Lesser, 1939: 575):

> . . . if a study is to be essentially descriptive, and is to take up only those questions which as a descriptive inquiry it itself suggests, what justification is there for studying primitive conditions rather than modern conditions? "Cultural relativity, the importance of cultural or social context, is already fully realized," such critics may say. "We recognize with you, and are happy to give you credit for making clear to us, the tremendous variation in patterning of social institutions and behavior, but, bearing that in mind, why not turn now to problems of contemporary civilization and make the point of view fruitful? And after all, if the application of knowledge to the solution of problems is to be regularly postponed until after the data are secured by means of descriptive methods, why not at least deal analytically with modern civilization, where the future for application is not so far removed, since the data we will be considering are closely related to our own life and time?"

Nearly half a century ago, Lesser told his colleagues that he could not see how an anthropological point of view could "carry conviction to others while we apparently remain a group of investigators endlessly curious about everything that has to do with man and his history and too consistently unwilling to set up our investigations in terms of decisive problems that can advance the science of society every time a thorough piece of research is carried out" (1939: 575). I believe that

Steward was right, when he referred to the effect of "the national and social upheavals of the 1930s" upon anthropological horizons. Pressure for new kinds of inquiry, focused upon the wider range of cultures which began to make themselves felt just before World War II, had real consequences after the war. But the space between primitive peoples and other peoples tended to be preserved as a space, nonetheless.

There is, lastly, the matter of historical perspective itself. I have suggested that American Indians were of interest to anthropologists for what they *had* been, rather than for what they had become by the time they were being studied. If one were to glance at our English contemporaries, beginning with Malinowski and Radcliffe-Brown, we would see that the present was, on the contrary, entirely suitable for study—but little effort was invested in linking it to the past. American historical anthropology, for the most part, meant the intact past, the supposedly precontact past if possible; British anthropology inclined to ignore as unknowable or irrelevant the pasts of the peoples studied. Far more could be said of this, for I am blurring the facts by these terse comments. Nonetheless, I believe what I say here is not unforgivably exaggerated. So far as anthropological studies of the peasantry by North Americans are concerned, we have already seen that they were generally viewed by those who did them as being entirely separate from studies of "primitive" peoples. I have meant to argue here, then, that anthropology's contribution to peasant studies has been both laggard and deficient. Let me suggest why I think that contribution has been insightful, nonetheless.

Anthropological studies of the peasantry begin with the monographs to which I earlier referred: Redfield's *Tepoztlán*, Fei's *Peasant Life in China*, and those falling between their dates (1930–1939). Since I have been critical of the anthropological perspective, I stress again the fact that Redfield's original study was made more than half a century ago. Its faults are well known. Its virtues, however, included a deliberate shifting of the anthropological focus away from so-called primitives to a radically different subject matter. But that shift preserved the traditional anthropological catechism: study what you can see and hear; record everything you can, do not expect it to be entirely consistent; listen; count the ancillary blessings of discomfort. If those items in the catechism do not add up to a methodology for other, sterner disciplines, so be it. They have, I believe, nonetheless helped to reveal worlds otherwise hidden or unimagined. I shall merely hint at one here.

Peasant revolts are often viewed as attempts to restore a world now lost, and the view has much to recommend it. But of course peoples and societies cannot faithfully retrace their steps as collectives. Aiming at going backward will always bring in its train some radical reorganization of preexisting social forms. What anthropology suggests, I think, is that revolutionary circumstances require an expansion of role playing by revolutionaries, often in order to meet the intensifying demands imposed by the conflict itself. The old may be led by the young; the female may command the male; the poor may direct the activities of the rich; the rural may teach the urban—but more important, such things happen under conditions that necessarily alter the way such new acts are regarded. We Americans who were astonished by photographs of young Vietnamese girls nudging giant American captive male pilots with the barrels of their kalashnikovs may be sure that young Vietnamese boys were engaged in the same labors. From the point of view of the revolutionary forces, the opportunity to prove oneself competent in new ways says something about how people regarded their own society before it became revolutionary. Doing things differently—particularly when this means allowing the culturally sanctioned prerogatives of particular statuses to be usurped by those systematically excluded from them in any social system—becomes *in itself* a revolutionary act. The possibilities of engineering new social arrangements according to new rules can come into view, which is a different thing from their coming to mind, only when older categories of status are thrown into doubt *by acts*.

As Wolf has pointed out (1969b), such testing by whole groups can take the form of failed insurrections, revolts, land riots, and jacqueries, which mark the trail leading up to a revolution that succeeds. New role playing, which is a part of these tests, is necessarily characterized by culture-specific traits and coefficients. Innovations of these kinds in everyday life may be extremely subtle—noticeable and important only to those whose knowledge of the culture is already detailed and sensitive. Indeed, innovations in speech, dress, etiquette, domestic decision making, and similar features of daily interaction can only be innovative if they are at once outside the range of expectable (normative) variation, yet more than merely whimsical or idiosyncratic. Their meaning to those to whom they matter, in short, must be associative—they must *mean* what they are intended to mean, beyond their content as behavior. Under what circumstances, then, does the wife dare to eat in her husband's presence; the child to command the energy of the elder; or the humble peasant to direct the effort of his betters? These occasions do not simply invert the past—they illuminate it as well. Anthropologists have been sensitive to such matters, and have contributed powerfully to our imaginative understanding of what peasant revolutions are, exactly because they have tried to observe and interpret cultures on their own terms, and because they are ready to assume that no act or statement is too trivial or irrational for their purposes.

It is in this light that the peasant yearning for a past perhaps now only imagined must be judged. A going back must, in certain regards, hinge upon a going forward; blind custom, as I have elsewhere suggested, is neither blind nor merely customary. The particularistic emphasis that so often marks anthropological study should not be perceived as mere enchantment with the relativistically unique. Anthropology on the level of rural regional or community study *must* be historical and particular, if it also aspires to be sociological and generalizing. (I daresay the other social sciences might benefit from a similar confinement.) And for all its limitations, I would still contend that anthropology has provided us with a rich body of descriptive and analytic material on a world of peasantry, largely ignored until quite recently by sociologists, historians, and political scientists alike.

Many of the papers at the conference on which the present volume is based were sensitive to the need to "reconstitute the unity of the historical process," to use Roseberry's phrase. Wasserstrom points out that the colonial society of eighteenth-century Mexico brought, in his words, "Spaniards and Indians together, not simply as distinct ethnic groups, but as members of antagonistic social classes." Skocpol emphasizes the manifold variety of contests within which peasant unrest can arise, and the need for their comparative study. Migdal, stressing the political mediation of external pressures, raises the issue of how such mediation is differentially experienced—but also, it seems to me, of how it may be *commonly* experienced—within the rural sector. All of these arguments promise more sophistication, as does Adas' assertion that commercial relationships often precede territorial occupation. In the modern world, the so-called "crisis of the peasantry" often means that additional levies upon local production may be imposed most effectively by increasing the consumption of new commodities, even at poverty levels in the rural social system. Powdered milk happens to be a timely example; but increases in the consumption of sucrose, particularly in the form of cold, carbonated, stimulant drinks, also exemplifies intensified outside claims on peasant productivity.

In conclusion, it may be worth mentioning the way typological exercises in history and the social sciences are often usefully followed by critical periods of reflection, when the categories themselves are examined with the aim of getting back to the study of process. In a recent work, Roseberry (1982) argues that the category of peasantry itself badly needs reexamination, and he presses for the worldwide examination of what he describes as the "uneven development of proletarianization" (cf. also Mintz, 1973; 1974). In this view, peasants represent points in a general worldwide process and are manifestations of it. I think this view is persuasive and powerful, even if I am not yet prepared to accept it unreservedly. It seems to me to represent the kind of opening argument that must always be aimed at our categories—categories which, once detached from their historical context, become abstractions more tenuous than our descriptions of particular cases. It is by a willingness to move from the general to the specific, and back again, that the work of social scientists and historians can be welded together analytically. I believe these papers suggest the promise of such cooperation.

Notes

1. Introduction

1. We acknowledge with thanks the participants in the symposium whose contributions are not included here. These include the discussants, Emily Ahern, David Harvey, Franklin Mendels, Orest Ranum, Richard Rubinson, and Kathleen Ryan, as well as Rod Aya and Susan Naquin, whose papers are not included here. We also want to thank Richard Price for his help during and after the symposium. Michael Adas's original paper has been published elsewhere (Adas, 1981), and the essay we include here is new.

2. We largely ignore relative deprivation theories (see, for example, Gurr, 1970), which see collective social movements as the discharge of tensions accumulated due to a gap between expectations and reality, or to the lack of synchronization between society and culture, or to some similar process. We agree with the criticisms of these theories Skocpol (1979) and Aya (1979) have made elsewhere, and we will not repeat them here. Frustration may indeed be an important correlate of rural unrest, but frustration alone is not a satisfactory explanation.

2. Conflicts and Peasant Rebellions

1. This was before the administrative regularization of the later seventeenth century. For information on the rivalry of Baltazar and Bosquet, although not on this particular conflict, see Beik (1974).

3. Uprisings under Spanish Colonialism

1. The *alcalde mayor* (governor) of Chiapas purchased his office for five years, during which he frequently realized a profit of as much as 100,000 pesos. In so doing, he forced native communities to purchase from him on credit a wide variety of goods which they often did not need and to repay these goods with highly valuable commodities such as cacao or cochineal. It was this system which in local parlance came to be known as the *repartimiento*. For a further discussion of the colonial economy, see Robert Wasserstrom (1978; 1982).

2. It would be fair to say that as long as they settled their accounts with the royal treasury, local governors could count upon the *audiencia* to turn a blind eye upon even the legitimate complaints of native communities. Only when their activities seemed likely to provoke a breakdown of public order were such officials investigated by superior authorities.

3. Naturally, such practices were condemned by Dominican authorities as idolatrous and pagan. It is ironic that many modern scholars accept these views, which hold that Indians in Chiapas had never truly understood or accepted Christianity and that they continued to practice their old rites whenever they could. In fact, native conversions appear to have been quite genuine, whereas allegations to the contrary almost invariably served to justify the misbehavior of their pastors. See Ximénez (1929, 3: 261) for a number of examples.

4. *Cofradías* were religious brotherhoods which collected funds to pay for communal religious celebrations. By the mid-sixteenth century, they also permitted local priests to engage in a sort of ecclesiastical *repartimiento*. For a more complete discussion of this situation, see Wasserstrom (1978; 1982).

5. In fact, Klein's view of Indian life and social organization in 1712 is anachronistic. To be sure, native officials such as *alcaldes, mayordomos* and *alfereces* had by that time assumed a variety of civil and religious functions within their communities. But these functions do not appear in the least to have been organized in a hierarchical fashion. Rather, they represent complementary and interdependent offices through which indigenous peoples undertook the critical task of reconstructing Indian life and custom after the Conquest.

4. Capitalist Penetration

1. "There had occurred already before 1850 significant technological advances in textiles, and to a lesser extent in coal, iron, and transport" (Bagwell and Mingay, 1970: 7). In the cotton industry, for example, the period from 1820–1850 saw powerweaving and steam power come to dominate the industry, and the productivity of workers rose rapidly (as much as 300 percent in hourly output per worker).

2. "The main incentive to mechanization in the industry seems to have been the growth of demand . . ." (Musson, 1978: 80). During the same period, the import of wool increased 400 percent; flax, almost 25 percent; hemp, 40 percent; and jute, about 1200 percent (Clapham, 1952: 225).

3. "*La obra de la Reforma desata un cambio extenso y profundo en el régimen de la propiedad de la tierra al favorecer la propriedad privada y crear un verdadero proletariado agrícola*" (The operation of the Reform unleashes an extensive and profound change in the system of land ownership by favoring private ownership and creating a true agrarian proletariat) (Cosío Villegas, 1965: 2).

4. Not all areas of Mexico experienced the same rush of land consolidation. In remote Oaxaca, for example, where a number of factors made export-oriented estates much less viable, it was not the case ". . . that the disamortized property got chiefly into the hands of those wealthy few who already possessed valuable real estate" (Berry, 1970: 286).

5. Another estimate is that 1 percent of the population owned 70 percent of the land (International Labour Office, 1953: 298).

6. The British adopted another type of land tenure (besides the *Zamindari* system), the *Ryotwari* system. This latter system was geared to create small landholders but largely failed, as we shall see momentarily, because of other aspects of the penetration of capitalism.

7. There had been some controversy over whether there really was an absolute decline in the standard of living in the second half of the nineteenth century (Thorner, 1955: 103–119; Morris, 1968: 1–15). It is especially unclear, given the falling value of the rupee and the lack of disaggregated statistics, exactly how much the standard of living varied for those directly or indirectly involved with farming through cultivation or services to cultivators (M. Mukeiji, 1965: 689–90). For the falling wages of industrial workers, see K. Mukeiji (1965: 656–60).

8. British foreign investments "made possible not only construction of railway but the digging of mines, the building of factories, the erection of public utilities, and the establishment of plantations (Johnson, 1939: 3; see also Simon, 1968). Large increases continued later. From 1874 until the outbreak of World War I, British gross foreign investments outstanding grew more than 300 percent (France's and Germany's increased even faster) (Kuznets, 1966: 322; Cairncross, 1953: 203; Feinstein, 1972: 205).

9. According to Sanyal, the beginning of road construction preceded that of railway construction by more than a decade, with 30,000 miles of road laid in the 1840s (Sanyal, 1930: 3). It is doubtful, however, how many of these roads were useful for commercial purposes.

10. Bose writes, "It was not until after 1857, however, that we find British capital flowing into India to any appreciable extent. And when it did, non-railway investment clearly went chiefly into raw material production for export, tea plantations becoming the most important, and later jute manufactures" (Bose, 1965: 506). About £150 million in British capital were invested in India between 1854 and 1869 and approximately £5 million per year during the 1870s (Jenks, 1927: 225).

11. In 1867, the date that C. E. Black marks as the beginning of Mexico's consolidating leadership, there were only 272.7 kilometers (López Rosado, 1968, 3: 54; Coever, 1977: 41– 62).

12. For an excellent contrast of peasants in Egypt, where commercialization occurred simultaneously in nearly all parts of the country, and in Turkey, where commercialization was much less homogeneous, see Rodrik (1979).

13. Coatsworth, for example, cautions against assuming stability once railways were built even where agricultural exports did not predominate. "Transport innovation was the cause of important shifts in crop structure, estate management, labor arrangements, land tenure patterns and rural welfare. Rural populations shared few of the benefits of this modernization and frequently suffered as a result" (Coatsworth, 1974: 49).

14. Exports had begun to grow even prior to 1857, but the total value exported in 1857 amounted only to £27 million. More important exports went from "drugs, dyes and luxuries" to foodgrains and other raw materials (Varshney, 1965: 445).

15. K. Mukeiji estimates 30 percent drop in that period (Mukeiji, 1965: 658–59). Others have estimated less.

16. The annual rate of growth of per capita crop production from 1877–1910 was −0.8 (Reynolds, 1970: 96).

17. Popkin calls this the "myth of the village" (Popkin, 1979).

5. Bandits, Monks, and Pretender Kings

1. J. S. Furnivall was one of the few writers to challenge these assumptions.

2. Following contemporary usage, Burman in this essay refers to the majority ethnic group of present-day Burma who speak Burmese and whose original home was in the Dry Zone of Upper Burma. Burmese refers to all of the ethnic groups (Burman, Mon, Karen, Kachin, etc.) which have come to make up the population of independent Burma. Because inter-ethnic clashes were often involved in protest movements in colonial Burma, the distinction is important in the context of this paper.

3. The best accounts of the post-1852 resistance can be found in the District gazetteers for Lower Burma, especially *Maubin*, 1931: 12; *Thayetmyo*, 1911: 12–13; *Toungoo*, 1914: 12; *Bassein*, 1916: 16–18; *Tharrawaddy*, 1920: 25–34; *Henzada*, 1915: 22–4; and *Syriam*, 1914: 17. See also Dunn, 1920: 16.

4. The prince had been saved from the purge of male members of the royal house after Thibaw's accession to the throne by the intercession of the Thathanabaing or head of the Buddhist Sangha in precolonial Burma.

5. The process of local reorganization and the replacement of hereditary *thugyis* had actually begun shortly before the 1886 disturbances. See Browne (1873: 63ff).

6. In precolonial Burma peasants and artisans were organized into military-style groupings that were divided between those who provided taxes (*athins*) and those who proffered labor services (*ahmudan*).

7. For excellent illustrations of these patterns see the articles by Max Harcourt, Gyanendra Pandey and Brian Stoddart in Low, 1977.

8. This discussion of the predepression rebellions is based upon relevant sections of the Bassein, Henzada, Akyab, Pakokky and Toungoo gazetteers; Collis, 1953; Heine-Geldern, 1942; Langham-Carter, 1939; Sarkisyanz, 1965; Cary, 1930; White, 1913; and *Report(s) on the Police Administration of Burma*, 1894: 60, 68; 1901: 10; 1909: iv; 1912: 14; 1914: 20–21.

9. References to bandit activities abound in British police and judicial reports. The patterns discussed here are based primarily upon evidence drawn from the following: *Report(s) on the Police Administration of Burma*, 1899: iv; 1901: iv, 10; 1902: 18; 1903: 9; 1906: 17; 1910: 3, 15; 1913: 22, 23; 1915: 7; 1917: 111 1918: 19, 25.

10. Unless otherwise noted, this discussion of the links between crime rates and socioeconomic conditions is based upon: *Report(s) on the Police Administration of Burma* 1895: 64; 1897: 25; 1899: iv; 1903: 7–8; 1904: ii; 1916: iii–viii, 2–3; 1917: iii, vii; 1919: 9–11; 1920: iv, 9–11; 1921: iii, 11, 13, 16.

11. The one person who has had access to the Burmese archival sources in Rangoon that are essential to a full understanding of this critical period, Patricia Herbert, is presently at work on her Ph.D. dissertation.

12. Because headmen were allowed to keep firearms for self-protection, their houses were often key targets of groups seeking to arouse popular risings. For sample references to attacks on headmen throughout this period see: Moscotti, 1951: 38–41. For earlier attacks on headmen see *Report(s) on the Police Administration of Burma*, 1908: 16; 1909: 17, 18; 1910: 16, 17, 18; 1915: 20; 1917: 10; 1918: 11; 1921: 18; 1922: 15–19.

13. Because I have discussed the 1930 risings in detail in other works, my major purpose here is to identify themes linked to the long-term patterns of protest under consideration and explore the ways in which the depression risings can help us in evaluating the usefulness of some of the main theories that have been set forth to explain the origins of anticolonial protest.

14. The concern to weaken or destroy bureaucratic control is amply attested by the choice in

most rebellions, including the Saya San, of telegraph and railway lines and the houses of village headmen as prime targets for assault. Though these measures were aimed at stunting the repressive capacity of the regime, the destruction of railway lines and telegraph stations and the atrocities often associated with attacks on headmen went far beyond the extent of damage or injury needed to deprive the colonizers of these critical means of social and political control.

15. For Scott's position on these issues see 1976: 92ff. For counter evidence and a different view see Adas, 1979: 201–2.

16. See, for example, the essays on peasant protest in Low, 1977; and the studies by Baker, 1976; Washbrook, 1976; Ranger, 1968, 1969; Ileto, 1979; and Kartodirdjo, 1973 cited in the text.

6. Peasants, Proletarians, and Politics

1. The "Introduction" occupies a problematic position within the Marxist literature. It was a rough draft, it is internally inconsistent, and Marx himself decided not to publish it. Its popularity, particularly among economic anthropologists who freely quote the section on production, distribution, consumption, and exchange, should therefore provoke skepticism. Martin Nicholas regards it as a "false start," which it certainly is, but it is an instructive one for many of the reasons to which Nicholas alludes. That is, we see in the "Introduction" Marx's search for a method. We can learn from the "Introduction," then, not with unproblematic citations, but with a critical examination of a method in formation (Nicholas, 1973; Echeverría, 1978).

2. This section of the "Introduction" could also be used to criticize the ahistorical notions of abstraction that come from the Althusserians or the "Hindessian revolution" in England. But that would be the subject of a different essay.

3. I am well aware that this criticism will seem strange to most readers, given the fact that Lukacs is usually labeled a Hegalian Marxist and that he himself claimed that he did not devote enough attention to economic matters (see his Preface to the 1971 edition of *History and Class Consciousness*).

4. See Cardozo (1965) for a more detailed treatment of this period.

5. Given the ethnic and regional composition of those who established the coffee economy, it is interesting to note that an 1882 instance of street violence in Boconó, which seems to have been directed against liberals, took the form of an attack on *forasteros* (outsiders). It is hard to reconstruct exactly what happened because I am depending on newspaper accounts written by the victim. Rather than describing the incident or naming the participants, the authors assumed general knowledge and contented themselves with reasserting their personal dignity (*El Progresista*, 1882).

6. The best evidence I have of this comes from the Indian reserve lands in Boconó (Roseberry, 1977: 93–94; 1982).

7. The end of another "constitutional period" was approaching, and Gabaldón was urging Gomez not to allow himself to be "re-elected."

8. It was constantly rumored that Eleazar Lopez Contreras, then head of the army brigade at Caracas and later the man who replaced Gomez as chief of state upon his death in 1935, was sympathetic to a rebellion Rangel, 1975: 315–28). Gabaldón was made to believe Lopez had already enlisted in the cause (Heredia, 1974: 86–89).

9. According to Gabaldón, "The utility of that battle (in Guanare, 7 May 1929) was only for morale, because we came out of it with more arms but less ammunition and incapacitated for a new encounter" (quoted in Heredia, 1974: 111).

10. A series of parties emerged in 1936 after the death of Gomez. One of these, the Movement of Venezuelan Organization (ORVE), was the direct ancestor of Acción Democrática (AD), the party which has enjoyed the longest reign since 1945, and which was officially founded in 1941 (when such parties were legalized). Many of the generation of '28 were active in its formation. The Venezuelan Communist Party (PCV) had been formed in 1931, a descendent of the Venezuelan Revolutionary Party, formed by Gustavo Machado, Salvador de la Plaza, Carlos Leon, and others in Mexico. They were members of an earlier student generation, who themselves had protested, been imprisoned, and exiled. The conflict between the PCV and AD began in their future leaders' years in exile. My concentration on the Generation of '28 is not intended to indicate that they were more admirable; that question is not addressed. I have concentrated on them because they were the ones who achieved power. And I think it is interesting to note (and indicative of the nature of their power once they captured it) that they were willing to compromise

with the forces of the past as they embraced a future. The future leaders of Acción Democrática turned to caudillos like José Rafael Gabaldón and Roman Delgado Chalbaud as the agents of struggle in 1929. For a representative history of AD written by a North American political scientist, see Martz (1966).

11. The primary sector is divided into agriculture and petroleum/mining. Of the total economically active population, the agricultural corps declined from 43 to 20.3 per cent. The petroleum/mining corps declined from 3 to 1.3 per cent.

12. This is not to indicate that the left totally failed to organize rural folk, but simply to say that the governing parties (e.g., Acción Democrática) were immensely more successful.

13. The democratic experiment was interrupted from 1948 to 1958 by the military rule of Pérez Jimenez.

14. In a remarkable example of the unproductive use to which public funds from the petroleum boom were put during the government of Carlos Andrés Pérez, the National Agrarian Institute (IAN), the organism responsible for instituting agrarian reform, built a chapel for the *caserío* in which I lived.

15. This is an accurate assessment of the formation of the two parties. COPEI was organized as a right wing reaction to the potentially progressive aspects of the social democratic Revolution of 1945. Class and party alignments have changed over the years, however, as state and society have changed.

16. A good example of this strategy was the nationalization of foreign petroleum companies. In the party and government publicity accompanying this and other state actions, an attempt was made to promote identification as Venezuelan rather than as a member of a particular class. Where class identity is emphasized (e.g., on May Day), organizations and unions controlled by the parties which can mobilize and channel protest are stressed.

17. In such circumstances, discussions of relative autonomy seem particularly inappropriate, regardless of the conclusions drawn from such discussions, because the structuralist premises from which they emerge do not apply.

8. What Makes Peasants Revolutionary?

1. The discussion of Scott's views in this essay will be based exclusively on his 1977 essay on revolutions as such. His book (Scott 1976) analyzes only cases of peasant rebellions, and it is very cautious (cf. p. 194) in what it suggests about peasant-based revolutions. "Hegemony and the Peasantry," however, suggests that Scott is moving toward a general, culturally oriented theory of the peasantry as a social class with inherent revolutionary potential.

2. By talking about "Old World" versus "Third World" frames of references, I do not mean to say that there is no overlap between the historical cases of peasant-based revolutions analyzed by Moore as opposed to those discussed by Wolf, Migdal, Paige, and Scott. Actually there is considerable shared interest in Russia and—especially—China. What I mean to suggest is that Moore approaches his cases as historically established "agrarian bureaucracies," analyzable in the same terms as Western European agrarian states, whereas the others tend to treat their cases as countries which have not long before fallen under the sway of Western Capitalist imperialism. For all four authors writing since Moore the Vietnamese Revolution is the touchstone case, whereas for Moore, Russia and China were the key cases of peasant-based revolution.

3. For reasons that will later become clear, Joel Migdal's reasoning on the issue of which peasants are most prone to revolution is tangential to this dispute over propertied versus property-less peasants. For the time being, therefore, I shall leave Migdal aside.

4. Actually, Paige's notion that the simple fact of income from capital gives upper classes room to make reformist concessions to farmers or laborers is very dubious. Market conditions can exert severe constraints on possible concessions. Moreover, the line between reforms and structural changes is not always easy to maintain. Paige's own discussion of Malayan rubber plantations (1975: 50–58) illustrates the inadequacies of his basic theory.

5. There is no avoiding the conclusion that Paige (1975) contradicts the arguments of Wolf (1969a) and Scott (1977a). At first glance one might suppose that the contrasting theories were intended to apply to separate kinds of situations—that is, Wolf and Scott primarily to traditional agrarian societies and Paige only to commercialized export zones. However, in practice, Paige applies his theoretical logic much more broadly. In his theoretical chapter, he often refers to agrarian class relations in non-export-oriented societies (or areas), and in his case history of

Vietnam, he seeks to explain class relations and peasant politics in the nonexport areas of central and northern Vietnam as well as in the export-oriented zones of southern Vietnam.

6. On the social origins of the leaders of modern Vietnamese political movements see Wolf (1969a: 178–81). The cultural and intellectual roots of these movements are thoroughly explored in Woodside (1976).

7. On the enormous importance of nationalism in Vietnamese Communism see McAlister (1971) and Dunn (1972: ch. 5). Quite inappropriately, in my opinion, Paige tries to draw a firm distinction between communally-oriented nationalist revolutionary movements such as the U.P.A. of Angola and class-oriented socialist revolutionary movements such as Vietnamese Communism. But the Vietnamese Communists were effective precisely because they *combined* nationalism with class-based appeals to the peasantry! And, indeed, it is hard to see how any successful revolutionary movement in the Third World could avoid having strong nationalist overtones.

8. On these sects see McLane (1971) and Popkin (1979). Popkin (1979: 193–213) is especially good in explaining how the Cao Dai and Hoa Hao appealed to southern peasants and thereby made themselves formidable organizational competitors to the Communists.

9. See Paige's statistical analysis of "world patterns" in *Agrarian Revolution*, chapter 2. He indicates (1975: 94–96) that the presence of Communist or Trotskyist parties at protests in export agricultural zones was used as a key indicator of "revolutionary-socialist events."

10. Paige posits (1975: 32, 37) that only conservative (i.e., landlord-dominated) solidarity should occur when a landed upper class coexists with a landed peasantry.

11. See also the excellent discussion in Popkin (1979: 133–70).

12. On the leftist revolutionary movements in Portuguese Africa (Angola, Guinea, and Mozambique) see Davidson (1974). On peasants in the Cuban Revolution, see Wolf (1969a: ch. 6).

13. James Scott (1977a) suggests that revolutionary outcomes are likely to be better for the peasantry if their revolts are autonomous and spontaneous in relation to the revolutionary leadership. But a clear counter instance was the Russian Revolution where, in large part *because* of the extreme spontaneity and local autonomy of the peasant revolts, the peasants in the end faced the coercive extension of Bolshevik state power into the countryside. Chinese peasants, by contrast, benefitted after 1949 from the fact that the Chinese Communists had found it necessary to mobilize their direct political support in order to achieve national power in the first place (see Skocpol, 1979: chs. 6–7).

14. Popkin (1979) effectively underlines the insecurities and exploitation built into many traditional agrarian structures, and points out that peasants have good cause to attempt to "remake" these structures through revolts or participation in political movements.

15. On the organizing activities of the Communists in Vietnam see Popkin (1979: 213–42); Pike (1966); and Race (1972).

16. I have not seen systematic investigations of such questions, but useful speculations can be found here and there in Dunn (1972) and Chaliand (1977).

17. Popkin (1979: chs. 5–6) has some very insightful things to say about the collective mobilization of peasants.

18. In "Hegemony and the Peasantry" (1977a), Scott concentrates almost exclusively on the peasantry itself, analyzing why it is a class capable of making revolutions. In his previous work on peasant rebellions (1976), Scott stressed the ways in which Western imperialism exploits or uproots traditional peasants, fundamentally undermining the security of their subsistence-oriented economic practices and moral customs. The will to revolt, according to Scott, grows out of this confrontation between peasant traditionalism and modernizing capitalist forces. Thus his views seem to closely parallel those of Wolf (1969a) and Migdal (1974).

19. Although Paige does not realize it, this comment about political conditions since World War II introduces explanatory variables into the picture that his ahistorical and apolitical theoretical model cannot handle. Moreover, the validity of Paige's statistical analysis (1975: ch. 2) of "world patterns" of agrarian politics between 1948 and 1970 is called into serious question once we realize that, during this time, decolonization was happening in Asia and Africa, but U.S. neocolonial hegemony over Latin America remained quite firm. Many of Paige's findings about revolutionary movements versus agrarian revolts may reflect not, as he argues, the inherent political potentials of migratory and sharecropper estates versus commercial haciendas. They may reflect instead the internationally conditioned differences between African and Asian politics versus Latin American politics during the post–World War II period.

References

Abbreviations for Archival Sources and Periodicals

AGCh–Archivo General de Chiapas, Tuxtla Gutiérrez.

AHA–Archives Historiques de l'Armée, Vincennes.

AMD–Archives Municipales, Dijon.

AN–Archives Nationales, Paris.

BCR–Government of Burma, *Report on the Prevention of Crime and The Treatment of Criminals in the Province of Burma*, Rangoon, 1926.

BN MC–Bibliothèque Nationale, Paris, Mélanges de Colbert.

Gazette–*La Gazette de Théophraste Renaudot* (title varies), 1931–0000.

Mercure–*Le Mercure françois*, 1605–1644.

PFP–Government of India, Political and Foreign Proceedings, Range 200, vol. 47, 30 December 1853, no. 60. India Office Records, London, England (IOR).

RAB–*Report(s) on the Administration of the Province of Burma*, Rangoon, 1862–1938.

RAP–*Report(s) on the Administration of the Province of Pegu*, Rangoon, 1853–1961.

RPAB–*Report(s) on the Police Administration of Burma*, Rangoon, 1888–1930.

R & A Proc.–Government of Burma, Revenue and Agriculture Proceedings, vol. 8633, Nov. 1911 (IOR).

SPC–Government of India, Secret and Political Correspondence, vol. 30, no. 83, 22 August 1856, paragraph 179.

Publications Cited

Adas, Michael (1972). "Imperialist Rhetoric and Modern Historiography: The Case of Lower Burma before and after Conquest," *Journal of Southeast Asian Studies* 3: 175–92.

———. (1974). *The Burma Delta: Economic Development and Social Change on an Asian Rice Frontier, 1852–1941*. Madison: University of Wisconsin Press.

———. (1977). "The *Ryotwari* in Lower Burma: The Establishment and Decline of a Peasant Proprietor System," in R. E. Frykenberg, ed., *Land Tenure and Peasant in South Asia*. New Delhi: Orient Longman.

———. (1979). *Prophets of Rebellion: Millenarian Protest Movements Against the European Colonial Order*. Chapel Hill: University of North Carolina Press.

———. (1980). "'Moral Economy' or 'Contest State'?: Elite Demands and the Origins of Peasant Protest in Southeast Asia," *Journal of Social History* 13: 521–546.

———. (1981). "From Avoidance to Confrontation: Peasant Protest in Pre-Colonial and Colonial Southeast Asia," *Comparative Studies in Society and History* 23: 217–247.

Adriani, Alberto (1937). *Labor Venezolanista*. Caracas: Tipografía La Nación.

Akyab District Gazetteer (1917). Rangoon: Government of Burma.

Alavi, Hamza (1965). "Peasants and Revolution," *The Socialist Register 1965*: 241–277.

———. (1973). "Peasant Classes and Primordial Loyalties," *The Journal of Peasant Studies* 1: 23–62.

Amherst District Gazetteer (1913). Rangoon: Government of Burma.

Arensberg, C. (1937). *The Irish Countryman*. New York: Macmillan.

Aya, Rod (1979). "Theories of Revolution Reconsidered: Contrasting Models of Collective Violence," *Theory and Society* 8: 39–99.

Bagwell, Philip S. and G. E. Mingay (1970). *Britain and America 1850–1939*. London: Routledge and Kegan Paul.

Baker, Christopher (1976). *The Politics of South India, 1920–1937*. Cambridge: Cambridge University Press.

Band, Claire and William Band (1948). *Two Years with the Chinese Communists*. New Haven: Yale University Press.

Banerjee, Tarasankar (1966). *Internal Market of India (1834–1900)*. Calcutta: Academic.

Baptista, Jose María (1962). *Crónicas del Boconò de Ayer*. Caracas: Ministerio de Educación and the Ateneo de Boconó.

Barth, Frederick, ed. (1970). *Ethnic Groups and Boundaries*. London: George Allen and Unwin.

Bassein District Gazetteer (1916). Rangoon: Government of Burma.

Baulant, Micheline (1968). "Le prix de grains à Paris de 1431 à 1788," *Annales; Economies, Sociétés, Civilisations* 23: 520–540.

Beals, Ralph L. (1975). *The Peasant Marketing System of Oaxaca, Mexico*. Berkeley: University of California Press.

Beik, William H. (1974). "Two Intendants Face a Popular Revolt: Social Unrest and the Structure of Absolutism in 1645," *Canadian Journal of History* 9: 243–262.

Berry, Charles R. (1970). "The Fiction and Fact of the Reform: The Case of the Central District of Oaxaca, 1856–1867," *Americas* 26: 277–290.

Bhatia, B. M. (1965). "Agriculture and Co-operation," in V. B. Singh, ed., *Economic History of India 1857–1956*. Bombay: Allied.

Bianco, Lucien (1971). *Origins of the Chinese Revolution, 1915–1949*. Stanford: Stanford University Press.

Bodey, Hugh (1975). *Twenty Centuries of British Industry*. London: David and Charles.

Boislisle, A. M. de, ed. (1874–1896). *Correspondance des Contrôleurs Gènéraux des Finances avec les Intendants des Provinces*. 3 vols. Paris: Imprimerie Nationale.

Bonney, Richard (1978). *Political Change in France under Richelieu and Mazarin, 1624–1661*. Oxford: Oxford University Press.

Bose, Arun (1965). "Foreign Capital," in V. B. Singh, ed., *Economic History of India 1857–1956*. Bombay: Allied.

Bravo de la Serna y Manrique, Marcos (1679). *Carta Pastoral*. Guatemala: Unpublished typescript in the Biblioteca Fray Bartolomé de Las Casas, San Cristobal, Chiapas.

Bridges, J. E. (1881). *Report on Settlement Operations in the Bassein District, 1880–81*. Rangoon: Government of Burma.

Brito Figueroa, Federico (1966). *Historia Económica y Social de Venezuela*. 2 vols. Caracas: Universidad Central de Venezuela.

Brohm, John (1957). "Burmese Religion and the Burmese Religious Revival." Unpublished Ph.D. dissertation. Ann Arbor: University Microfilms.

Browne, Horace A. (1873). *Statistical and Historical Account of the District of Thayetmyo, Pegu Division of British Burma*. Rangoon: Government of Burma.

Butterfield, Herbert (1981). *The Origins of History*. New York: Basic Books.

Carincross, A. K. (1953). *Home and Foreign Investment 1870–1913*. Cambridge: Cambridge University Press.

Campbell, George (n.d., originally published 1881). "The Tenure of Land in India," in J. W. Probyn, ed., *Systems of Land Tenure*. London: Cassell, Petter, Galpin.

Cancian, Frank (1965). *Economics and Prestige in a Maya Community*. Stanford: Stanford University Press.

Cardoso, Fernando Henrique and Enzo Faletto (1979). *Dependency and Development in Latin America*. Berkeley: University of California Press.

Cardozo, Arturo (1965). *Proceso de la Historia de Los Andes*. Caracas: Biblioteca de Autores y Temas Tachirenses.

Cary, B. S. (1930). "Hints for the Guidance of Civil Officers in the Event of the Outbreak of Disturbances in Burma," Government of India, *Political and Judicial Correspondence*, File 7347, India Office Records, London.

Chaliand, Gérard (1977). *Revolution in the Third World: Myths and Prospects*. New York: Viking Press.

Chen Han-sheng (1936). *Landlord and Peasant in China*. New York: International Publishers.

Ch'en, Jerome (1967). *Mao and the Chinese Revolution*. London: Oxford University Press.

Ch'en, Jerome, Edward Friedman, Maurice Meisner, Tang Tsou et al. (1980). "Ideology and History: A report on the China Study-Tour of Seven Leading North American China Scholars." Unpublished manuscript.

Cheng Siok-Hwa (1968). *The Rice Industry of Burma, 1852–1940*. Kuala Lumpur-Singapore: Oxford University Press.

Chesneaux, Jean, Marianne Bastid, Marie-Claire Bergere (1976). *China From the Opium Wars to the 1911 Revolution*. New York: Pantheon.

Clamageran, J. J. (1867–1876). *Histoire de l'impôt en France*. 3 vols. Paris: Guillaumin.

Clapham, Sir John (1952). *An Economic History of Modern Britain*. Cambridge: Cambridge University Press.

———— and Eileen Power, eds. (1978). *The Cambridge Economic History of Europe*. 9 vols. Cambridge: Cambridge University Press.

Clément, Pierre, ed. (1861–1869). *Instructions et mémoires de Colbert*. 6 vols. Paris: Imprimerie Impériale.

Coatsworth, John (1974). "Railroads and the Concentration of Landownership in the Early Porfiriato," *Hispanic American Historical Review* 54: 48–71.

Coever, Don M. (1977). "The Perils of Progress: The Mexican Department of Fomento during the Boom Years 1880–1884," *Inter-American Economic Affairs* 21: 41–62.

Cole, John W. and Eric R. Wolf (1974). *The Hidden Frontier: Ecology and Ethnicity in an Alpine Valley*. New York: Academic.

Collis, Maurice (1953). *Into Hidden Burma*. London: Faber & Faber.

Córdova, Armando (1973). *Inversiones Extranjeras y Subdesarrollo: El Modelo Primario Exportador Imperialista*. Caracas: Universidad Central de Venezuela.

Cosío Villegas, Daniel (1965). *Historia Moderna de México*. 7 vols. Mexico City: Editorial Hermes.

Couper, Thomas (1924). *Report of Inquiry into the Condition of Agricultural Tenants and Labourers*. Rangoon: Government of Burma.

Crosthwaite, Charles (1912). *The Pacification of Burma*. London: Macmillan.

Davidson, Basil (1974). "African Peasants and Revolution," *The Journal of Peasant Studies* 1: 269–90.

Donovan, Peter (1976). *The Red Army in Jiangxi, 1931–1934*. Ithaca: Cornell University East Asia Papers, no. 10.

Draper, Hal (1977). *Karl Marx's Theory of Revolution: State and Bureaucracy.* New York: Monthly Review Press.

Driver, Peshotan Nasserwanji (1949). *Problems of Zamindari and Land Tenure Reconstruction in India.* Bombay: New Book Company.

Dubey, Vinod (1965). "Railways," in V. B. Singh, ed., *Economic History of India 1857–1956.* Bombay: Allied.

Dunn, Charles S. (1920). *Studies in the History of Tharrawaddy.* Cambridge: Cambridge University Press.

Dunn, John (1972). *Modern Revolutions.* Cambridge: Cambridge University Press.

Dutt, Romesh (1969). *The Economic History of India.* 2 vols. New York: Augustus M. Kelley.

Echeverría, R. (1978). "Critique of Marx's 1857 Introduction," *Economy and Society* 7: 333–66.

Elvin, Mark (1973). *The Pattern of the Chinese Past.* Stanford: Stanford University Press.

Embree, E. (1939). *Suye Mura.* Chicago: University of Chicago Press.

Engels, Frederic (1967). *The German Revolutions.* Edited by Leonard Krieger. Chicago: University of Chicago Press.

———. (1973 [1850]). *The Peasant War in Germany.* New York: International Publishers.

Fei, Hsiao Tung (1939). *Peasant Life in China.* London: Kegan Paul.

Feigon, Lee (1982). *Chen Duxiu and the New Youth of the Chinese Revolution.* Forthcoming from Princeton University Press.

Feinstein, C. H. (1972). *National Income, Expenditure and Output of the United Kingdom 1855–1913.* Cambridge: Cambridge University Press.

Feuerwerker, Albert (1977). *Economic Trends in the Republic of China.* Ann Arbor: Michigan Papers in Chinese Studies.

Flores Galindo, Alberto (1976). *Tupac Amaru II.* Lima: Retablo del Papel Ediciones.

Fourastie, Jean (1969). *L'évolution des Prix à Long Terme.* Paris: Presses Universitaires France.

Friedman, Edward (1975). "The German Peasant War," *The Journal of Peasant Studies* 3: 17–23.

Furnivall, J. S. (1939). "The Fashioning of Leviathan: The Beginnings of British Rule in Burma," *Journal of the Burma Research Society* 29: 1–37.

———. (1956). *Colonial Policy and Practice.* New York: New York University Press.

———. (1957). *An Introduction to the Political Economy of Burma.* Third edition. Rangoon: Peoples' Literature Committee and House.

Garavente, Anthony J. (1978). "He Long and the Rural Revolution in West-Central China, 1927–1935." Unpublished Ph.D. dissertation, Los Angeles: University of California.

Garlan, Yvon and Nières, Claude (1975). *Les révoltes bretonnes de 1675. Papier Timbré et Bonnets Rouges.* Paris: Editions Sociales.

Geary, Grattan (1886). *Burma after the Conquest.* London: Sampson, Low & Co.

Golte, Jürgen (1980). *Repartos y rebeliones. Tupac Amaru y las contradicciones de la economía nacional.* Lima: Instituto de Estudios Peruanos.

Gregory, James R. (1976). "The Modification of an Interethnic Boundary in Belize," *American Ethnologist* 3: 683–708.

Gurr, Ted Robert (1970). *Why Men Rebel.* Princeton: Princeton University Press.

Hall, D. G. E. (1964 [1955]). *A History of South-East Asia.* London: Macmillan.

He Long Tongzhi degushi (The Story of Comrade He Long) (1978). Hunan: Hunan Renmin Chubanshe (The Hunan People's Press).

Heine-Geldern, Robert (1942). "Conceptions of State and Kingship in Southeast Asia," *Far Eastern Quarterly* 2: 15–30.

Henzada District Gazetteer (1915). Rangoon: Government of Burma.

Heredia, A. Cipriano (1974). *El Año 29: Recuento de la Lucha Armada.* Caracas: Ediciones Centauro.

Hidalgo, Manuel (1735). *Breve explicación de la lengua tzotzil.* Manuscript in the Archivo Histórico Diocesano de San Cristobal, San Cristobal, Chiapas.

Hirshman, Albert O. (1979). *Exit, Voice, and Loyalty: Responses to Decline in Firms, Organizations, and States.* Cambridge: Harvard University Press.

Hobsbawm, Eric J. (1959). *Primitive Rebels.* New York: Norton.

_____ . (1969). *Bandits.* New York: Delacorte Press.

_____ . (1971). "Class Consciousness in History," in I. Meszaros, ed., *Aspects of History and Class Consciousness.* London: Routledge and Kegan Paul.

Hsieh, Winston (1972). "Triads, Salt Smugglers, and Local Uprisings: Observations on the Social and Economic Background of the Waichow Revolution of 1911," in Jean Chesneaux, ed., *Popular Movements and Secret Societies in China 1840–1950.* Stanford: Stanford University Press.

Htin Aung, Maung (1965). *The Stricken Peacock: Anglo-Burmese Relations 1752–1948.* The Hague: Nijhoff.

_____ . (1967). *A History of Burma.* New York: Columbia University Press.

Huang Dazhi (1980). *Peng Dehuai Pingzhuan* (A Critical Biography of Peng Dehuai). Hong Kong: Bo Wen Book Company.

Hugo, Victor (1964). *Les Misérables.* Translated by Charles E. Wilbur. New York: Simon and Schuster.

Huizer, Gerrit (1973). *Peasant Rebellion in Latin America.* Harmondsworth: Penguin.

Ileto, Reyaldo (1979). *Pasyon and Revolution.* Quezon City: Ateneo de Manila University Press.

International Labour Office (1953). *Indigenous Peoples.* Studies and Reports, New Series, no. 35. Geneva: International Labour Office.

Ireland, A. (1907). *The Province of Burma.* Cambridge: Harvard University Press.

Jenks, Leland Hamilton (1927). *The Migration of British Capital to 1875.* New York: Alfred A. Knopf.

Johnson, Chalmers A. (1962). *Peasant Nationalism and Communist Power: The Emergence of Revolutionary China, 1937–1945.* Stanford: Stanford University Press.

Johnson, E. A. J. (1939). *An Economic History of Modern England.* New York: Thomas Nelson and Sons.

Kartodirdjo, Sartono (1973). *Protest Movements in Rural Java.* Singapore: Oxford University Press.

Katz, Friedrich (1974). "Labor Conditions on Haciendas in Porfirian Mexico: Some Trends and Tendencies," *Hispanic American Historical Review* 54: 1–47.

Khurso, A. M. (1965). "Land Reforms Since Independence," in V. P. Singh, ed., *Economic History of India 1857–1956.* Bombay: Allied.

Klein, Donald and Anne B. Clark (1971). *Biographic Dictionary of Chinese Communism, 1912–1965.* Cambridge: Harvard University Press.

Klein, Herbert (1970). "Rebeliones de las Comunidades Campesinas: La República Tzeltal de 1712," in N. McQuown and J. Pitt-Rivers, eds., *Ensayos antropológicos.* Mexico: Instituto Nacional Indigenista.

Koenig, William (1978). "The Early Kon-baung Polity, 1752–1819: A Study in Politics,

Administration and Social Organization in Burma." Unpublished Ph.D. dissertation. Ann Arbor: University Microfilms.

Kumar, Dharma (1965). *Land and Caste in South India.* Cambridge: Cambridge University Press.

Kuznets, Simon (1966). *Modern Economic Growth.* New Haven: Yale University Press.

Landsberger, Henry A. (1974). "Peasant Unrest: Themes and Variations," in Henry A. Landsberger, ed., *Rural Protest: Peasant Movements and Social Change.* London: Macmillan.

Langham-Carter, R. R. (1939). "A Rebellion in Upper Burma," *The Burman Police Journal* 2: 15–29.

Lesser, Alexander (1933). *The Pawnee Ghost Dance Hand Game.* Columbia University Contributions to Anthropology, XVI. New York: Columbia University Press.

———. (1939). "Problems versus Subject-Matter as Directives of Research," *American Anthropologist* 41: 574–582.

Lévi-Strauss, Claude (1966). "Anthropology: Its Achievements and Future," *Current Anthropology* 7: 124–127.

Liagre, Charles (1934). "Les hostilités dans la région de Lille," *Revue du Nord* 20: 111–130.

Lieberman, Victor (1976). "The Burmese Dynastic Pattern, Circa 1590–1760: An Administrative and Political Study of the Taung-Ngu Dynasty and the Reign of Alaung-hpaya." Unpublished Ph.D. dissertation. Ann Arbor: University Microfilms.

Liublinskaya, A. D. (1966). *Vnutriennaia politika frantsuskovo absolutismo.* Moscow/Leningrad: Izdatel'stvo "Nauka".

López Rosado, Diego G. (1968). *Historia y Pensamiento Económico de México.* 6 vols. Mexico City: Universidad Nacional Autónima de Mexico.

López Sánchez, Hermilio (1960). *Apuntes históricos de San Cristobal de Las Cases, México.* 2 vols. Mexico: published by author.

Low, D. A. (1977). *The Congress and the Raj.* London: Heineman.

Lukacs, Georg (1971 [1922]). *History and Class Consciousness.* Cambridge: MIT Press.

McAlister, John T., Jr. (1971). *Vietnam: The Origins of Revolution.* Garden City: Double-day Anchor.

McAlpin, Michelle Burge (1974). "Railroads, Prices, and Peasant Rationality: India 1860–1900," *The Journal of Economic History* 34: 662–684.

McBride, George McCutchen (1971). *The Land Systems of Mexico.* New York: Octagon Books.

McDonald, Angus (1978). *The Urban Origins of Rural Revolution.* Berkeley: University of California Press.

McLane, John R. (1971). "Archaic Movements and Revolution in Southern Vietnam," in Norman Miller and Roderick Aya, eds., *National Liberation: Revolution in the Third World.* New York: The Free Press.

MacPherson, W. J. (1955–56). "Investment in Indian Railways, 1845–1875," *Economic History Review*, Series 2, 8: 177–86.

Madan, T. N. (1965). "Social Organization," in V. B. Singh, ed., *Economic History of India 1857–1956.* Bombay: Allied.

Majumdar, R. C. (1963). "Burma and Assam," in R. C. Majumdar et al, eds. *British Paramountcy and the Indian Renaissance*, part 1. Bombay: Bharatiya Vidya Bhavan.

Malavé Mata, Hector (1974). "Formación Histórica del Antidesarrollo de Venezuela," in D. F. Maza Zavala et al, eds., *Venezuela: Crecimiento sin Desarrollo.* Mexico: Editorial Nuestro Tiempo.

Malinowski, B. (1965 [1935]). *Coral Gardens and Their Magic*, vol. 1. Bloomington: University of Indiana Press.

Mao Zedong (1954). *Selected Works*. vol. 1. London: Lawrence and Wishart.

———. (1965–1967). *Selected Works*. vols. 1–4, Beijing: Foreign Languages Press.

Marshall, H. I. (1922). *The Karen People of Burma*. Columbus: Ohio State University Press.

Martz, John (1966). *Acción Democrática: Evolution of a Modern Political Party*. Princeton: Princeton University Press.

Marx, Karl (1964 [1895]). *Class Struggles in France 1848–1850*. New York: International Publishers.

———. (1973a [1857–58]). *Grundrisse*. Middlesex: Penguin Publishers.

———. (1973b [1852]). *The Eighteenth Brumaire of Louis Bonaparte* in David Fernbach, ed., *Karl Marx: Surveys from Exile*. New York: Vintage.

Matthews, H. M. S. (1890). *Report on Settlement Operations in the Bassein and Thongwa Districts, 1888–89*. Rangoon: Government of Burma.

Maubin District Gazetteer (1931). Rangoon: Government of Burma.

Maung, U Maung (1980). *From Sangha to Laity: Nationalist Movements of Burma, 1920–1940*. New Delhi: Hind Kitab.

Mead, Margaret (1932). *The Changing Culture of an Indian Tribe*. New York: Columbia University Press.

Meek, C. K. (1949). *Land, Law and Custom in the Colonies*. London: Oxford University Press.

Meisner, Maurice (1967). *Li Ta-chao and the Origins of Chinese Marxism*. Cambridge: Harvard University Press.

———. (1977). *Mao's China*. New York: Free Press.

Mendelson, E. M. (1975). *State and Sangha in Burma: A Study of Monastic Sectarianism and Leadership*. Ithaca: Cornell University Press.

Migdal, Joel S. (1974). *Peasants, Politics, and Revolution: Pressures Toward Political and Social Change in the Third World*. Princeton: Princeton University Press.

Mintz, Sidney W. (1968). "Tribesman and Villager in Southwestern Iran." Unpublished manuscript. New Haven: Yale University.

———. (1973). "A Note on the Definition of Peasantries," *Journal of Peasant Studies* 1: 91–106.

———. (1974). "The Rural Proletariat and the Problem of Rural Proletarian Consciousness," *Journal of Peasant Studies* 1: 291–325.

Montchrestien, Antoine (1889 [1615]). *Traité de l'économie politique*. Paris: Plon.

Mooney, J. (1896). *The Ghost Dance Religion. Fourteenth Annual Report of the Bureau of American Ethnology*, vol. 2. Washington: Government Printing Office.

Moore, Barrington, Jr. (1966). *Social Origins of Dictatorship and Democracy*. Boston: Beacon Press.

Morris, Morris D. (1968) "Towards a Reinterpretation of Nineteenth-Century Indian Economic History," *The Indian Economic and Social History Review* 5: 1–15.

Morris, R. C. (1930). "Report on the Causes of the Tharrawaddy Rebellion," Government of India, *Political and Judicial Correspondence*, File 7347.

Moscotti, Albert (1951). "British Policy in Burma, 1917–1937." Unpublished Ph.D. dissertation. Ann Arbor: University Microfilms.

Mousnier, Roland (1978). *Paris Capitale au Temps de Richelieu et Mazarin*. Paris: Pédone.

Mukeiji, K. (1965). "Levels of Living of Industrial Workers," in V. B. Singh, ed., *Economic Economic History of India 1857–1956*. Bombay: Allied.

Mukeiji, M. (1965). "National Income," in V. B. Singh, ed., *Economic History of India 1857–1956*. Bombay: Allied.

Musson, A. E. (1978). *The Growth of British Industry*. New York: Holmes and Meier.

Mya Khan (1969). "Village Administration in Upper Burma," *Journal of the Burma Research Society* 52: 58–77.

Mya Sein, Daw (1938). *Sir Charles Crosthwaite and the Consolidation of Burma*. Rangoon: Zabu Meitswe Pitaka Press.

Myrdal, Jan (1965). *Report from a Chinese Village*. New York: Signet.

El Nacional (1975). Caracas Newspaper. 16 July 1975.

Nagata, Judith (1974). "What is Malay? A Situational Selection of Ethnic Identity in a Plural Society," *American Ethnologist* 1: 331–350.

Nash, Manning (1970). "The Impact of Mid-Nineteenth Century Economic Change Upon the Indians of Middle America," in Magnus Morner, ed., *Race and Class in the Americas*. New York: Columbia University Press.

Nicholas, Martin (1973). "Forward," in Karl Marx, *Grundrisse*. Middlesex: Penguin Publishers.

Nisbet, John (1901). *Burma under British Rule and Before*. London: Archibald Constable.

North, Robert C. (1953). *Moscow and the Chinese Communists*. Stanford: Stanford University Press.

Orozco y Jiménez, Francisco (1911). *Documentos inéditos relativos a la Iglesia de Chiapas*. San Cristobal: Imprenta de la Sociedad Católica.

Paez Celis, Julio (1975). *Ensayo Sobre Demografía Económica de Venezuela*. Caracas: Eduven.

Paige, Jeffery M. (1975). *Agrarian Revolution: Social Movements and Export Agriculture in the Underdeveloped World*. New York: Free Press.

Pakokku District Gazetteer (1913). Rangoon: Government of Burma.

Pang, Shouxin (1980). "Henan Interviews." Unpublished manuscript.

Perkins, Dwight H. (1969). *Agricultural Development in China, 1368–1969*. Chicago: Aldine.

Perry, Elizabeth J. (1980). *Rebels and Revolutionaries in North China 1845–1945*. Stanford: Stanford University Press.

Pike, Douglas (1966). *Viet Cong*. Cambridge: M.I.T. Press.

Plant, Colonel (1886). *Narrative of the Insurrection in the Tenasserim Division during 1885–86*. Rangoon: Baptist Mission Press.

Platelle, Henri (1964). "Un village du Nord sous Louis XIV: Rumégies," *Revue du Nord* 46: 489–516.

Polachek, James M. (1982). "Mao's 'Moral Economy' and the Jiangxi Soviet (1927–1934)," *Journal of Asian Studies* (forthcoming). Pages cited refer to Davis Center Seminar Paper, 16 October 1981.

Popkin, Samuel L. (1979). *The Rational Peasant: The Political Economy of Rural Society in Vietnam*. Berkeley and Los Angeles: University of California Press.

Powell, John Duncan (1969). "Venezuela: The Peasant Union Movement," in Henry Landsberger, ed., *Latin American Peasant Movements*. Ithaca: Cornell University Press.

————. (1971). *The Political Mobilization of the Venezuelan Peasant*. Cambridge: Harvard University Press.

El Progresista (1882). Bocono Newspaper. 21 July through 18 August 1882.

Race, Jeffrey (1972). *War Comes to Long An: Revolutionary Conflict in a Vietnamese Province*. Berkeley and Los Angeles: University of California Press.

Raj, Jagdish (1965). *The Mutiny and British Land Policy in North India 1856–1868.* Bombay: Asia Publishing House.

Rangel, Domingo Alberto (1969). *Capital y Desarrollo: La Venezuela Agraria.* Caracas: Universidad Central de Venezuela.

———. (1970). *Capital y Desarrollo: El Rey Petroleo.* Caracas: Universidad Central de Venezuela.

———. (1974). *Los Andinos en el Poder,* 2nd ed. Caracas: Vadell Hermanos.

———. (1975). *Gomez: El Amo del Poder.* Caracas: Vadell Hermanos.

Ranger, T. O. (1968). "Connections between 'Primary Resistance' Movements and Modern Mass Nationalism in East and Central Africa," *Journal of African History* 9: 437–53, 631–41.

———. (1969). "African Reactions to the Imposition of Colonial Rule in East and Central Africa," in L. H. Gann and Peter Duignan, eds., *Colonialism in Africa, 1870–1960.* Cambridge: Cambridge University Press.

Rangoon Gazette (Weekly Budget) (1929–30). Rangoon.

Rao, G. N. (1978). "Political Economy of Railways in British India, 1850–1900," *Artha Vijāna* 20:368–419

Redfield, R. (1930). *Tepoztlán.* Chicago: University of Chicago Press.

Reinhard, Marcel, André Armengaud and Jacques Dupâquier (1968). *Histoire Générale de la Population Mondiale.* Paris: Editions Montchrestien.

Reynolds, Clark W. (1970). *The Mexican Economy.* New Haven: Yale University Press.

Ricardo, Lou (1982). "Letter from Changsha," *Far Eastern Economic Review,* 115, 3, (January 15–21): 62.

Rodrik, Dani, (1979). "Peasants in Distress: Agrarian Transformation and Rural Mobilization in Egypt and Turkey." Unpublished Honors Thesis. Cambridge: Harvard College.

Roseberry, William (1977). *Social Class and Social Process in the Venezuelan Andes.* Ann Arbor: University Microfilms.

———. (1978). "Peasants as Proletarians," *Critique of Anthropology* 11:3–18.

———. (1979). "On the Economic Formation of Boconó," in Luise Margolies, ed., *The Venezuelan Peasant in Country and City.* Caracas: Ediciones Venezolanas de Antropología.

———. (1980). "Capital and Class in Nineteenth Century Boconó, Venezuela," *Antropológica* 54 (forthcoming).

———. (1982). *The Development of Capitalism in the Venezuelan Andes.* Austin: University of Texas Press (forthcoming).

Sanyal, Nolinaksha (1930). *Development of Indian Railways.* Calcutta: University of Calcutta.

Sarkisyanz, Emanuel (1965). *Buddhist Backgrounds of the Burmese Revolution.* The Hague: Nijhoff.

Saw, U (1931). *The Burmese Situation, 1930–1931.* Rangoon.

Schram, Stuart (1966). *Mao Tse-tung.* Baltimore: Penguin Books.

Schwartz, Benjamin I. (1951). *Chinese Communism and the Rise of Mao.* Cambridge: Harvard University Press.

Scott, James C. (1976). *The Moral Economy of the Peasant: Rebellion and Subsistence in Southeast Asia.* New Haven: Yale University Press.

———. (1977a). "Hegemony and the Peasantry," *Politics and Society* 7: 267–96.

———. (1977b). "Protest and Profanation: Agrarian Revolt and the Little Tradition," *Theory and Society* 4: 1–38, 211–246.

Scott, James G. and John P. Hardiman (1900). *Gazetteer of Upper Burma and the Shan States*. Rangoon: Government of Burma.

Selden, Mark (1971). *The Yenan Way in Revolutionary China*. Cambridge: Harvard University Press.

Selected Stories of Lu Xun (1972). Beijing: Foreign Languages Press.

Semo, Enrique (1973). *Historia del capitalismo en Mexico*. Mexico: Editorial Era.

Shaoshan Fengyun (The Shaoshan Storm) (1979). Beijing: New China Youth.

Shwebo District Gazetteer (1929). Rangoon: Government of Burma.

Silverman, Sydel (1975). "Bailey's Politics," *The Journal of Peasant Studies* 2: 111–120.

———. (1979). "The Peasant Concept in Anthropology," *Journal of Peasant Studies* 7: 49–69.

Simon, Matthew (1968). "The Pattern of New British Portfolio Foreign Investment, 1865–1914," in A. R. Hall, ed., *The Export of Capital from Britain 1870–1914*. London: Methuen.

Singh, V. B., ed., (1965). *Economic History of India 1857–1956*. Bombay: Allied.

Skinner, G. William (1964–65). "Marketing and Social Structure in Rural China," *Journal of Asian Studies* 24: 3–43, 195–228, 363–99.

Skocpol, Theda (1979). *States and Social Revolutions: A Comparative Analysis of France, Russia, and China*. Cambridge and New York: Cambridge University Press.

Smedley, Agnes (1956). *The Great Road: The Life and Times of Chu Teh*. New York: Monthly Review Press.

Smith, Donald E. (1965). *Religion and Politics in Burma*. Princeton: Princeton University Press.

Snow, Edgar (1938). *Red Star Over China*. New York: Random House.

Spence, Jonathan D. (1981). *The Gate of Heavenly Peace*. New York: Viking.

Steward, Julian H. (1950). *Area Research: Theory and Practice*. Social Science Research Council Bulletin 63. New York: Social Science Research Council.

Stinchcombe, Arthur L. (1961). "Agricultural Enterprise and Rural Class Relations," *American Journal of Sociology* 67: 165–176.

Syriam District Gazetteer (1914). Rangoon: Government of Burma.

Tadaw, Saw Hanson (1959). "The Karens of Burma," *Journal of the Burma Research Society* 42: 31–40.

Taylor, William (1972). *Landlord and Peasant in Colonial Oaxaca*. Stanford: Stanford University Press.

Terray, Emmanuel (1972 [1969]). *Marxism and "Primitive" Societies*. Translated by Mary Klopper. New York: Monthly Review Press.

Tha Aung, Maung and Maung Mya Din (1941). "The Pacification of Upper Burma: A Vernacular History," *Journal of the Burma Research Society* 31: 80–136.

Tharrawaddy District Gazetteer (1920). Rangoon: Government of Burma.

Thaxton, Ralph (1981). "The Peasants of Yaocun: Memories of Exploitation, Injustice, and Liberation in a Chinese Village," *The Journal of Peasant Studies* 9: 3–46.

———. (1982). *China Turned Rightsideup*. New Haven: Yale University Press.

Thayetmyo District Gazetteer (1911). Rangoon: Government of Burma.

Thein Pe, Maung (1973). "Her Husband or Her Money," in P. M. Milne, trans., *Selected Short Stories of Thein Pe Myint*. Ithaca: Cornell University Press.

Thomas, P. J. (1934). *The Problem of Rural Indebtness*. Madras: Diocesan Press.

Thomer, Daniel (195). "Long-Term Trends in Output in India," in Simon Kuznets, Wilbert

E. Moore and Joseph J. Spengler, eds., *Economic Growth*. Durham: Duke University Press.

Thompson, E. P. (1978). *The Poverty of Theory and Other Essays*. New York: Monthly Review Press.

Thompson, J. Eric, comp. (1958). *Thomas Gage's Travels in the New World*. Norman: University of Oklahoma Press.

Tilly, Charles (1975). "Food Supply and Public Order in Modern Europe," in C. Tilly, ed., *The Formation of National States in Europe*. Princeton: Princeton University Press.

Toungoo District Gazetteer (1914). Rangoon: Government of Burma.

Toynbee, Arnold et al. (1968). *Man's Concern with Death*. London: Hodder and Stoughton.

Trens, Manuel (1957). *Historia de Chiapas*. Mexico: Talleres Gráficos de la Nación.

Usher, Abbott Payson (1920). *An Introduction to the Industrial History of England*. Boston: Houghton Mifflin.

Van Slyke, Lynman P. (1968). *The Chinese Communist Movement*. Stanford: Stanford University Press.

Varese, Stefano (1978). "El estado y lo multiple," unpublished manuscript. Mexico: El Colegio de México.

Varshney, R. L. (1965). "Foreign Trade," in V. B. Singh, ed., *Economic History of India, 1857–1956*. Bombay: Allied.

Velsen, J. van (1964). *The Politics of Kinship: A Study in Social Manipulation among the Lakeside Tonga of Malawi*. Manchester: University of Manchester Press.

Venezuela, Banco Central (1971). *La Economía Venezolana en los Ultimos Treinta Años*. Caracas.

Venezuela, Ministerio de Fomento (1971). *X Censo de Población y Vivienda. Resumen General*. Caracas.

Wallace, Anthony (1966). *Religion: An Anthropological View*. New York: Random House.

Wallerstein, Immanuel (1973). "The Two Modes of Ethnic Consciousness: Soviet Central Asia in Transition?" in Edward Allworth, ed., *The Nationality Question in Soviet Central Asia*. New York: Columbia University Press.

―――. (1974). *The Modern World-System*, vol. 1. New York: Academic.

Washbrook, D. A. (1976). *The Emergence of Provincial Politics in the Madras Presidency, 1870–1920*. Cambridge: Cambridge University Press.

Wasserstrom, Robert (1978). "Population Growth and Economic Development in Chiapas, 1524–1975," *Human Ecology* 6: 127–43.

―――. (1982). *Ethnic Relations in Central Chiapas, 1528–1977*. Berkeley: University of California Press.

Weber, Adna Ferrin (1963). *The Growth of Cities in the Nineteenth Century*. Ithaca: Cornell University Press.

Wemyss, Alice (1961). *Les Protestante du Mas-d'Azil. Histoire d'une résistance 1680–1830*. Tououse: Privat.

White, Herbert T. *Herbert Thirkell White Collection*, India Office Records, London. European Mss.E. 254.

―――. (1913). *A Civil Servant in Burma*. London: Edward Arnold.

White, Robert A., S. J. (1969). "Mexico: The Zapata Movement and the Revolution," in Henry A. Landsberger, ed., *Latin American Peasant Movements*. Ithaca: Cornell University Press.

Williams, F. F. (1923). *The Vailala Madness and Destruction of Native Ceremonies in the*

Gulf Division. Port Moresby: Papuan Anthropology Reports, 4.

Wolf, Eric (1969a). *Peasant Wars of the Twentieth Century.* New York: Harper & Row.

———. (1969b). "On Peasant Rebellions," *International Social Science Journal* 21: 286–293.

Wolfe, Martin (1972). *The Fiscal System of Renaissance France.* New Haven: Yale University Press.

Woodman, Dorothy (1962). *The Making of Burma.* London: Crescent Press.

Woodside, Alexander B. (1976). *Community and Revolution in Modern Vietnam.* Boston: Houghton Mifflin.

Worsley, P. (1957). *The Trumpet Shall Sound.* London: MacGibbon and Kee.

Wu Yuzhang (1981). *The Revolution of 1911.* Beijing: Foreign Languages Press.

Ximénez, Francisco (1929–1931). *Historia de la provincia de San Vicente de Chiapa y Guatemala.* 3 vols. Guatemala: Biblioteca "Goathemala" de la Sociedad de Geografía e Historia.

Yamethin District Gazetteer (1922). Rangoon: Government of Burma.

Yi Yi (1961). "Life at the Burmese Court under the Konbaung Kings," *Journal of the Burma Research Society* 44: 85–129.

Zhandou Yingxiong Gushi Xuan (1978) (A Selection of Stories of War Combat Heroes). Beiking: The People's Press.

Zhang Ermu (1979). *He Long Zai Xiangexi.* Hubei Province: Changjiang wenyi chubanshe (The Changjiang Literary and Arts Press).

Zhang Kaiyuan and Lin Zengping (1980). *Xinhai Geming Shi* (History of the 1911 Revolution). Beijing: Renmin chubanshe (The People's Press).

Zheng Weisan (1941). *Kangri zhanzheng yu nongmin yundong* (The War of Resistance and the Peasant Movement). New Fourth Army Political Department.

Zhongguo Jianshi (A Simple History of China) (1979). Tianjin: Tianjin Shrfan xueyuan Lishixi (The Tianjin Normal History Department).

Index

Elbeuf, Duke of, 14, 15
Elder Brothers Society, 141, 147, 151, 152, 153
Engels, Frederic, 9, 132, 152–53
Ethnicity, 9, 56, 89, 92, 98, 102, 115, 181–82, 191
Evara, 183
Exploitation, 6, 43, 54, 87–88, 95–96, 129, 195
Exports: 59, 60, 64, 76, 174, 177, 194; in India, 71, 190, 191; in Mexico, 72; in Burma, 80, 88–89, 91; in Venezuela, 111–13, 117–20 passim, 124–25, 129; in China, 135, 136

Federalist War, 112
France: peasant unrest in 17th century, 13–15, 17–18; taxes, 14–15, 23–27, 31–32, 39–40; wars, 19–20, 22–23, 29–30, 36–39, 40, 41; peasants, 19, 114–17; state officials, 23, 26–27, 35–36; protests against the state, 27–29; capitalism, 28; civil wars, 30, 38–39. *See also* Camisard Rebellion.
French Revolution, 115–18, 169, 177
Fronde Rebellion, 26–27, 38, 39

Gabaldón, Joaquin, 123
Gabaldón, José Rafael, 120–23, 192, 193
Gabaldón Rebellion, 111, 120–21, 123
Gage, Thomas, 45
García, Juan, 51, 54
Gaung Gyi, 81
Geary, Grattan, 83, 89
General Council of Burmese Associations (GCBA), 99, 100, 101
General Council of the *Sangha Samettgyi* (GCSS), 99–100
Generation of '28, 121, 192
Ghost Dance, 183
Gomez, Juan Vincente, 117–24 passim, 192
Gómez, Sebastián, 50–52, 53
Gorant, Etienne, 34
Gran Registro de la Propridad, 61
Great Revolution of 1925–27 (China), 146
Guerrillero Episode, 125
Guomindang, 132–34, 148, 151, 155–56
Guzmán Blanco, 112, 113

Harnel, Philippe, 34
Hegel, Georg Wilhelm Friedrich, 106
Hegelian Marxism, 192
He Long, 140–43, 148, 150–51, 153, 154
Henry IV, 21, 22
He Shidao, 141
Hidalgo, Father Manuel, 53
Hoa Hao, 165–66, 194
Huguenots, 21, 37–38

India: land tenure, 62, 190; taxes, 63–64; markets, 71; exports, 71, 190, 191
Indian Civil Service, 76
Indian immigrants in Burma, 89–90, 103

Japanese Imperial Army, 156
Jimenez, Pérez, 193
Juárez, Benito Pablo, 61

Kachin (Burma), 89
Karen (Burma), 85, 87, 89, 98, 102
Kautsky, K., 144
Konbaung State (Burma), 79–80

Labor, 54, 58, 84, 138
Land consolidation, 61–63, 103, 190
Land reform, 60–63, 193
Land tenure, 8–9, 18–19, 54–55, 77, 91, 97, 114, 119, 174; laws, 59–63; in Mexico, 60–62; in India, 62–63, 190
de Lara, Father Simon, 49, 51, 54
La Rochelle, 22
Leaders, local: 9, 190, 191; in Burma, 80–81, 83, 84–85, 92–95 passim, 100–101, 104; in China, 139–43
Lenin, V. I., 144
Leon, Carlos, 192
Ley de desamortización (Ley Lerdo), 60–62
Ley de Exvinculación de Tierras, 60
Li Dazhao, 143–46 passim, 150
Liu Zhen-hua, 146
Liu Zhidan, 152
Lopez Contreras, Eleazar, 192
Loret, Jean, 13, 14
Louis XIII, 22, 27, 30, 37, 39
Louis XIV, 13, 14, 24–30 passim, 37–39 passim
Lumpenproletarians, 147, 148, 150
Lustucru War, 14–15, 40
Lu Xun, 135, 148

Machado, Gustavo, 121, 192
Magic, 87, 103
de Maisterra, Manuel, 43
Malinowski, Bronislaw, 182
Mao Zedong, 132–35 passim, 139, 143–47 passim, 148–54 passim
Markets: 6, 7–8, 71, 73, 115, 174, 193; in India, 71–72
Márquez, Joaquin Gebaldón, 121
Marx, Karl, 9, 106–7, 115, 116, 139, 142–44 passim, 152–53, 192
Maung Gui, Joseph, 102
May Fourth Movement, 132, 143
Mazarin, Cardinal, 13, 22, 24, 26, 39
Mayenne, Duc de la, 37
Mexican Revolution, 169
Mexico: taxes, ecclesiastical, 42, 45–46; colonialism, 18th century, 43–44, 54; state officials, 43–45; 54–55; religious officials, 44–45, 48; peasant unrest, 48–50; religious state, 50–52; capitalism, 54–56; land tenure, 60–62; exports, 72
Migdal, Joel S., 157–58, 108–77 passim
Military: 11, 73, 158, 164, 166, 169, 172,

Notes on Contributors

Michael Adas (Ph.D., Wisconsin) is Professor of History at Rutgers University. His publications include *The Burma Delta: Economic Development and Social Change on an Asian Rice Frontier, 1852–1941* (University of Wisconsin Press, 1974) and *Prophets of Rebellion: Millenarian Protest Movements Against the European Colonial Order* (University of North Carolina Press, 1979). He is currently working on a book concerning colonial relations during World War I.

Scott Evan Guggenheim is a graduate student in Anthropology at The Johns Hopkins University. His interests include the social history of the Spanish Empire, world systems analysis, and land tenure in the Philippines. His publications include "Estrategias de Adaptacion en Almolaga, Hidalgo" (*Cuadernos de Trabajo de CIS-INAH*, forthcoming) and "Compadrazgo, Baptism and the Devaluation of Natural Birth" (with Maurice Bloch; *Man*, forthcoming).

Joel S. Migdal (Ph.D., Harvard) is Chairman of the International Studies Program in the School of International Studies, University of Washington (Seattle). His publications include *Peasants, Politics, and Revolution* (Princeton University Press, 1974) and *Palestinian Society and Politics* (Princeton University Press, 1980). He is currently interested in state-society relations in the Third World, U.S. training and equipping of Third World police forces, and the political economy of post–World War II international orders.

Sidney W. Mintz (Ph.D., Columbia) is Professor of Anthropology at The Johns Hopkins University. His interests include rural economy and the relation between anthropology and history. His publications on peasants include *Worker in the Cane* (Yale University Press, 1960), "The Rural Proletariat and the Problem of Rural Proletarian Consciousness" (*The Journal of Peasant Studies* 1:291–325, 1974), and *Caribbean Transformations* (Aldine, 1974). He is currently completing *Sweetness and Power*, a history of sugar consumption in the United Kingdom.

William Roseberry (Ph.D., Connecticut) is Assistant Professor of Anthropology at the Graduate Faculty of the New School for Social Research. His contribution to this volume is based on a case study which is presented in greater detail in his forthcoming book, *The Development of Capitalism in the Venezuelan Andes* (University of Texas Press). His other publications include "Peasants as Proletarians" (*Critique of Anthropology* 11:3–18, 1978) and "Capital and Class in Nineteenth Century Boconó, Venezuela" (*Antropológica*, forthcoming).

Theda Skocpol (Ph.D., Harvard) is Associate Professor of Sociology and Political Science at the University of Chicago. Her current research interests include methods of historical sociology, patterns of state interventions and politics during the New Deal, and mobilization for World War I in Britain, France, and the United States. Her publications include "Wallerstein's World Capitalist System: A Theoretical and Historical Critique" (*American Journal of Sociology* 82:1075–1090, 1977), *States and Social Revolutions* (Cambridge

University Press, 1979) and "Rentier State and Shi'a Islam in the Iranian Revolution" (*Theory and Society*, forthcoming, 1982).

Ralph Thaxton (Ph.D., Wisconsin) is Assistant Professor of Politics at Brandeis University. His major research interests include peasant mobilization, theories of revolution, and Chinese politics. His forthcoming book, *China Turned Rightsideup* (Yale University Press, 1982) concerns the rise of peasant revolution and Communist power in North China during the anti-Japanese war of resistance. His publications include "Tenants in Revolution: The Tenacity of Traditional Morality" (*Modern China* 1:323–358, 1975) and "The Peasants of Yaocun: Memories of Injustice, Exploitation, and Liberation in a Chinese Village" (*The Journal of Peasant Studies* 9:3–46, 1981).

Charles Tilly (Ph.D., Harvard) is Professor of History, Theodore M. Newcomb Professor of Social Science, and Director of the Center for Research on Social Organization at the University of Michigan. His publications include *The Vendée* (Harvard University Press, 1964), *The Rebellious Century* (with Louise A. Tilly and Richard Tilly; Harvard University Press, 1975) and *From Mobilization to Revolution* (Addison-Wesley, 1978). His chief current research concerns the formation of national states, the development of capitalism, and the forms of conflict in Europe since 1500.

Robert Wasserstrom (Ph.D., Harvard) is currently Special Advisor, Office of Planning and Research, Inter-American Foundation. Among his current research interests are the social effects of economic development in Latin America, and the unforeseen consequences of agricultural technology. His publications include "Revolution in Guatemala: Peasants and Politics under the Arbenz Government" (*Comparative Studies in Society and History* 17:443–478, 1975), "A Caste War That Never Was: The Tzeltal Conspiracy of 1848" (*Peasant Studies* 7:73–85, 1978) and *Ethnic Relations in Central Chiapas, 1526–1977* (University of California Press, 1982).

Robert P. Weller (Ph.D., Johns Hopkins) is Assistant Professor of Anthropology at Duke University. His current research interests include religion and rural revolt, the relation between ideologies and political economy, and the influence of Western industry in China. His publications include "Unity and Diversity in Chinese Religious Ideology" (University Microfilms, 1980) and "Sectarian Religion and Political Action in China" (*Modern China*, forthcoming, 1982).